MONUMENTAL AMBIVALENCE

MONUMENTAL
AMBIVALENCE

The
Politics of
Heritage

LISA BREGLIA

UNIVERSITY OF TEXAS PRESS
Austin

JUN 2 1 2007

Requests for permission to reproduce material from this work should
be sent to:
   Permissions
   University of Texas Press
   P.O. Box 7819
   Austin, TX 78713-7819
   www.utexas.edu/utpress/about/bpermission.html

⊗ The paper used in this book meets the minimum requirements
of ANSI/NISO Z39.48-1992 (R1997) (Permanence of Paper).

LIBRARY OF CONGRESS CATALOGING-IN-PUBLICATION DATA

Breglia, Lisa, 1972–
   Monumental ambivalence : the politics of heritage / Lisa Breglia.
— 1st ed.
      p.   cm. — (Joe R. and Teresa Lozano Long series in Latin
American and Latino art and culture)
   Includes bibliographical references and index.
   ISBN-13: 978-0-292-71427-4 (cloth : alk. paper)
   ISBN-10: 0-292-71427-0 (alk. paper)
   ISBN-13: 978-0-292-71480-9 (pbk. : alk. paper)
   ISBN-10: 0-292-71480-7 (alk. paper)
      1. Mayas—Mexico—Yucatán (State)—Ethnic identity.   2. Mayas—
Mexico—Yucatán (State)—Government relations.   3. Cultural prop-
erty—Protection—Mexico—Yucatán (State)   4. Cultural property—
Government policy—Mexico—Yucatán (State)   5. Privatization—
Mexico—Yucatán (State)   6. Contracting out—Mexico—Yucatán
(State)   7. Yucatán (Mexico : State)—Ethnic relations.   8. Yucatán
(Mexico : State)—Government relations.   9. Yucatán (Mexico : State)—
Antiquities—Collection and preservation.   I. Title.   II. Series.
   F1435.3.E72B74   2006
   305.8'0097265—dc22

                                               2006015000

In memory of Pedro "Puas" Aguilar

CONTENTS

LIST OF ABBREVIATIONS

CAM	Comisión Agraria Mixta
CIW	Carnegie Institution of Washington
CNCA	Consejo Nacional para la Cultura y las Artes
CONAPO	Consejo Nacional de Población
CREP	Chunchucmil Regional Economy Project, also known as Pakbeh Project
CRM	cultural resource management
CULTUR	Patronato de las Unidades de Servicios Culturales y Turísticos del Estado de Yucatán
ICOMOS	International Council on Monuments and Sites
IMF	International Monetary Fund
INAH	Instituto Nacional de Antropolgía e Historia
INEGI	Instituto Nacional de Estadística Geografía e Informática
INI	Instituto Nacional Indigenista
PAN	Partido de Acción Nacional
PROCAMPO	Programa de Apoyos Directos al Campo
PROCEDE	Programa de Certificación de Derechos Ejidales y Titulación de Solares Urbanos
RAN	Registro Agrario Nacional
RPP	Registro Público de Propiedad
SECTUR	Secretaría de Turismo
SEDESOL	Secretaría de Desarollo Social
SEP	Secretaría de Educación Pública
SRPMZA	Subdirección de Registro Público de Monumentos y Zonas Arqueológicas
UNESCO	United Nations Educational, Scientific, and Cultural Organization

ACKNOWLEDGMENTS

The arguments and ideas I present in this book are thoroughly shaped by my fieldwork experiences in and around archaeological sites in Yucatán. There are countless people to thank for providing support and guidance in the accomplishment of this work. Though there are a few to whom I cannot express here the extent of my gratitude and appreciation, I offer the following acknowledgments.

In Yucatán, I first wish to thank the former and current directors of the Instituto Nacional de Antropología e Historia, Centro Regional Yucatán (INAH-CRY), Alfredo Barrera Rubio and Luis Millet Cámara. Also at the INAH-CRY, Licenciado Luis Parra Arceo provided much-needed clarification on key matters, even after I left the field. At Chichén Itzá, the support of site manager Licenciado Villevualdo Pech Moo was vital to my research. I also extend warm thanks and appreciation to all of the INAH *custodios* and their families, who were quite open to my presence and questions as well as very generous with their time.

In Pisté, Tere Castillo and her family are dearly thanked, as is her late husband, Pedro Pablo "Puas" Aguilar, to whom I dedicate this work. I thank Doña Racquel Castillo de Cocom for the use of her lovely house and Don Ezequiel and his family for taking such good care of it while I was away (and also for coming in the middle of the night to kill tarantulas). Rey and Edy Mis, Doña Elda, Don Oligario, and their family were my own away from home, and I will not soon forget our Yucatecan barbecue on the eve of Hurricane Isidore. I also thank Victor Olalde for his friendship and companionship.

I especially would like to thank Traci Ardren, co-director of the Pakbeh Project, and Aline Magnoni, Scott Hutson, and other project members who were very kind to invite me to share their work and their lives in Chunchucmil. Other members of the Chunchucmil community deserve special attention, including Gualberto Mena, Aida, Guadalupe, Juventino, and all of their family. I also extend thanks to the many residents of the town of Kochol who were warm and welcoming to my presence and research. I could not have accomplished this research in the field without the friendship and advice of Juan Castillo Cocom and Liana Chatzigeorgiou, Fernando Armstrong Fumero, Carlos Bojórquez, Quetzil Castañeda, and Jorge Ortíz.

My friends and colleagues at Rice University deserve special merit. George Marcus, James Faubion, Stephen Tyler, and Beatriz González-Stephan were kind and supportive in their suggestions and guidance and, perhaps most importantly, patient and good-humored while this project was in its dissertation stage. Angela Rivas, Michael Powell, Nahal Naficy, and Timothy Wood have provided a stimulating, if far-flung, network of intellectual camaraderie for several years now. This book was completed at Wesleyan University, and I especially thank Elizabeth Traube and my colleagues in the Department of Anthropology for providing me with a comfortable and collegial environment in which to teach and write. Thanks also to John Hammond for his technical assistance preparing the images that appear in this book.

Special thanks to Theresa May and the University of Texas Press for their support and hard work in making this book a reality. Lynne Chapman, Tana Silva, and two anonymous reviewers took extraordinary care with this work. I deeply appreciate their efforts.

The research presented here was made possible through the financial support of the Rice University Department of Anthropology, the Ora N. Arnold Graduate Research Fellowship, a Dissertation Improvement Grant from the National Science Foundation, and a Dissertation Research Grant from the Wenner-Gren Foundation for Anthropological Research.

And final thanks to Paul Smith, whose heart, humor, patience, and generosity are truly monumental.

MONUMENTAL AMBIVALENCE

"That which is everybody's is nobody's," according to a Spanish aphorism, and nowhere are rights of ownership over the public domain more hotly contested than in the increasingly fraught debates over the preservation and privatization of cultural and artistic heritage around the globe. Far from being an issue exclusive to natural resources (such as water or energy) or social programs (including education and pensions), the deregulation and divestiture of state-owned enterprises has now reached the realm of culture. Shrinking state coffers have left even some of the most privileged houses of cultural and artistic treasures in precarious financial conditions. More tentative still is the fate of hundreds of thousands of archaeological and historic monuments, many of which remain undocumented and unprotected. After decades of highly centralized control over key heritage resources—whether monuments, museums, or archaeological zones— governments are demanding accountability, efficiency, and profit from their cultural institutions.

In turn, citizens have become disillusioned, fed up, and even incensed as states move to divest cultural properties. Public debates over privatization of national patrimonies have intensified in the past few years in countries around the world. Recently, for example, cultural workers from across Italy demonstrated in front of the Colosseum bearing "No to Privatization" signs following Prime Minister Silvio Berlusconi's approval of plans to grant concessions for heritage properties to the private sector. In China, infrastructural development aimed at linking heritage sites with high-volume tourism networks is proceeding at a pace alarming to conservationists, academics, and the United Nations Educational, Scientific, and Cultural Organization (UNESCO). Visitors to the Taj Mahal were almost left in the dark as a direct result of the Indian government's outsourcing of maintenance responsibilities to a private firm. Meanwhile, in Mexico, local Maya working at the archaeological site of Chichén Itzá revealed their uncertainty toward a guaranteed constitutional protection of national cultural patrimony by half-expecting the construction of a McDonald's at the

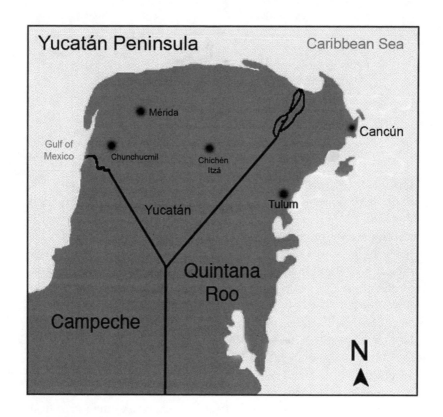

Yucatán Peninsula

Caribbean Sea

Mérida

Gulf of
Mexico

Chunchucmil

Chichén
Itzá

Cancún

Yucatán

Tulum

Quintana
Roo

Campeche

N

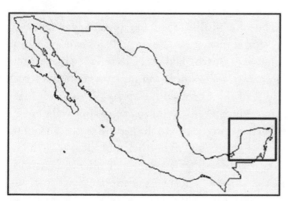

MAP O.I. *The Yucatán Peninsula. Map by John Hammond.*

top of the Castillo. As neoliberalism becomes the order of the day, citizens, national agencies, and international organizations each, in turn, wonder about the fate of "their" cultural heritage. The public-good guarantees of modern nations are quickly becoming merely artifactual. The ambivalence of "that which is everybody's is nobody's" produces a seemingly irresolvable tension between a state that needs to sell off its patrimony to be in line with global circulations of capital, and its citizenry, which heavily invests in the monuments and symbols of national patrimony as a way of defining its social identities and place in the global landscape.

For communities around the world residing in landscapes of ruins, the stuff of contemporary everyday life continually trespasses upon privileged sites of ancient civilization. Yet, monuments are not isolated in time or space from the social and political lives of citizens. Nor are the monuments immune from changing economic agendas affecting the global marketplace. While privatization programs—especially those implicating symbolically rich resources—make splashy international headlines, it is nearly impossible to discern sentiments toward ownership, custodianship, stewardship, or other forms of possession of cultural heritage on the ground. Most notably absent are the views and opinions of local communities as they go about their workaday lives in the midst and shadows of some of the most famous and fabulous instances of heritage spaces in the world.

I offer this study as an ethnographic foray into the intimate politics of monumental heritage and the contingencies of claiming cultural patrimony in Yucatán, Mexico. Perhaps this project resonates with contradiction. After all, the very notion of monumentality suggests—and perhaps even requires—the univocalization and ossification of meaning in material cultural icons. Through archaeological science and the project of nation building, what is commonly understood as Mexican heritage signals a "glaciation of the past" (Foucault 1967/1986). Thus, the invocation of monumentality, it would seem, necessarily effaces the subtle, personal, contingent practices, expressions, and claims enacted in negotiating both the meaning and content of the stuff of heritage. Yet as Knapp and Ashmore (1999, 1–2) suggest, "We know from modern peoples that meaning in a landscape is not directly related to how obtrusively it has been marked in material, archaeologically detectable ways." Indeed, monumentality strives to erase—and thus assumes the erasure of—ambivalence. But once we begin to look for the fissures in monumentality, we find that ambivalence abounds.

FIGURE 1.1.   *A banner like many others strung up in heritage sites across Mexico in the summer of 1999:* No to the privatization of cultural patrimony and archaeological zones. *Photograph by author.*

ON THE OCCASION OF "PRIVATIZATION"

April 28, 1999: Mauricio Fernández Garza, senator from the conservative National Action Party (PAN), presents to the Mexican Senate Committee on Cultural Affairs a proposal to amend Section XXV of Article 73 of the Mexican Constitution.[1] This article guarantees federal jurisdiction over "all matters concerning archeological, artistic, and historic monuments, the conservation of which is of national interest." No matter that the actual proposal cleverly stepped around the notion of outright divestiture of state-held and regulated cultural properties by encouraging nongovernmental participation in the work of preservation and promotion (Fernández Garza 1999), the senator's initiative immediately became known in opposition circles as the cultural patrimony "Privatization Proposal." Widely perceived as a profane intrusion of both party politics and free-market economics into the sacred sphere of national cultural heritage, the proposal presented a monumental threat not only to the integrity of the nation's patrimony but to the very fabric of Mexican nationalism itself.

Given the continued acceleration and intensification of Mexico's neoliberal program of the past two decades, Fernández Garza's proposal to formally open the field of cultural patrimony to the private sector might have been expected, yet it was received by many as a shock. Since the 1980s, privatization has arisen as an essential component of Mexico's neoliberal economic structural reform package that entails trade liberalization and deregulation, increased direct foreign investment, and transformation of communal agricultural lands (*ejidos*) into private property.[2]

Under pressure from international financial institutions including the World Bank and the International Monetary Fund (IMF), Mexico has attempted to institute an "open economy" in which the state's intervention is limited by a new legal and institutional framework. Under this new economic model, "the tendency is for the market to replace regulation, private ownership to replace public ownership, and competition, including that from foreign goods, to replace protection" (Lustig 1998: 1). Under President Salinas de Gortari (1988–1994), the privatization program underwent an unprecedented expansion involving such previously untouchable sectors of the economy as telecommunications, pensions and insurance, commercial banking, agriculture, television and radio, ports and airports, potable water distribution, and mining (Salinas-León 1996: 177).[3] The revocation of protectionist measures, the unleashing of market forces, and the creation of a national environment generally hospitable toward all forms of private investment left the field of cultural heritage especially vulnerable. Was it not just a matter of time before the sacred realm of cultural heritage would be affected?

Though the proposal to open the realm of cultural heritage to the private sector could have been expected, it certainly was not welcomed. Following the proposal to amend constitutional protection of national heritage properties, cries of "Our cultural patrimony is not for sale" echoed across multiple constituencies of academics and intellectuals, heritage administrators, journalists and cultural critics, and ordinary citizens. Conferences and forums hastily sprang up, international news outlets covered the story, and demonstrations erupted from Mexico City to Chiapas. Yet after its initial huge splash on the public scene in summer 1999, the proposal has rested, with an eerie quiet, under the myriad problems faced by the administration of Vicente Fox—whose election a year later coincided with the last public gasps of the cultural patrimony privatization protest movement. Fernández Garza's amendment never passed. As far as the Constitution now stands, cultural heritage remains the inalienable property of the nation. Yet the introduction of the proposed amendment and the subsequent public outcry it engendered mark a significant moment for both reflecting upon as well as newly imagining the place of "heritage" in the modern nation state.

Throughout this study, I will point toward the specificity of the Mexican case regarding the national custodianship of cultural properties and the intervening role of the private sector in transforming these properties into monumental heritage. But Mexico's heritage crisis is far from unique. Across the globe, nations are constantly facing new problems concerning the logically or discursively opposed projects of protection or preservation on the one hand and promotion or development of national or global heritage on the other. To address these "monumental" issues, I track ambivalence toward archaeological ruins as it is articulated by a series of social actors and institutions. These include international organizations, national agencies, bureaucrats, academic researchers, and significantly—populations residing within landscapes of ruins.

Ambivalence is articulated by different kinds of agents in relation to each other, for example between an international heritage convention and a national law, or may be internal to a particular kind of agent, such as within a community of site residents. I also locate ambivalence between and within different kinds of interests: among these, the scientistic projects of archaeology and ethnography in contrast to governmentalistic development projects. On the ground, these multiple expressions of ambivalence feed the (often unproblematic) coexistence of de jure and de facto policies and practices affecting both the daily operations of heritage sites and the expressions of nationalism, ethnicity, and descent that they embody. I argue that the preeminent "site" of monumental ambivalence is located not within the ruins themselves (as material cultural icons) but rather in the historical interplay between the territorial assertions of the nation over its patrimonial resources and the interventions of private interests seeking to benefit from those same resources.

While the term "heritage" readily evokes the past, it often obscures the everyday reality that archaeological zones are active, dynamic, contingent spaces of the production of social relations. In order to critically engage the everyday lives of archaeological zones, I draw upon ethnographic and historical evidence from two archaeological sites—Chichén Itzá and Chunchucmil—and the Maya communities that overlap their borders—Pisté, Chunchucmil Pueblo,[4] and Kochol—on the Yucatán Peninsula. Rather than an analysis of changes wrought in the cultural sector by the de jure implementation of a cultural patrimony privatization policy, I am instead concerned with documenting both the fallout of the as yet unsuccessful proposal to privatize cultural patrimony I describe above and the host of other kinds of privatization already intervening in the production of heritage sites across the Mexican national landscape.

Archaeological zones are peculiar assemblages organized as strategic ways of making sense of time and space. The two case studies presented in this book clearly illustrate how archaeological sites are historically produced social spaces. At Chichén Itzá, a site internationally renowned for archaeology and tourism for nearly a century, successive generations of federally employed site guards and custodians regard the site as inheritable family patrimony. They claim that the mandate of caring for the site, as well as the right to benefit from it economically, is in their blood. At Chunchucmil, farmers with land tenure rights within the heritage site strongly assert patrimonial claims over what has only recently become an official archaeological zone. In this case, the patrimonial significance of the site is not founded upon the ruins themselves but on the farmland where they sit.

The perspective I take throughout this book is based on the following premise: archaeological ruins in Mexico, although juridically mandated as national property, are in practice sites of multiple, coexisting claims on ownership, custodianship, and cultural inheritance. Given the public debates surrounding heritage during my fieldwork, I am particularly interested in the relationship between public- and private-sector interventions into the "territory" of heritage over the course of more than a century. I set out to demonstrate how de jure policies and de facto practices of privatization have affected local Maya communities in terms of the ownership, use, and tenure of land within archaeological zones in Yucatán. Using a diverse range of sources—from onsite interviews with archaeological zone workers to property records—I show how local patrimonial claims to and understandings of "ruins" are highly contingent. Rather than finding a stable basis in ethnic or indigenous identity claims, patrimony claims are instead situated in complex relation to (1) state policy regarding the ownership and custodianship of cultural materials, (2) issues of jurisdiction and access within archaeological zones, and (3) the ongoing efforts of U.S. and Mexican interest groups to develop archaeological sites and to promote scientific knowledge of ancient Maya civilization as well as international cultural tourism.

The big picture both backgrounding and occasioning this book is the question of how neoliberal privatization affects the field of cultural heritage. As an ethnography, this study cannot completely account for the multiple ways in which governments, citizens, archaeologists, bureaucrats, organizations, and others practice heritage across the globe. After all, it is the specificity of history, geography, and the unique structure of social and economic relations in a heritage landscape that carries the fundamental weight of this discussion. What this work does present, however, are experiences with heritage at two Maya archaeological sites and their adjacent or overlapping residential communities in Yucatán, Mexico. In my quest to trace the multiple iterations of heritage at the Maya archaeological sites of Chichén Itzá and Chunchucmil, I find that the workaday definitions of "heritage" or "patrimony" simply cannot account for the variety and contradiction evident in how local residents, state officials, archaeologists, and others used (and abused) heritage on the ground. Ethnographic and historical research into the everyday lives of archaeological sites and their associated residential communities in Yucatán reveals an insistent repetition of multiple forms of ambivalence toward cultural patrimony. I call this historically, politically, economically, and culturally produced condition "monumental ambivalence."

I initially developed the concept of monumental ambivalence drawing upon a subtle yet distinctive invocation of heritage articulated among Maya excavation workers hired by mostly foreign archaeologists at the site of Chunchucmil. At the local level, archaeological site workers and residents are ambivalent as to whether archaeological ruins represent national cultural patrimony rather than usufruct-based land inheritance. Maya residents of one small agricultural community are ambivalent as to whether the ancient mounds archaeologists have recently begun to excavate are indeed monuments at all. One might have thought that the introduction of an archaeological excavation project in a tract of dry, rocky, uninhabited land would be the most exciting or at least noteworthy change in the surrounding communities for the past several generations. Yet, as I discuss in depth in Chapters Five and Six, the prospects of tourism development at the site instead met lukewarm reception.

Not only are local residents ambivalent about tourism development and archaeology—they project a decided ambivalence as to whether the mounds on their farmland are indeed "heritage" at all! These indigenous agriculturalists and entrepreneurs find themselves—rather than rejecting univocal state ideologies of heritage—fashioning patrimonial claims based upon what is already present in the multivocal ensemble of heritage objects, practices, and procedures as they are continually shaped and reproduced across time and space. We will see how various social actors and institutions—from bureaucrats to site custodians to Maya farmers—are able to exploit the ambivalent character of heritage to serve multiple and continually renegotiated ends. In and around the archaeological sites of Chichén Itzá and Chunchucmil, social actors willingly and unwittingly engage in the regional, national, or international discourse on heritage. In doing so, they demonstrate their ambivalence toward heritage not as indifference, but as a practiced non-acceptance of heritage as a unified, privileged sphere dominated alternately by the state, archaeological science, and the tourism industry.

Kept and protected under the custodianship of the nation, cultural heritage is "everybody's." Yet under the care of the big bureaucracies of the old-style liberal state, the responsibility for the protection and preservation of heritage properties, whether tangible or intangible, seemingly falls on "nobody's" shoulders. National custodianship of cultural patrimony rhetorically assures "everybody's" access to heritage in the name of the public good, but privatization threatens to draw heritage out of public hands, leaving "nobody" accountable for its future.

In the space between "everybody" and "nobody" sits a crucial dilemma for national heritage institutions but also for local social actors who live deeply within the spaces marked by the production and consumption of heritage across the national landscape. Who has the right to possess heritage properties as material goods and the legitimate bases on which to claim benefits from the same? To what extent is this ambivalence of everybody's and nobody's a problem for the preservation or promotion of heritage sites? What are the implications of monumental ambivalence on the ground: for archaeologists, administrators, landowners, or local indigenous communities?

My assertion of the fundamental ambivalence of heritage is specifically designed to counteract the notion of the univocality of heritage. Both despite and because of the particularities of Mexican nationalism, heritage is not univocal: it is monumentally ambivalent. The 1999 proposal for privatization reform in the cultural sector is at once part of a long historical narrative of Mexico's past and a rupture in the imaginary of the state as patrimonial custodian of the possessions of the key resources of the national territory. In other words, Mexico is a state preoccupied with fulfilling the incomplete project of becoming modern while already jumping ahead to imagining itself as neoliberal. Mexico demonstrates ambivalence toward its own modernity, as the state seems to want to maintain an older, liberal form of exclusive possession over its resources and participate deeply and decisively in a globalizing world. Thus this study of monumental heritage lends insight into a bigger picture: how nations imagine themselves vis-à-vis the ancient past in a rapidly changing world presumably oriented toward the future.

THE HERITAGE ASSEMBLAGE

The Mexican state, its institutions, and a range of social actors with competing interests develop and orchestrate a variety of strategic operations that organize not only meaning, but the very system of value around objects of cultural patrimony. At the site level, farmers, small business entrepreneurs, and federal heritage site employees enact tactical maneuvers sometimes supporting but often thwarting the strategic logic of the state's discourse of monumentalization. Over and against the predominant image carried by the rather static, structured concept of monumentalization, with its penchant for, in Foucault's (1967/1986) words, "the glaciation of the past," I argue that understanding the contemporary everyday life of heritage is not to be found in examining material culture as such. Rather, I am suggesting that we imagine heritage as an assemblage, a term I borrow from archaeology.

In archaeological parlance, an assemblage is a group of artifacts representing a culture, related to each other based upon their recovery from a common archaeological context. The archaeological assemblage refers to a collection of objects and their association. Instead of a concatenation of objects defined by their physical environment, my conceptualization of the heritage assemblage accounts for social actors, institutions deeply involved in both the production and reproduction of heritage.[5] We might also think of the assemblage as a multi-sited object of study (Marcus 1998) through which we may interrogate how ruins or other landscape features become heritage, for whom, and why this is important for the state and its multiple audiences and constituencies.

HERITAGE AS PRACTICE

"Why," asks David Lowenthal, "does heritage loom so large today?" (1996: 5). Whether fundaments of imperialist nostalgia, cornerstones of identity-based social movements, or one more tourism marketing ploy, current interest in heritage, appropriately characterized by Lowenthal as "the Heritage Crusade," is a strictly modern search for origins. Indeed, "only in our time has heritage become a self-conscious creed, whose shrines and icons daily multiply and whose praise suffuses public discourse" (1). At the same time, we can also think of heritage as a particular kind of social relationship, a postmodern search for origins, if you like, that references—without being predicated upon—material culture. The contemporary preoccupation with heritage reflects, as Stuart Hall puts it, "not the so-called return to roots but a coming-to-terms with our 'routes'" (1996: 4).[6]

A critique of the univocality of heritage takes these understandings as necessary givens, intervening deeply into the very composition of heritage discourse and practice—the heritage assemblage—particularly those elements that imbue heritage with a distinctly territorializing character. Ethnography of heritage, as I will further describe, moves us along the routes of contemporary heritage practice without becoming mired in questions of archaeological interpretations of the material remnants of the past.

Studies of heritage sites around the world have concentrated, for the most part, on the material cultural aspects of heritage sites and objects.

Most critical heritage studies can be situated into two general categories, both of which have a strong disciplinary affiliation with archaeology. In the first category we find studies primarily oriented toward cultural resource management (CRM).[7] The second category, which includes works from the fields of museum studies[8] and heritage tourism,[9] is more relevant to my own concerns in this book. I also place in this category a smaller body of studies of heritage sites carried out by archaeologists concerned with the social contexts and multiple audiences—or "publics"—of their work.

Certain heritage sites and museums have become prototypes in this second category. Colonial Williamsburg (Greenspan 2002; Handler and Gable 1997) is a key site for studying the articulation between heritage- and meaning-making processes (between institutional practices and ideologies) in a history museum setting. Stonehenge and Çatalhöyük are prototypes of conflict and contestation among various users of the heritage spaces.[10] Barbara Bender's (1998) study of the meanings and usages of Stonehenge as a "contentious contemporary symbol" pays close attention to the site's competing users, their practices, and their beliefs. Hodder (1998: 125) describes the "kaleidoscope of interests that have converged on Çatalhöyük" based on different experiences of the past for different constituencies engaged with the site. Himpele and Castañeda (1997) approach a similar "convergence" through a different angle and medium in their ethnographic film portrayal of New Age tourists attending the spring equinox event at Chichén Itzá. Generally speaking, these works concern the multivocality of the past and, consequently, the multivocality of heritage. Yet it seems to me that illustrating the multivocality of heritage—or the multiple meanings infused and suffused within a heritage object—does not necessarily imply a critique of the univocality of heritage as a social, cultural, political, and economic process. As part of a new approach to heritage, I propose that multiplicity is not opposite of univocality: rather, it is ambivalence.

Skeates (2000; 9–10) finds that a definition of archaeological heritage carries two registers, "the material culture of past societies that survives in the present" and "the process through which the material culture of past societies is re-evaluated and re-used in the present." What these registers of archaeological heritage share is a grounding reference to material culture. Analyses of heritage based on unquestioned assumptions of the stability of material-cultural referents take what I call a "heritage-as-artifact" approach. This approach is exemplified by most of the work I have cited above in the established fields of heritage and museum studies

and is finding new life in the emergent fields of social and public archaeology. The heritage-as-artifact framework carries specific ideologies and
biases. Most importantly, as I will address in this chapter, the heritage-as-
artifact approach emphasizes the nonrenewability of cultural resources.
Grounded as it is in material culture, this approach sits rather conserva-
tively in place in the disciplinary history of anthropology.[11]

The definition and framework I use for analyzing how heritage works
is somewhat unconventional. For the most part, I am interested in what
can be understood about heritage when we, at least momentarily, sever
heritage from the realm of material culture (thus deviating significantly
from the archaeologically oriented studies) and develop instead an ethnographic understanding of heritage practice. Certainly I am not the first
cultural anthropologist concerned with the social and cultural genealogies of historic places. Yet as recently as 1996 Michael Herzfeld has stated
that "studying the local politics of heritage—that is, ethnographically—
is still in its infancy" (122).

Now, a decade later, ethnographic studies are still few, while their im-
port and even necessity are greater. The ever-increasing interpellation of
heritage sites into the international tourism market is transforming these
"local" spaces into investment sites for global capital. In this process, what
was formerly understood as "the commons" is continually reterritorialized
through privatization of heritage properties. As I will detail, however, heritage studies per se has not quite been able to grasp the on-the-ground implications of heritage practices in this key moment of transformation.
Speculation on meanings of the past is perhaps becoming less important
both to nations and to local communities facing questions of the future of
"their" heritage.

Only a handful of studies have focused ethnographically on the living
communities coexisting with heritage sites.[12] Herzfeld's *A Place in History*
(1991) focuses on the constitution of history in the town of Rethemnos in
Crete. The author examines, in part, interventions of archaeology and its
practitioners in the daily lives of residents whose homes are targets of historic preservation. David Shankland (1996, 1999, 2000) and Ayfer Bartu
(2000) work as social anthropologists in an archaeological heritage environment. In these studies, the social anthropologists leave the excavation
site at Çatalhöyük to conduct, in Shankland's words, an "anthropology of
an archaeological presence" (1996: 349).

Caftanzoglou (2001) examines an "inappropriately located" residential
community, Anafiotika, adjacent to Greece's most prestigious monument,
the Acropolis. My study complements these latter forays of social or

cultural anthropologists into "archaeological" environments through my examination of the sociocultural/historical significance of heritage sites beyond the parameters of both archaeology and monumentality. What does the site mean for local people—Maya and non-Maya—who live around or inside its borders? How is the site both sacred and mundane? How can ancient ruins be a natural feature of the landscape and the built environment of an ancient people?

In this study I offer an alternative approach that releases heritage from its own confines of monumental materiality exemplified in the heritage-as-artifact approach. For simplicity I call this understanding "heritage-as-practice."[13] In this approach, I understand heritage as first and foremost a particular kind of social relationship among all kinds of users of a heritage site—for example, between local populations and state agencies or between archaeologists and site laborers. Understood as a practice, heritage is an endlessly renewable resource, not some "thing" to be extracted from the contexts of its users or locked away for its own good. This distinction helps us to understand from the top down and the bottom up, so to speak, how the invention of heritage is an ambivalent process used by the state to create national identity and collective belonging and how citizens, in turn, ambivalently engage in the produced spaces of heritage.

THE SITES

As I watched protestors at Chichén Itzá bearing "No to Privatization" signs in the summer of 1999, I was confronted with a twin dilemma: the novelty of cultural-sector privatization in Mexico and the specifically neoliberal character of this process. Once the flare-up of protest died down, I came to understand that privatization's "neoliberal" qualifier, while indicating perhaps an intensification of speed and scope, masks the long-term involvement of the private sector in the field of cultural heritage. I also found that although the Mexican state has constitutionally held jurisdiction over archaeological heritage properties since Independence, private hands have had their grip on Chichén Itzá for centuries.

Realizing that private-sector involvement in cultural patrimony was perhaps an old phenomenon dressed up in a new suit, I shifted my research question to exploring how current endeavors by archaeologists and local communities to develop and preserve cultural heritage promote alternative privatizations of archaeological zones. I argue that private-sector intervention in lands containing ruins is hardly a new phenomenon, having historical precedents dating back over the course of nearly a century.

Privatization might be effected through property ownership of the land itself (regardless of the presence of ruins), through the establishment of private economic enterprises within the official territory of these national properties, or via other forms of intervention into the federal jurisdiction of archaeological zones. All these forms that privatization takes, alternative as they are to standard neoliberal privatization, illustrate the competing interests in archaeological zones and at the same time speak to the competing meanings produced by different social actors regarding archaeological heritage.

The 1999 privatization debate sparked my initial interest in studying cultural patrimony in Mexico. Already in the midst of summer fieldwork, I turned my attention to the local participants in the protests, the *custodios* (guards and caretakers) of Chichén Itzá. Chichén's custodios are federal employees of the National Institute of Anthropology and History (INAH), the state agency responsible for the identification, investigation, and protection of the nation's archaeological, historic, and artistic heritage. These workers at Chichén, many of them second- and third-generation workers in the archaeological zone, comprised one of the links joining this international tourist destination and World Heritage site to national politics through their expressions of ownership of the ruins.

It did not take much investigation for me to discover that this group of workers, most from the nearby town of Pisté, constituted a special enclave within the larger community. Other residents and on-site personnel regarded them with both open and veiled hostility. This was due in large part to their steady, salaried employment, their strong unionization, and their entrepreneurial activities inside the archaeological zone, from which they received exclusive economic benefits within a federal public space.

Meanwhile at Chunchucmil on the other side of the Yucatán Peninsula but within the same state, the national cultural heritage privatization proposal had little relevance. What, then, did privatization threaten if not the ownership or custodianship of the ruins? The complex, very local politics of patrimony and privatization indeed call for an ethnographic study of the meanings of living in and around ruins in Yucatán that moves well beyond implications of the usual suspects in studies of heritage sites: archaeological science, the nation, and tourism.

To disentangle the complex politics of patrimony at the local level, I create micro-level spatial genealogies of these two archaeological sites, Chichén Itzá and Chunchucmil, and their associated living communities, respectively Pisté and Chunchucmil Pueblo and Kochol. These oral and archival histories highlight the sites' archaeological development and the ends to which this development has been directed, notably tourism; the status of private landownership and communal land tenure in the property comprising the official archaeological zones; the relationships between the zones, specifically in terms of their value as natural and cultural resources, and their neighboring communities; the roles of Maya workers and their families in the historical development and daily maintenance of these zones. Chapters Three and Four address these issues at Chichén Itzá, while in the final two chapters of the book I consider the same for Chunchucmil.

I use ethnographic description, oral histories, and analysis of archival documents related to the land tenure history of the sites now deemed federal heritage properties. While I would insist upon the multiple contingencies of these case studies, I think they offer a provocative insight into larger processes beyond the local. In addition to inspiring new ways to understand heritage as a social and economic phenomenon, these local ethnographic portraits offer an empirical grounding for often vague concepts such as neoliberalism. These case studies also provide a useful grounding for my ongoing investigations into the politics of global heritage. I address the wider implications and future directions of this research in the Conclusion.

Pisté is a predominantly Maya community of about 4,000 residents within the municipality of Tinum, which at the time of my fieldwork had a total population of 9,548 (INEGI 2000). The town is situated near two main highways 120 kilometers southeast of Mérida and 200 kilometers from Cancún. As a tourist service center with hotels, restaurants, and souvenirs, Pisté is an economic nucleus of a mini-region that encompasses eleven neighboring municipalities. The archaeological zone of Chichén Itzá, just 2 kilometers from Pisté, was named a World Heritage Site in 1987 by the United Nations Educational, Scientific, and Cultural Organization (UNESCO). While hundreds of sites throughout Mexico are declared official *zonas arqueológicas*, Chichén Itzá is one of the few so designated by presidential decree. As a major national and international tourist destination, the site receives nearly one million visitors per year. Chichén Itzá is the third most heavily visited archaeological attraction in México, after Teotihuacán and Xochimilco, near the capital metropolis of Mexico City.

Chunchucmil Pueblo, population 951, and Kochol, population 1,237, are located within the municipality of Maxcanú, which had a total population of 18,771 during my fieldwork (INEGI 2000). Like Pisté, they are predominantly Maya communities, though smaller and with much less economic activity. The two towns are seven kilometers apart and more than twenty kilometers from the municipal seat. Situated between the towns of Chunchucmil and Kochol is the archaeological zone, which officially carries the name Chunchucmil. This zone covers approximately sixteen square kilometers of ejido land. Ejidos are federal lands granted to rural communities in the 1930s for agricultural production. The ejido constitutes the backbone of social and economic structures throughout Yucatán and in fact most of rural Mexico. No large architectural structures have been excavated or reconstructed at Chunchucmil, and many *ejidatarios* (participants in the cultivation of ejido land) use this land, including even the site center, to cultivate corn and other crops.

The federal government only recently declared Chunchucmil an official archaeological zone, demarcated its boundaries, and granted a U.S.-based archaeology team permission to work there. Site excavation during the time of my research employed approximately twenty laborers from Kochol for two-week rotations. The archaeological project directors, of whom I was a guest in 2001, maintained that the residents of Chunchucmil Pueblo and Kochol demonstrated an active interest in the site's development as a basis for a community program of sustainable tourism where presently there is none. Unlike Pisté, where tourism at nearby Chichén Itzá grew throughout the twentieth century, these two former henequen haciendas have been in serious economic decline for decades.

Archaeologists initiated surveying and mapping activities at Chunchucmil in 1993 and broke ground for excavation work in 1998. The site has proven to be a challenge for researchers, not just in an intellectual sense but also in everyday excavation and other site work. The project's relationships are strained and tense with surrounding communities, especially Kochol, that hold communal farming rights to the land upon which the archaeological zone sits. The tensions have multiple underlying causes, most with deep historical roots that predate the archaeological project and lie in the history of the regional political economy and the prominent role land has played in it. Old tensions also originate between de jure and de facto "ownership" by private interests and the state and usufruct rights of local residents.

Before the establishment of the ejido system in the 1930s, settlements like Chunchucmil Pueblo and Kochol were henequen haciendas, valuable fiber-producing plantations relying on the labor of Maya people through a system of debt peonage. Through a federal program of communal land distribution, the indigenous populations were "liberally" endowed with a free relation to land. In this manner the formerly subjected peoples were putatively enabled to participate in the Mexican nation re-imagining itself as modern and progressive—as a nation in which indigenous people, once a "problem," could now, with their land, be self-sufficient. This system, dependent on huge state and federal subsidies, left little room for new agricultural or industrial initiatives on the part of the Maya people.

Neoliberal reforms introduced on the federal level in 1992 have made possible the privatization of the ejido. Significantly, most of the Chunchucmil archaeological zone is made of ejido land parcels pertaining to no less than five nearby communities. As the ejido parcels are opened to privatization, the land containing the ruins of the ancient trading center of Chunchucmil is simultaneously receptive to reterritorialization. The contemporary situation I present in this ethnographic study, based on research I carried out in 2001 and 2002, locates Chunchucmil on the brink of privatization, as it stands to affect two registers of heritage: land and monuments.

Though this ethnographic research touches on many social agents and actors, both Mexican and international, the focus of my work is on two specific but not identical groups. I have been working with the first group, the INAH custodios at Chichén Itzá, since the summer of 1999. Comprising the second group are residents of the former hacienda and contemporary town of Kochol who are employed as rotating seasonal workers in the Pakbeh Project, a U.S.-based archaeological project carrying out excavations in the Classic Maya site of Chunchucmil. In the ethnographic study of the archaeological zones and their nearby contemporary Maya communities, I am concerned with the involvement of local residents in the Mexican and U.S. as well as other foreign archaeological projects at these sites and with the intervention of the Mexican state in developing these sites as tourism destinations. How have Maya people from these communities assumed positions as heritage workers in archaeological zones understood as local, regional, national, and international cultural patrimony? Historically, how has this form of labor affected the local economies, and how are these workers positioned in the contemporary tourism industry vis-à-vis the community as a whole?

THOUGHTS ON COMPARATIVE ETHNOGRAPHIC RESEARCH

Following my introduction to the politics of heritage at Chichén Itzá, I got the opportunity to extend what I was learning about the relationships among contemporary Maya communities, the archaeological past, and local political economy. I was invited to live and work as a guest researcher some two hundred kilometers away with the Pakbeh Project in rural north-western Yucatán. The Chunchucmil archaeological zone and the fieldwork experience proved to be an ethnographically and historically rich—if in some ways awkward—source of comparison. I say that Chunchucmil pro-vided an awkward comparison for several reasons, two of which I will men-tion here.

At Chunchucmil there is no rebuilt or restored monumental architec-ture, only a handful of itinerant visitors to the site, and no INAH custodios patrol the completely unfenced zone. Thus in terms of archaeological and infrastructural development, Chunchucmil is decades, if not a century, be-hind Chichén Itzá. The second factor is very much related to my own situatedness as a researcher. At Chichén Itzá INAH officials granted me nearly unfettered access to the archaeological zone and to site workers. Following the establishment of this arrangement, I conducted my daily re-search activities independent of assumed associations with other anthro-pologists, archaeologists, or Mexican state or federal institutions. My in-terlocutors were primarily the site workers and their families. While at Chunchucmil, on the other hand, during the initial phase of my research I lived with the members of the Pakbeh archaeological project.[14] My ethno-graphic interlocutors included the project's archaeologists and students, locally hired excavation workers, and nearby community residents. Given these differing conditions, it would be disingenuous (and more than slightly irresponsible) to suggest that this study compares perfectly analo-gous sites. Instead, each site served as a foil for the other.

As much as I was traveling in the course of my fieldwork between Mérida, Pisté, Maxcanú, Kochol, and Chunchucmil Pueblo, the "great distance" between the two study areas did not occur to me until people in Kochol, Chunchucmil Pueblo, and Pisté pointed it out. "Well, it's not too bad," I would answer in terms of the geographic distance I regularly trekked. After all, if one times the buses right, the whole trip to either area, always via Mérida, the state capital and regional urban center, might only take five hours. But the sense of distance between the two sites was greater than could be measured in kilometers or travel time.

The sites I chose were connected in various ways, through the activi-ties of anthropological research and through the peripatetic workaday lives of Yucatán's residents. At the same time, they were brought into new juxtaposition through my own research and presence. Anecdotal ev-idence I will relate helps give a more distinct flavor to the distance be-tween Chichén Itzá and Chunchucmil and their associated communities.

Following this, I consider how my experience of moving back and forth between the two geographical sites prompted my own methodological reflections on comparative research and multi-sited ethnography.

One existing connection is located within the work experiences of my informants. In each research population, at least one person knew of the other place. Manuel is a mostly monolingual Maya-speaking day laborer from the former henequen hacienda of Kochol, a community redefining its economic infrastructure in the past five to ten years through developing export crops of papaya and habanero peppers. He knows of Pisté from his experience in constructing the Mérida-Cancún highway in the 1980s. He never visited Chichén Itzá. Among the custodios at Chichén Itzá, two know of Kochol and Chunchucmil Pueblo. Don Marcelo, a former employee of the Mexican census bureau, worked with social scientists in various mapping and demography projects. As an essential component of his job, Marcelo traveled throughout Yucatán gaining familiarity with many of the region's smaller settlements unattached to the state's rather anemic highway system. The second is Don Julio, who worked as a bus driver for several years on routes between Mérida and Campeche. It was Don Marcelo who knew of Kochol and the pig-raising industry that made it locally (in)famous. But the empirical knowledge that each of these individuals acquired about Pisté, Chichén Itzá, Kochol, or Chunchucmil town and archaeological site could not be matched by the depth, scope, and detail of how members of their communities imagined the "other" place. The literal connectedness between the sites became rhetorically subsumed as the residents of one site who had never visited the other constructed surprisingly consistent and coherent images of the "unknown" place.

The articulation of another series of connections between Pisté/Chichén Itzá and Kochol/Chunchucmil was occasioned as I relayed information about my research within the different communities. I told various friends and informants in Pisté whom I had met and grown to know over the course of several summer fieldwork seasons where I spent those weeks when I disappeared from Pisté. Most of them assumed I was doing work at the university in Mérida, but I explained that I was doing a comparative research project requiring my presence in two other towns. I often discussed the matter of my second site of research around the archaeological zone of Chunchucmil. Depending on the precise circumstances of our meeting and the length of time I had been away, usually ten days to two weeks, I would follow this up with either a short or detailed report on my recent activities (and, embarrassing as it seems now, show off the excavation-induced blisters on my hands). After the first few encounters of this nature

I came to expect the soon typical response to any mention of Chunchucmil: *Chunchuc—¿cómo se llama?* (What do you call that place?).

"It might as well be Mars!" I exclaimed to an anthropologist colleague of mine. "And it's just the other side of the same state!" In my time living and working in these communities, I came to understand that the residents, through cable and satellite television, usually knew more about national and global affairs than very local ones. Regional newspapers are sold and avidly read in Pisté, while in Kochol and Chunchucmil Pueblo the rare copy encountered in someone's home was usually several days old, having passed through many hands. I wondered how different from mine were the perspectives of the inhabitants of each place toward the other, especially as people from Pisté began to ask what might be considered anthropological questions about the communities of Chunchucmil and Kochol and offer equally anthropological commentary. For instance, Pisté residents often assumed that the more rural inhabitants of Kochol and Chunchucmil Pueblo must be more traditional in dress, language, and agricultural practices and must speak more authentic Maya, less infused with Spanish. As if going down a cultural attribution checklist, Pisté residents asked: Do the women all wear *huipiles* (traditional white cotton smock with colorful embroidery)? Do all of the men make *milpa* (corn plots)? I started to wonder if there was a copy of Redfield's *Folk Culture of Yucatán* (1941) floating around town.

Questions about Pisté and Chichén Itzá ensued from the other side of Yucatán as well. The impression of Pisté as a more developed, sophisticated, and even cosmopolitan pueblo stressed the differences between the two places yet produced nearly identical assumptions: "In Pisté, they must speak very good Maya," supposing that the larger town must have better educational opportunities. Other perceived differences were noted with a hint of smug satisfaction that my experience in Yucatán would be culturally richer for my stay in the Chunchucmil area: "Surely," noted one of my hosts, "you won't get a handmade tortilla in Pisté!"

For the next several months, each of the two sites I researched served as a catalyst for asking questions of the other. I would regularly mention Pisté to my more recent acquaintances in Kochol in order to explain something about myself and what my work was about. The people of Kochol wanted to know what effects tourism had brought to Pisté. They also wanted to know how the people of Pisté learned languages such as English to improve their skills and thus their marketability in the tourism industry. Some comments about Pisté contradicted the most commonly held opinion of the pueblo as an unattractive, tacky tourist town, an empty receptacle of "zero-degree culture" (Castañeda 1996). "The people in Pisté must speak *Hach Maya*," said one Kochol resident. The term *hach* (very) or *verdadero* (true) Maya is the name given by many contemporary Yucatecs referring to the Maya language of the *antiguos*, the ancient Maya. Along the same lines, another Kochol resident speculated that in Pisté perhaps the people even knew how to write Maya. He lamented they could not do so in his community.

As these case studies unfold, it becomes apparent that each geographical site references the other. At the same time, a complementary host of other "sites" reveals itself. These are the sites unaccounted for in the strictly geographical reckoning of space and place. These sites consist of traces of official history or local memory, constructions of a cultural imaginary, and even the ethnographic record. The interactions I describe above demonstrate that Yucatán is far from homogeneous and that perhaps mine was a particular kind of comparative study, rendering it *not* a comparative study in the classic disciplinary sense but a multi-sited ethnography. In his essay "Ethnography in/of the World System" Marcus (1998: 90) states: "Multi-sited research is designed around chains, paths, threads, conjunctions, or juxtapositions of locations in which the ethnographer establishes some form of literal, physical presence, with an explicit, posited logic of association or connection among sites that in fact defines the argument for ethnography." Each geographical site carried valences of the other, evoked through history, memory, the discourse of anthropology, as well as my own person as researcher-traveler-resident going between one place and the other.

Thus each town has an image of the other as a place or a repertoire of practices that make up what is commonly understood as Maya Culture. This repertoire includes language, customs, traditions, food, celebrations, work activities, and the ways in which they are done. It also consists, in a deeper symbolic sense for some, of material cultural artifacts, most significantly, ancient Maya ruins. We will see, implicitly and explicitly, how residents of Pisté, Kochol, and Chunchucmil use this image of Maya Culture as a standard to judge their own lives and their cultural heritage. Furthermore, we will see that this standard is treated with a certain ambivalence—sometimes sought after and embraced and at other times rejected or denied.

The image of Maya Culture I refer to here emanates from specific sources and yet is not solely determined by these sources or methods of deployment. Its genealogy might be traced, but as a text, it circulates beyond its origins. Castañeda (1996) demonstrates that in Pisté and Chichén

Itzá, Maya Culture is constructed through discourses of archaeology and the state. He writes, "It seems that the category of 'Maya culture' has become embodied with meanings and references—with a life all its own—that takes the notion beyond any temporal, spatial, and social anchorage" (13). Is it not, then, the task of contemporary ethnographers working in the Maya area to find those anchorages? It is necessary to empirically contribute to a project of not only reevaluation of the realities of daily life experiences of Maya people but also the methodological strategies and theoretical frameworks employed in their description and analysis.

Chichén Itzá is historically situated in the milpa, or corn-growing, area of Yucatán, while Chunchucmil Pueblo and Kochol are in the heart of an area formerly dominated by henequen fiber production. The two agricultural areas represent quite different histories within a geopolitical region often homogenized when speaking of "the Maya" or "Maya Culture," and we will further examine the distinctions within this overbroad regionalization. Robert Redfield's seminal ethnographies such as *Chan Kom: A Maya Village* (with Alfonso Villa Rojas 1934) and *A Village That Chose Progress: Chan Kom Revisited* (1950) have defined the Yucatec Maya culture-civilization yet focus on the milpa area, excluding the hundreds of Maya settlements on the henequen haciendas in the northwestern part of the peninsula. Comparative work between the two areas has not significantly contributed to the canon of anthropology of the Maya of Yucatán. When not explicitly participating in the homogenizing project of Redfield's continuum model, ethnography in Yucatán has been so local as to isolate the particular area or community under study. One near-exception to this might be found in Re Cruz's *The Two Milpas of Chan Kom* (1996), a study of the movement of workers between Chan Kom in eastern Yucatán and Cancún, on the peninsula's eastern coast in the state of Quintana Roo. I say near-exception because the study relies on the concept of Maya Culture of the milpa area. Ethnographers of the henequen area have thus consistently faced the task of relating their analyses of its cultural practices and expressions to the dominant Maya culture of the milpa area. Where ethnography is beginning to question the category of Maya culture there is room to also question how cultural description and analysis have followed regional historical and socioeconomic distinctions.

Anthropology is certainly not the only culprit in the problem of using otherwise determined categories as appropriate for unquestioned redeployment. Government agencies such as the Instituto Nacional Indigenista (INI) and nongovernmental cultural foundations, along with local institutional academic production and popular media representation, consistently pose certain areas of Yucatán as centers of "culture." While the southern and eastern quadrants of the state are described as traditional or culturally conservative, the northern and western parts of Yucatán— dominated as they were by henequen haciendas—are tagged as regions of culture loss. Even as the milpa area has a political economy diversified beyond subsistence corn cultivation and henequen is no longer grown as a mass-scale export product, this distinction in the cultural character of the two areas remains.[15] In a study of local understandings of cultural heritage, these "inherited" distinctions are discourse for critical analysis. Although not based on full-scale ethnographic community studies, this study does present a comparison that is greatly needed in the ethnography of Yucatán, particularly as the region, easily influenced by the rises and dips in the international tourism industry, is changing so rapidly.

In order to bring the ethnographic and historical analysis of these two very different sites into a meaningful comparison, I have developed a comparative study that takes as its baseline criteria not an exact set of shared circumstances, but rather a set of ethnographic homologues. For example, custodios at Chichén are not the same kind of social actors as the excavation laborers at Chunchucmil—not socioeconomically, in terms of education, or in their knowledge of the bureaucratic apparatus structuring the everyday life of a heritage site. But what they share is the experience of living and working amid ruins. Thus the sites are linked through such conditions as well as through the questions I bring to each concerning the role of Maya labor in the production and maintenance of cultural heritage, local economic conditions, and the presence and degree of private initiative development.

A crucial component of the analysis of the circulation of heritage discourse on a local level is a commitment to understanding the spatiality of the archaeological zone as a place in which these discourses are produced, manipulated, and redeployed with relation to the space or place itself. While I take as a primary "location" of study two archaeological zones in Yucatán, I am at least as interested in the nonarchaeological dimension of life amid ruins, that is, the social relations within heritage sites partially shaped by but not wholly accounted for in the discourse of archaeology. Thus, I look toward theories of the production of space to help illustrate the processes and dynamics at work in my analysis of heritage as a social relationship.

This approach echoes a growing scholarly concern among social theorists, cultural geographers, and others emerging alongside critiques of the intensification of capitalism and the contradictions of modernity. This literature suggests that non-Cartesian understandings of space highlight lived experience, relationships between spaces, and the situatedness and heterogeneities of sites or localities (Elden 2001: 117). In his now-classic *The Production of Space* (1974/1991), Lefebvre suggests that we focus attention on the production of space rather than assume its pre-existing givenness. He calls for a critical approach to analyze "not things in space but space itself, with a view to uncovering the social relationships embedded in it" (89). I agree. And what is more, this emphasis away from "things in space"—monuments themselves—toward the space of social relations fills an ever-widening gap in our understandings of the past, present, and future of heritage.

Working in tandem with this theoretical approach is a methodological complement to our analysis of social space—genealogy, defined as "the union of erudite knowledge and local memories which allows us to establish a historical knowledge of struggles and to make use of this knowledge tactically today" (Foucault 1980: 83). Genealogy runs counter to the linear, regularized production of historical knowledge. While history relies on origin, genealogy assumes a heterogeneity of origin in a multiplicity of coinciding factors. It investigates, as Judith Butler (in Colwell 1997) elucidates, "the political stakes in designating as origin and cause those identity categories that are in fact the effects of institutions, practices, discourses with multiple and diffuse points of origin."

As a method, genealogy does not search for origins or a chain of causality; genealogy instead isolates points of coincidence in power and knowledge as problems to be unraveled. Colwell (1997: 26) begins with the distinction between genealogy and history in order to demonstrate the process of the former:

[G]enealogy does not invent, discover or emphasize new or different events nor does it re-interpret events in order to discover hidden or sedimented meanings that have been neglected by the tradition. It is the attempt to counter-actualize the event, to return, in one form or another, to the virtual structure of the event in order to re-problematize the event. The goal is not to find a new solution, to "fix" history, to offer a better or truer history or account of the past. The goal is to make the problem problematic, to make it a real problem once again, a problem we no longer know the answer to but for which we are compelled to find solutions.

Through genealogy we arrive at a "history of the present," in this case a history of the present-past as represented or signified through "heritage."

Genealogy and ethnography go hand in hand in the examination of local, flexible, and provisional discourses of cultural patrimony, within and without institutional ordering.

To bring Foucault's genealogical method to a new arena of study, I suggest a new use for an old term that currently circulates in the language of archaeology and heritage: "provenance." A provenance, or "record of the ultimate derivation and passage of an item through its various owners" (*Oxford English Dictionary* 1989), is most typically used in establishing the authenticity of a work of art or artifact. Here I employ the term in reference to the archaeological site as a whole, as a social space. In this application, the provenance of the archaeological site is a kind of genealogy. This kind of examination moves us toward the provisional establishment of a history of the present of Chichén Itzá and Chunchucmil. Historical contextualization in the mode of spatial genealogy—bringing the archaeological zones together with their surrounding communities—helps us to account for the monumental ambivalence toward archaeological heritage in Yucatán.

Instead of moving right into the case studies, however, I want to address two important issues. First, if I am claiming to offer this study as a new approach to understanding the politics of heritage, what are the theoretical and methodological machinations inspiring this endeavor? I have offered a series of concepts and ideas for the study of heritage sites and practices. Some of these, most notably the distinction between heritage-as-artifact and heritage-as-practice, arise as critical responses to the ways in which others have undertaken in the cross-disciplinary field of heritage studies. Others, for instance my emphasis on the spatial dimensions of heritage, are drawn from my own engagements with other work in anthropology and social theory. In the chapters that follow, I test both the possibilities and limits of approaching heritage anew as I work through the historical and ethnographic evidence drawn from case studies in Yucatán.

In the next chapter I will introduce the terms for a spatial analysis of heritage. I emphasize the spatial, territorial dimensions of heritage practice, isolating the spatial tendencies of heritage policy and legislation in the Mexican national arena as well as on the international stage. It does not take an arsenal of scholarly devices to figure out that heritage implicates questions of time. For most, heritage is intrinsically about the past. What is more, heritage is primarily composed of an array of material cultural objects constituting irrefutable "evidence" of the past. Yet an ethnography of the political dimensions of patrimony must locate heritage in space as well as time. A spatial analysis looks beyond heritage as a discrete set of objects waiting to be mapped onto the national territory by legislative procedures and then orchestrated into routes and itineraries. Indeed we should work toward understanding a new, emergent cartography of heritage that reflects ambivalence rather than univocality.

In subsequent chapters I interweave these concepts and approaches into my own ethnographic study of heritage practices in and around the two Maya archaeological heritage sites. In Chapter Three I present a case study in the genealogy of cultural sector privatization of archaeological heritage in the case of Chichén Itzá, a key site in the Mexican national cultural patrimonial landscape that has been privately owned for decades. Over and against the dominant popular representation of the crisis of possible privatization of 1999, I utilize local and state governmental archives, oral history, and ethnographic interviews to argue that the protests over the contemporary threat of privatization fail to acknowledge that the modern history of Chichén Itzá is shaped by different interests as they compete for control over the archaeological zone. I argue that these alternative privatizations may read as counterpoint to the juridical frameworks and represent business as usual within the archaeological zone that is based on extralegal interpretation of the laws and policies governing cultural patrimony.

Chapter Four presents an in situ ethnographic study at Chichén Itzá of the social actors who participate in the local-level negotiation of laws, policies, and ideologies within the historical circumstances. The themes of this ethnographic account emanate from two simple questions: what are the daily activities of maintaining a World Heritage archaeological zone, and who does this work? These questions help to fill in the larger framework of local, everyday perspectives on cultural heritage. The main research subjects at Chichén Itzá are its custodians—the guards, wardens, and groundskeepers. This analysis discerns the strategies and tactics employed by the family groups of these workers as they insert their interests into the social, juridical, and economic matrix undergirding the everyday functioning of the archaeological zones. I demonstrate that while within the larger discourse of national cultural patrimony and World Heritage, local meanings of the site of Chichén Itzá are produced through their manipulation. As such, national patrimony comes to signify and justify family patrimony.

Using oral and written historical sources, in Chapter Five I introduce the study's second case and narrate how the land itself serves as patrimony for the people of Kochol and Chunchucmil Pueblo. For them the archaeological ruins, possibly a rich resource indeed, are no more than secondary in importance to the land upon which they sit. Oral histories from Chunchucmil Pueblo and Kochol focus mostly on the decades of henequen cultivation. Nearly every informant gives details of life under the debt peonage system, the social and economic backbone of the hacienda. These histories shed light on another kind of patrimony—the insurmountable debts to the hacienda store, passed from father to son as a terrible inheritance. From this local, historical perspective, we will see how economic systems are intricately tied with social systems and how management of land resources was dependent on an equal management of labor resources.

In Chapter Six I question the role of archaeology in positioning the residents of Chunchucmil and Kochol as communities descendant from the ancient Maya. How, I ask, does this assertion affect the interpretive strategies of local people in understanding and assigning significance—cultural, historical, economic, or even political—to the ruins in their midst? I interrogate the politics of patrimony for people who explicitly do not consider themselves descendant communities of the ancient Maya. Rather than arguing from the standpoint of the politics of identity, I consider the multiple "territories" that comprise an archaeological zone and how they are created and recreated on an everyday basis by local residents, representatives from governmental agencies, and foreign archaeologists.

From these case studies, I conclude that claiming patrimony is a historically contingent practice that is as much related to the changing field of social relations as it is to material culture. Looking toward the larger picture of the fate of cultural heritage under neoliberalism, I find that privatization does not always appear in a singular guise, nor has it threatened intervention in the field of cultural patrimony only of late. Indeed, an array of alternative privatizations accompanies the contemporary management, development, and occupation practices in heritage sites. As a contribution toward future research, I explore the possibilities of bringing the heritage-as-spatial-practice approach to the study of global heritage.

The typically modern practice, the substance of modern politics, of modern intellect, of modern life, is the effort to exterminate am-bivalence: an effort to define precisely—and to suppress or elimi-nate everything that could not or would not be precisely defined. Modern practice is not aimed at the conquest of foreign lands, but at the filling of the blank spots in the compleat mappa mundi. *It is the modern practice, not nature, that truly suffers no void.*

BAUMAN 1991: 7–8

LOCATING CULTURE ON THE MAP

In January 2003 Mexico's Ministry of Tourism (SECTUR) announced plans to create La Cartografía de Recursos Culturales (the Cartography of Cultural Resources), designed to locate and identify the tangible and intangible cultural resources upon the map of Mexican national territory. According to its promoters, the project was designed to create a foundation of information for touristic development, handicraft production, and cultural industries in Mexico. Originally presented in the proceedings of the Indigenous International Tourism Forum in the city of Oaxaca in March 2002, the project represents the participation of several agencies: the Office of Cultural Heritage and Tourism of the National Council of Arts and Culture (CNCA), the Ministry of Tourism, and UNESCO. This mapping project defines among its objectives the fostering of link-ages between the promotion of cultural tourism and the protection of the tangible and intangible national patrimony. The project goals are to ex-plore the means and methods through which the material and spiritual benefits of Mexico's cultural heritage fall upon the communities to which the patrimony most directly pertains and upon all of society.

The Cartografía de Recursos Culturales project raises several questions objectively pertinent to broader concerns in the fields of preservation, conservation, and cultural resource management. As we will see, the codification of cultural resources—for the most part tangible resources such as archaeological and historic monuments—has long been a practice of the patrimonial Mexican state. In its objective to locate resources geographically, economically, and socially, the project maps a space of ambivalence. This is evident in the double-faceted intention of the project. On the one hand, the Cartografía is designed to show tangible and intangible resources while avoiding the sanctification of the former and the objectification of the latter. The goal here, stated CNCA President Sari Bermúdez, is to keep cultural resources accessible so that their "values and uses are understood and appreciated" (cited in Paul 2002). When an astute reporter asked the president, "What would happen if one of the communities disagreed with the promotion of cultural tourism behind the map project?" she responded: "These are simply the maps. Tourism policy corresponds to another agency. . . . Our specific task is to create the map and to locate culture upon it" (ibid.). Given such a turn of phrase, we can safely assume not only that "the map is not the territory" (Korzybski 1941: 58) but indeed, as Baudrillard (1983: 2) claims, that the map precedes the territory.

According to Harvey (2001: 220), "Cartography is about locating, identifying and bounding phenomena and thereby situating events, processes, and things within a coherent spatial frame." Whether we are talking about political maps, military maps, or cultural resource maps, mapping represents a strategic logic of representation in a conceptual sense and practical sense and seeks to spatially locate, fix, and define resources across the national social, cultural, and economic landscape. Driven by the modern impulse to head off ambivalence through a proper inventory of a nation's patrimonial resources, state agencies and the private-sector tourism industry employ mapping as an unambivalent, unambiguous practice.[1] International organizations, most notably UNESCO's World Heritage program, carry out this mapping on a global scale. The territorial and territorializing practice of heritage seeks to encompass everything into, as Bauman suggests, the complete *mappa mundi*—a vision of a world made coherent through the ideal of humanity's common heritage.

The notion of locating cultural resources or, in the words of the CNCA president, locating culture itself is one tactic in a strategic plan of resource exploitation on a national scale. While the Cartografía project's promoters claim to be only the mapmakers, mere technicians removed from questions of policy, one author points out, "The limitations of the map-medium are more than 'technical' and non-controversial; the questions involved are more than merely a matter of which projection or scale to select, and with such choices seen as 'technical,' rather than as involving wider issues" (Black 1997: 17). Thus, mapmaking is only one procedural aspect of defining culture-as-resource, set within the dual parameters of the very local arrangements at any particular cultural resource site and hooked into the global circulations of people, capital, and ideas.

The Cartografía de Recursos Culturales represents a strategic way of identifying resources and articulating them to certain regions in an actively imagined, constructive, and productive process. The representational power of such a map works to invent territory and, in turn, to construe the cultural accoutrements thereby defined as resources. In the course of more than a century of nation building, Mexico has sought to align natural and cultural resources in accord with the interests of the nation. As such, the map of cultural resources is an inherently political document working at the intersections of patrimony or heritage on the one hand and the ongoing tension between privatization and nationalization on the other.

The intensification of the coincidence of these phenomena—how they are becoming "mapped" onto each other—provides the occasion for my study of the different forms in which the private sector has intervened in formal and informal ways in Mexican cultural patrimony over the course of the past several decades. Proceeding from this image of the cultural map, then, I seek to interrogate the discursive representations of space implicit in the laws, policies, and institutions that define, regulate, and give meaning to heritage. I trace out the territorializing aspects of heritage with special attention to the effects of national and international legislation on the governance of indigenous populations. By highlighting the territorial tendencies of cultural patrimony policy and legislation, I argue that the Mexican state—as primary custodian of national cultural heritage—works in conjunction with other social actors and institutions to manage its heritage properties not by exterminating ambivalence, but by sustaining it.

THE TERRITORIAL HERITAGE ASSEMBLAGE

When we approach a heritage site—through a guarded entrance gate, an Internet site, or a tourism brochure—we have some understanding of the "locatedness" of the site in actual time and space. When I visit Chichén Itzá, for example, I know I am in the state of Yucatán in Mexico. I know, in other words, the geographical coordinates of my visit to Chichén Itzá. But this is not the primary location of the heritage site, so to speak. In tourism promotion, preservation activities, archaeological interpretations, and so on, heritage is first and foremost located in time. After all, heritage is "the present past" (Hodder 1983) as well as "the presented past" (Stone and Molyneaux 1994). Indeed, how many tours of ancient places promise to take you "back in time"?

While the idea of heritage, in its preoccupation with the past, calls immediately to mind the question of time and history, here I put those issues aside for the moment to think of heritage primarily as a question of space and territory.[2] I am not referring here exclusively to Cartesian space (the typical mechanism for representing the boundaries of a heritage site), but more toward what Lefebvre (1974/1991) calls "the production of space." For Lefebvre, space is "not a thing but rather a set of relations between things (objects and products)" (83). If heritage is a contextual, contingent social practice, it follows that a spatial analysis of heritage must proceed from a distinction between analysis of "things in space" (85) versus an analysis of space in and of itself.

Take the example of an archaeological mound. An analysis of a mound as a thing in space would distinguish the mound as an archaeological monument rather than a natural topographical feature,[3] one of a certain number of like objects in a particular environment or landscape. As such, it is defined, classified, and subject to certain regimes of knowledge and coded by law, science, ethics, and tourism. But an analysis of the mound in Lefebvre's terms is quite different. As a produced space, the mound participates in any number of relationships—with human action, history, and political economy—understood as spatial relations. Lefebvre uses a trialectic of space—spatial practice, representations of space, and representational space—to sort out the operations within these relations (38–39).[4] Perceptions and appropriations of the spatial patterns of everyday life are *spatial practices*, the ways that space, along with its users, is appropriated and dominated. The transformation of mounds situated in communally held agricultural land into monuments comprising national and World Heritage sites is one example of a spatial practice. The organization of mounds-cum-monuments into archaeological sites creates a *representation of space*. Representations of space such as archaeological zones or World Heritage Sites identified by UNESCO are the realm of professional practitioners including archaeologists and other heritage specialists. A mound or archaeological site is a *representational space* directly lived not only by local residents but by visitors as well. Mounds are representational space where symbolic meanings are enacted in spatial form. They are affective spaces where elements of the folkloric spill over into contemporary lived experience. As representational spaces, mounds become monuments: proper and uncontested symbols of Mexican nationalism.

As heritage practices territorialize a landscape, the social character of that landscape is transformed: into an archaeological zone, a historical place, or a monument site. How can we describe the assemblage of the social space of a heritage site? The heritage site is an assemblage of such "things" as monuments, entrance gates, ticket booths, visitors, workers, refreshments, and so on, as well as "territories" including land tenure and property ownership regimes, social codes of behavior for locals and visitors, archaeological science, ideologies of nationalism, ethnicity, and development, and so on. As the cases I present clearly demonstrate, the conjunction of spatial practices specific to the political economy of a given site—Chichén Itzá or Chunchucmil—and heritage legislation do not meet in a clean intersection. Rather, their coincidence is disjunctive, producing a space of ambivalence between law and territory.

Legal frameworks and institutions governing heritage properties in Mexico are inseparable from issues of property ownership, land tenure policies, and jurisdiction—all spatial practices. As we will see, the general tendency in heritage legislation through the nineteenth and most of the twentieth century highlighted control of things in space. This has begun to shift just in the past decade as the state endorses contemporary management and utilization practices of heritage sites. This new orientation toward exploitation of patrimonial resources is infused with the language and logic of neoliberalism. Rather than controlling things in space according to the logic of territorial sovereignty, the territory of neoliberalism intervenes in the field of social relations, altering notions of citizenship and identity over and above the material embodiments of heritage. As I previously suggested, the critical moment of this transformation is not, as one might expect, the debt crises of the past two decades and Mexico's integration into neoliberalism. Rather, the genealogy of this transformation can be traced back further to the liberal reforms of the 1920s and '30s. It was at this time that the seeds of ambivalence were planted on two linked fronts: the codification of land and the categorization of subnational (specifically indigenous) identities. Heritage is a point of intensification on both these fronts.

From Spanish colonialism onward, the heritage assemblage has operated across multiple spatial and spatializing planes: geographical, territorial, and ideological. The ability of the heritage assemblage to operate as a spatial and spatializing practice is its key source of ambivalence. This is especially apparent in the relationship between unmarked land and marked ruins. Land containing ruins has the both-and quality that is the primary feature in the ambivalent character of modern heritage: it may be simultaneously the property of the nation and privately owned; it is federally granted agricultural land, yet also the raw material for state-sponsored or private-sector tourism development. Landscapes of ruins are spaces in which, historically, wage labor was introduced to certain resident indigenous communities as locals were employed in excavation and reconstruction efforts throughout the past century and into the current one.

NATIONAL PATRIMONY: DE JURE

> The state and each of its constituent institutions call for spaces—but for spaces which they can organize according to their specific requirements; so there is no sense in which space can be treated solely as an *a priori* condition of these institutions and the state which presides over them. (Lefebvre 1974/1991: 85)

Did heritage exist before the modern nation-state? Set within the heritage-as-artifact approach, the answer seems obvious: Of course it did. After all, Chichén Itzá, Palenque, and Teotihuacán are older than the Mexican nation. Indeed, these edifices have existed for a thousand years. But they have not, across these thousand years, been either "ruins" or "heritage." As Lefebvre suggests, space does not exist before it is organized through specific sets of practices abiding by specific sorts of logics and rationales. Building—or producing—the space of heritage across the national landscape has been part and parcel of building the modern Mexican nation. Though this process unfolds over the course of more than a century, one hundred or so years is not quite one thousand.

Thus far I have been most concerned with adjusting our perspective on heritage away from time and toward space. In terms of the two kinds of approaches to heritage—artifact and practice—the former is preoccupied within abstractions of time ("ancient" time is perhaps our best example), while the latter allows for understanding heritage as a contingent practice situated in actual time and space. In discussing heritage as a territorial assemblage, I pointed out that a primary element of the assemblage is the legal discursive frame that underlies heritage practice. I now look closely at the genealogy of Mexico's laws and policies regarding protection and custodianship of the objects of national cultural patrimony. I demonstrate that heritage legislation is an eminently spatial practice meant to define a particular kind of map of Mexican national territory.

As we will see, the statist cartography of heritage in Mexico seeks to define the quality and extent of patrimonial possessions within national borders. Historically, maps, museums, atlases, and even guidebooks determine, establish the importance of, and thus manage the material embodiments of heritage. These representations of the space of heritage "profoundly shaped the way in which the . . . state imagined its dominion—the nature of the human beings it ruled, the geography of its domain, and the legitimacy of its ancestry" (Anderson 1983: 164).

Since the Conquest, the orchestration of heritage resources has had two aims: to know both the extent and the quality of its territory. While ruins were certainly components of colonial geography of New Spain, they became part of the wealth of the nation only through their "resourcing" under conditions of Mexican modernity after Independence. The resourcing of heritage required a body of laws that could, at least on paper, regulate not just the objects of heritage in and of themselves, but the relationship between the stuff of heritage and wider social, political, cultural, and economic contexts. Though not constituting an exclusive framework, legislation and policy regarding ruins in Mexico since the colonial period contribute significantly to the heritage assemblage.[5]

Thus it is worth focusing on the de jure treatment and understanding of heritage for two reasons. First, a synopsis of heritage legislation in Mexico provides a crucial backdrop for reading the intricacies of the everyday workings of the heritage assemblage in the case studies to follow. The second reason I am interested in official legal discourse is because of the very curious nature of the categories that manipulate and domesticate the ambivalent spaces and objects of heritage. Through a heritage-as-artifact approach, the legal discursive arm of the heritage assemblage has sought to regulate things in space (Lefebvre 1974/1991: 104). This is evidenced, for example, by a great concern in the body of legislation for explicating the relationship between monuments and land proprietorship. But in its heritage-as-practice approach, the legal appendage of the heritage assemblage has also sought to model social relationships. I refer here to relationships among groups of social actors as well as institutional structures and ideals of Mexican modernity.

LEGISLATIVE GENEALOGY

With the coming of Mexican Independence from Spain in 1810, the prehispanic cultural heritage that had been considered royal patrimony passed into the hands of the newly independent nation (Sánchez Caero 1995: 188) and thus became the cultural patrimony of the *patria*, the nation or home-land.[6] Post-Independence, Mexico's interest in understanding, protecting, and conserving its archaeological and historical heritage dates back to the presidency of General Guadalupe Victoria, who passed the first law related to "antiquities," the term used at that time to designate archaeological her-itage. We can read much of the subsequent legislation—even up to the contemporary period—as an effort to territorialize the nation in terms of geography and ideology. Rather than provide a comprehensive chronology of cultural heritage legislation, I will focus my on distinguishing how par-ticular laws, institutions, and ideologies are woven together to form the fundament of the statist cartography of heritage. We will look at legislative discourse as a spatial practice that defines patrimony within and across the national borders; classifies and categorizes heritage properties (movable or immovable, for example) and properties of heritage (archaeological or historic, tangible or intangible); and links heritage to the territorializa-tion of other resources across the Mexican national landscape, most significantly land.

Lefebvre (1974/1991: 85) contends that space is a social relationship "inherent in property relationships (especially ownership of the earth, of land) and also closely bound up with forces of production (which impose a form on that earth or land)." Before looking at how the Mexican state be-gan to build the official legal structure of the heritage assemblage, it is nec-essary to question the constitution of property relationships with regard to cultural heritage. The very concept of heritage property is ambivalent. When we say "property" (or the Spanish *propiedad*), we refer to either some entity such as a piece of land, to ownership of that entity, or both. The con-cept of heritage property is the same: an entity (whether tangible or intan-gible, movable or immovable), its context of ownership or custodianship, or both. Cultural heritage does not only and always refer to a distant (whether ancient or colonial, in the case of Mexico) monumentalized past. Rather, it incorporates sets and subsets of definitions and materials and is categorized into two broad types, tangible and intangible, in accordance with standard schema used by Mexico and UNESCO. Under the category of tangible heritage are movable and immovable properties. Heritage legislation, as we will see, has as its primary task the negotiation of the ambivalence of property through the schematization of the material and symbolic landscapes according to these types.

Before the Mexican state could begin to specify the spatialization of heritage across the national landscape, it first had to confront the task of transferring colonial conceptions of property and ownership to the new national territory. Early legislation following Independence balanced the young nation's concerns for external sovereignty and internal coherence. The 1827 Arancel de Aduanas (a legal code dictating customs tariffs) officially prohibited exportation of archaeological finds. In asserting control over the flow of artifacts across its borders, this legislation discursively linked the concept of the territorial integrity of a modern sovereign nation with the objects of cultural heritage. While the Arancel de Aduanas demonstrates the nation looking toward the outside world, other pieces of early legislation reflect a concern with internal coherence—again played out through heritage properties. A key example of this type of legislation is the Ley de Terrenos Baldíos (1894) that prohibited the transfer of properties upon which archaeological monuments were found.[7]

Amid the internal struggles, the foreign interventions, and the political and economic chaos that the nation faced in the post-Independence period, a rising nationalism created both an atmosphere and a necessity for the establishment of more precise legislation regarding the nation's cultural patrimony. Although cultural heritage legislation for most of the nineteenth century most often was linked to larger issues such as property ownership, a few key pieces aimed at codifying heritage. The Mexican Constitution of 1857 set a new framework for conceptions of property and ownership that affected the legislation of cultural heritage. Based on a model inspired by French liberalism, the spirit of this legislative framework placed the rights of the individual over that of the collective such that property ownership came to be seen as a natural right.[8] This reform had a profound effect on proprietorship of archaeological materials for its implication of "vertical ownership." The right to vertical ownership means that the subsoil and whatever is found beneath it is the property of the surface owner. This was not changed until the Ley de Minas, or Mining Law, of 1884 reasserted national custodianship over subsoil resources (Olivé Negrete 1995: 35).[9] In 1868 President Benito Juárez codified the cultural heritage of the nation in the Ley General de Bienes Nacionales. The patrimony under the auspices of this legislation included castles and forts, historic cities, weapons storehouses, and other buildings that through sale, donation, or any other manner became national property (Olivé Negrete 1995: 21). This was broadened in the law of May 11, 1897, that for the first time formally declared national custodianship over all "immovable heritage properties" (*bienes inmuebles*), or monuments.[10]

It was not until 1930 that the concept of the archaeological zone appeared in Mexican heritage legislation. Following this, in 1934, legislation was passed that continues to serve as the basis for the official declaration of archaeological zones (Melé 1998a: 74). These pieces of legislation thus reterritorialized both the concept of categorizing what constitutes heritage and the spatial practice of marking and bounding heritage across geographical space. In effect, they shifted the legislative discourse away from treating archaeological and historic monuments as discrete *objects* toward treating them as discrete *spaces.* Through introduction of the archaeological zone concept, heritage sites became "packaged" representational spaces. As "zoning" implicated a shift from objects toward spaces, land-monument assemblages (a monument proper and the land on which it is situated) became the foci for the spatialization of heritage.

HERITAGE NATIONALIZATION

The initiative for privatizing, or even concessioning, cultural patrimony in Mexico cannot be properly understood outside the historical trajectory of the nation's assertions and reassertions of custodianship over natural and cultural resources. After more than a decade now of neoliberal reforms, two key resources in Mexico remain under the patrimonial custodianship of the nation: oil and cultural heritage. These two resources, representing the fields of both the natural and the cultural, have come to be identified as key components to the wealth of the Mexican nation economically, historically, and culturally.

The coalescence of oil and archaeological patrimony as *ur*-symbols of the Mexican nation can be traced through two foundational stories. The first is the Mexican national mythology of the ancient past, which incorporates the legacies of multiple ancient civilizations: Olmec, Mixtec (popularly known as Aztec), Maya, and others. Archaeological remains as the material embodiments of this mythic past have been utilized within the nation to rally diverse populations into a vision of a unified nation, as Bartra (2002: 6) has noted: "'Official culture' has taken a great leap across the centuries to search for the foundations of the modern state in ancient Mesoamerica."

The second foundational story is that of a historically embedded yet relatively recent reassertion of the postrevolutionary Mexican state's control over its territory and resources through nationalization programs, most notably of the petroleum industry in 1938. Petroleum is Mexico's most valuable natural resource. Mexico's state-owned oil company, Petróleos Mexicanos, or Pemex, holds a constitutionally established monopoly for the exploration, production, transport, and marketing of the nation's oil. Significantly, the two foundational stories merge in a year's time, as archaeological patrimony and Mexican cultural heritage in general became consolidated as national property through the creation of the National Institute of Anthropology and History (INAH) in 1939.

The heritage assemblage, as I have described now in various ways, does not act in an isolated sphere, nor does it act solely upon what we typically think of as heritage objects. The heritage assemblage, with its autopoetic territorializing drive, attracts and captures bits of other discourse and practice. Its most significant attachments are drawn from two linked sources: national identity and custodianship of resources. The historical project of "forging" the Mexican nation, or *Forjando Patria* (Gamio 1916/1960), refers not to the state's immediate post-Independence nation-building project but rather to the formation of the liberal state brought about by the 1910 Revolution. Aided and abetted by anthropology, the twentieth century forging of the Mexican nation was a scientistic, governmentalistic effort to incorporate diverse ethnicities across the national landscape by tying together the natural and cultural, populations and territory. It was, in other words, an attempt to create a national fabric. Forging the Mexican nation is eminently a process of resource mobilization by the state, that is, through rationalizing activities of classification and instrumentalization, orchestrating population and territory into resources. Heritage became a key site for the modern Mexican state to make sense of its uneven topography. The identification of cultural resources (monuments) alongside natural resources (oil and minerals) offered one more way in which the state could carry out territorial assertions across national space, and subsequently, into the national imaginary.

Beginning in the 1930s Mexico accelerated its nationalization of foreign companies in the petroleum, railroad, and mining sectors and instituted more protectionist measures. Among the resources brought into the newly secured fold of the nation's patrimony was cultural heritage. Part of the nation's strong protectionist strategy involved holding private property rights away from the majority of Mexico's population. Access to land for the primarily agriculturalist majority population was provided by the patrimonial state in the form of ejido land grants. The ejido system was designed as a transitional measure to keep the countryside subsisting until the national economy could support the transformation from collectively held commons to individual property rights.[11]

It is crucial to note that these nationalizations were reassertions of territorial control rather than fresh assertions of the nation's control over its natural and cultural wealth. Mexican political and legislative history tells of the ongoing tensions across more than a century regarding national sovereignty over resources, made most explicit in actions of the dictatorial President Porfirio Díaz. His opening of Mexican oil resources to foreigners in the late nineteenth century may be read as a compromising blow to national sovereignty that was not fully restored until well after the 1910 Revolution, by President Lázaro Cárdenas.

As I have also suggested, to properly understand the genealogy of heritage legislation in Mexico it is necessary to track land policies through liberalism into neoliberalism. In addition to recognizing the wealth of possibility as well as the possibility of wealth in oil resources, the postrevolutionary liberal state reshaped land into a multiply signifying resource. The postrevolutionary Constitution of 1917 and its subsequent amendments mark the coincidence of land and cultural property as intertwined issues under the nation's solidification of its liberal agenda. Before the Revolution, many archaeological sites were part of the large tracts of land that formed haciendas and as such were legally held by private interests. Throughout Yucatán, no special provisions were made to treat archaeological ruins as juridically marked spaces.

Article 27 of the 1917 Constitution broke up the large landholdings, redistributing communal agricultural tracts to the (mostly indigenous) population through the *ejido* land-grant system. In parceling ejido lands, little heed was given, at least officially, to the presence of archaeological ruins on these lands. Then, in the 1920s and 1930s, monuments throughout Mexico were reterritorialized into a new arrangement with the state: by virtue of the ejido system, hacienda land containing monuments stood to move from private to public holding. As the ejido system was one of land tenure and not ownership, the recipients of ejido land rights did not own the monuments. While the liberal ejido distributions allowed the state to secure national custodianship of sites of cultural patrimony, the neoliberal land "re-reform" that took effect in 1992 has the potential to dramatically alter both ownership and usufruct practices in ejido lands, including those containing archaeological monuments. It remains to be seen whether this privatization of the ejido will be accompanied by privatization of cultural patrimony.

Today, a tract of land containing monuments has a curious ownership regime: while a parcel of land may be held by a private owner, the portion of land that contains monuments or artifacts is under federal custodianship. Needless to say, this makes for some amount of trouble and confusion for archaeologists, federal authorities, private landowners, and those with usufruct land rights. In terms of questions of ownership and/or custodianship, the land-monument assemblage packaged through the practice of archaeological zoning becomes rather complicated to disentangle, as Mexican archaeologist José Luis Lorenzo (1998: 81) points out:

> Some foreign colleagues have trouble understanding how archaeology is administered in Mexico. The reason for this is that they do not fully understand the Latin legal traditions inherited from the colonial period which gave the state sovereignty over the land. Private ownership of the land and the subsoil and all that it contains is neither a Latin nor a Hispanic concept, but an Anglo-Saxon one.

According to the 1982 Ley General de Bienes, land containing monuments is divided into two categories (Olivé Negrete 1995: 23). The first is public-domain property of the federation. In general, "public domain" refers to natural resources, subsoil resources, and territorial waters. With respect to items of cultural patrimony, it refers to artistic, archaeological, and historic monuments, whether movable or immovable. The second category is property including land containing archaeological monuments that is specified as private-domain property of the federation (ibid). Chichén Itzá is a prime example: the archaeological site is *propiedad particular* (private property), yet the monuments are federal properties. As the monuments are grouped within an officially declared archaeological zone, the entire site is treated as property under federal jurisdiction. In the case of Chichén Itzá, we will see that the federal jurisdiction does not prevent either access to or conduct of private-sector activities within the archaeological zone.

The distinction between the categories state-public and state-private demonstrates a monumentally ambivalent position of the state toward private ownership. Perhaps we might read this position as anticipating what presently is thought of by many as the future threat to cultural patrimony: privatization. We will see how the state's ambivalent position allows for different interpretations of how a heritage site may be used by different kinds of social actors and how different kinds of claims for inheritance may be made upon a patrimonial site. Although modern cultural heritage legislation has several distinct features, this distinction between a cultural property per se, such as a monument, and the land upon which it sits is the most pertinent to the discussion of the archaeological zones of Chichén Itzá and Chunchucmil in the following chapters.

NATIONAL/IST ARCHAEOLOGY

The legislation of Mexico's cultural patrimony, especially regarding ancient heritage, could work neither effectively nor responsibly without the means and methods by which to identify the material components of heritage and to determine their significance. Archaeology supplied both the means and methods. On June 3, 1896, legislation was passed to regulate authorizations and permissions to carry out archaeological explorations, with the caveat that objects found even on private property would be the domain of the national government (Olivé Negrete 1980: 35; Sánchez Caero 1995: 189). By the last third of the nineteenth century, the ruins of ancient civilizations in Mexico and Central America piqued the curiosity of travelers. Legislation responded to the new pathways being etched through the jungles of Chiapas and Yucatán by formalizing old ways and establishing new policies and regulations to contain heritage properties within the national borders, coffers, and imagination. By the mid- and late nineteenth century, amateur and early professional scientific interest in the vestiges of ancient civilization greatly extended Mexico's heritage landscape. The explorations and discoveries in Yucatán and Chiapas by proto-archaeologists including John Lloyd Stephens and Frederick Catherwood, among others, set the stage for identifying, categorizing, then incorporating heritage properties onto the national cultural and political map.

The value of the "newly discovered" heritage properties was enhanced through the professionalization of archaeological practice, a field in which Mexican institutions were little prepared to participate. The seventeenth and eighteenth centuries saw the emergence of investigators interested in the indigenous past who took up tasks such as the conservation of documents and relics. "Professional" investigation did not begin until the late nineteenth century. Through the establishment of national anthropology in that period, the Mexican state fused ideology, institution, and policy into a long-lasting relationship. The articulation of archaeology to nationalist projects such as we find in the case of Mexico is becoming increasingly well-documented. The proliferation of studies of particular nations and their institutional archaeological heritage is connected to the emergence of historians of archaeology and those interested in documenting its social, political, and economic contexts.[12] While most of the work covers Europe and the Middle East, authors such as Kohl and Fawcett (1995: 3) claim that "the issues associated with the relationship between archaeology and nationalist politics, whether considered historically or in terms of contemporary developments, are ubiquitous." These relationships may be overt, subtle, "in service to the state," or less politicized and may change according to sociopolitical and historical conditions.

Nationalist archaeologies emerged throughout the world across the nineteenth and twentieth centuries. Of course, just as nation formation itself was a different process for European imperialist states than for emergent postcolonial nations, so too was the role of archaeology—more broadly, the past—in their ideologies, sentiments, and imaginations. Rife with political rhetoric and propaganda, archaeology was tied up in questions of civilization and development, the international prestige of a nation's prehistoric civilizations, and the construction of ancient civilizations as the ancestral forebears of modern national or ethnic groups. This is a particularly salient feature of the Mexican case. Diverse peoples within a national territory are united through a national myth based in the ancient past, typically through archaeology. In the Mexican nationalist myth, as embodied in the diagrams, dioramas, and displays of the National Anthropology Museum in Mexico City, the modern Mexican state has its origins in the region's "Aztec" (not Maya) past.

In Mexico, archaeology has figured as both a "national" and "nationalist" enterprise, as Kohl (1998: 226) carefully distinguishes them:

> The former refers to the archaeological record compiled within given states. The latter refers more inclusively not only to that record but also to policies adopted by the state that make use of archaeologists and their data for nation-building purposes, and such policies may extend beyond the borders of the state. Nationalist archaeology is frequently involved in the creation and elaboration of national identities, processes that occur not only within states but also as states expand and interact with other states.

Between 1885 and 1942, archaeology in Mexico developed out of a loosely defined proto-state endeavor characterized by incorporating the explorations of mostly foreign amateurs into a state institutional model of museums, professional training institutions, and a centralized government agency to manage all heritage properties.[13]

Heritage is implicitly a question of governance as it territorializes the Mexican national landscape through laws and institutions and thus through the orchestration not only of spatial relations but also of social relations. Next we will see how governance through heritage is an ambivalent spatial practice. Over the course of the twentieth century, the heritage assemblage has incorporated this ambivalence into the discourse on ruins themselves and into the relationship between indigenous people and cultural patrimony. Anthropology—as a primary discourse through which heritage is legitimized—was brought into the service of the state to pull together the monumental symbols of national heritage and Mexico's diverse living populations for the purposes of "good governance."

The nationalistic fervor following the Mexican Revolution marked a time of "deep-seated changes in the way of looking at and dealing with the living Indian which, in turn, affected attitudes toward the dead Indian" (Lorenzo 1998: 79). Heritage thus took center stage as Mexico's route of addressing the nation's "indigenous problem." A nationalist project known as *indigenismo* sought to integrate diverse populations of indigenous people into a singular Mexican nation by "substituting their ethnic identity for a Mexican identity" (Guillermo Bonfil Batalla 1997: 45), which required a double movement. The first movement was constructing a national culture from above that would draw on the "best elements" from each of the existing heterogeneous populations and cultures to create a common national patrimony. The second movement was the "transmission or imposition of this new culture on the majority" (ibid). Of course, as Bonfil Batalla points out, creation of a new national culture would be an artificial construction emanating from Mexico City and an implicitly spatial practice. The centrifugal power of national culture redefined indigenous cultural practices at the margins of the nation. In the case of Maya culture, the margins were not only ideological but geographical, given the distance of Yucatán, Chiapas, and other Maya cultural centers from Mexico City.

In its identification, description, and analysis of tangible and intangible forms of heritage, anthropology played a key role in placing indigenous people in a role appropriate to the nation's new modernity. Manuel Gamio, often referred to as the father of Mexican anthropology, developed the idea that scientific archaeology had a "practical end" beyond the increase of knowledge.[14] He contended that nationalist and political ends were equally infused in the goals of archaeological endeavors (Vázquez 1994: 80). This ideology played out in archaeological excavation projects, most notably at Teotihuacán, near Mexico City. Gamio built into Mexico's national heritage institution the notion that anthropology could be applied toward good governing. Although by 1925, Gamio had practically abandoned archaeology, many of his ideas persisted, and are reflected in the functions of goals assigned to the contemporary INAH.

While archaeology and nationalism have an obvious—though variable—articulation, the mere positing of the fact that they are related is insufficient to understand the historical complexity of the ways that the state has, over time, intervened in as well as invented cultural heritage.

I argue that certain characteristics of the historical development and current status of cultural patrimony legislation are certainly not weak, timid, or particularly liberal. It depends on perspective: from an institution in Mexico City or from inside an archaeological zone or Maya community in Yucatán. As we have seen thus far, the legal roots as well as the spirit of cultural patrimony legislation predate the liberal state that institutionalized a particular understanding of cultural heritage and how it should be administered, protected, and promoted.

THE NATIONAL INSTITUTE OF
ANTHROPOLOGY AND HISTORY

The consolidation of legislation concerning the custodianship, protection, and investigation of cultural heritage sites throughout Mexico's national territory is insufficient without a regulatory institution to carry out its policies. The INAH was created in 1939 during the presidency of Lázaro Cárdenas as a subsection of the Ministry of Education (Secretaría de Educación Pública, SEP). The INAH has under its purview archaeological zones, historic monuments and areas, and museums. As a centralized federal agency, the INAH has a complex and wide-reaching infrastructure. Through a network of state bureaus, it administers all archaeological, historical, and artistic national heritage in the thousands of monument zones and in various museums, including the National Museum in Mexico City, the INAH's premier showcase of Mexican heritage. The inventory of archaeological and historically significant sites and materials is a primary responsibility of the INAH. The institute is responsible for more than 110,000 historical monuments (built between the sixteenth and nineteenth centuries) and for 29,000 archaeological zones (sites of prehispanic civilization). Of these 29,000 archaeological zones, 150 are open to the public. In addition to historic and archaeological monuments, the INAH supervises more than 100 museums categorized according to the extent and quality of their collections, geographical situation, and number of visitors. The INAH coordinates and participates in excavation activities, public openings of archaeological sites, and the rescue and recovery of historical monuments. The agency also registers historical monuments and archaeological pieces in the care of individuals.

Today, all sites of archaeological patrimony are under the governance of two pieces of legislation: the Ley Federal Sobre Monumentos y Zonas Arqueológicas, Artísticos e Históricos of 1972, last modified in 1993, and the Ley Orgánica del Instituto Nacional de Antropología e Historia.[15] The founding legislation is the Ley Orgánica, which was approved on December 31, 1938, and went into effect on February 3, 1939 (*Diario Oficial de la Federación*). The 1938 law reflected a long national experience in legislating the protection of archaeological and historical monuments and marked the "federal government's absolute control of the management and fate of cultural resources" (Robles García 2000). Unlike a nationalization brought about through a threat of foreign intervention, as with oil, the cultural patrimony legislation was created with a more internal focus, toward the hierarchy of the federal system. By implication, the power of the state or local governments was limited, as Robles García (2000) explains: "In practice, this avoided the possibility that state, municipal, or local governments could issue permits to explore or loot archaeological sites, or that they could otherwise have decision power over the use of historical or archaeological monuments."

The Ley Federal of 1972 establishes in Articles 27 and 28 that all archaeological, historic, and artistic monuments are property of the nation. As such, they are inalienable and imprescriptable. This law asserts jurisdiction over "moveable and immovable properties produced by cultures preceding the Hispanic within national territory, including human, plant, and animal remains related to these cultures" (INAH 1995). The Ley Orgánica, on the other hand, establishes the institute and defines the agency's "patrimony," or that which pertains to the INAH, including the artistic, archaeological, and historic monuments already supervised by the Department of Monuments under SEP's administration, as well as any monuments discovered through exploration that would conform to cultural patrimony legislation. Article 5 confirms that objects found within monuments or museum collections may not be sold, loaned, or alienated from the custodianship of the INAH. Article 4 reassures that the custodianship granted to the INAH does not detract from the national character held by the cultural heritage. Article 3, Item VII provides that that INAH will maintain in its control the income obtained through admission fees paid by visitors to monuments and museums as well as income generated through the sale of publications, reproductions, posters, and so forth.

The Ley Orgánica was modified in 1985 to reflect the complex organizational structure of the INAH as well as a more nuanced understanding of cultural patrimony. Cultural patrimony in the 1939 version of the law is material, understood in its embodied or objectified form. In addition to monumental heritage, the INAH has followed UNESCO in extending its mandate to the jurisdiction of what might be called nonmonumental and intangible heritage: languages, traditions, music, dance, handicrafts, and so on.

Besides changing its vision of defining heritage as influenced by UNESCO, since the 1970s the INAH has reenvisioned itself as a national institution in service to the public. This populist strain was most evident in the ways in which museums were fashioned at the time, oriented as they were toward disseminating information to the general public through exhibitions (Vázquez Olvera 1995: 188). In a document solicited by the Vicente Fox transition team in fall 2000, just before the president-elect was to take office, the Colegio Mexicano de Antropólogos contributed its opinions on the institutional restructuring of the cultural sector in Mexico. With regard to the zonas arqueológicas, the Colegio (2000: 5) advised: "The monuments grouped as archaeological zones should carry out a primarily didactic function, for both Mexicans and foreigners. And their proper use as a touristic resource should always be subordinated to preliminary and adequate investigation." Concentrating most directly on the INAH, the Colegio's document raised several points that contributed toward a general consensus that the institute needed to reconstitute its scientific character and reinforce its legal framework. The first point concerns the 1972 Ley Federal. This esteemed academic body argued that the law was neither obsolete nor ineffective. Instead, it was not being followed or, in some cases, was being misapplied by authorities.

The current official vision of the INAH includes and indeed relies upon the participation of civil society. Carlos Vázquez Olvera (1995: 185) notes a growing awareness in recent years of the relationship between social phenomena and cultural patrimony. Social scientists have recognized the importance of the participation of civil society in the cultural field. This marks a change in thinking and practice, as previously in Mexico it was the exclusive realm of the state to determine what cultural patrimony is and how it would be used. However, we might also read this use of "civil society" as a euphemistic cover for encouraging the participation of the private sector in the heritage field.

As a centralized agency controlled from Mexico City, the INAH is a metonymy of the monumental approach the Mexican state has taken toward its patrimonial resources since the liberal reforms of the 1917 Constitution. The creation of a single centralized institution acted as a strong show of force for national sovereignty. This territorialization of heritage through institutionalization was another layer in the statist cartography of heritage. The affirmation of state control over monuments—powerful emblematic symbols of national cultural identity—could only reinforce the twin ideologies of the strength of the Mexican state and the value of its patrimonial resources. We will see how the statist cartography of heritage comes into play with the international discourse on World Heritage.

NATIONAL PATRIMONY AS WORLD HERITAGE

> The protection of a heritage site is not solely incumbent on the State in whose territory is a work to preserve, but, instead, is a duty commonly shared by humanity as a whole, that indivisible depository of all of the great creations that constitute landmarks in the universal adventure. (Former UNESCO Director General Federico Mayor 1988: 4)

World Heritage, or Patrimonio de la Humanidad as it is called in Mexico, promotes the ideal of the importance of sites with "outstanding cultural value" not solely to the nations in whose territory they are found or their descendant cultural groups but to every living person on the planet. At what point does the universalism of World Heritage efface national/ist agendas and/or the local particularities of a heritage site? What roles do communities that live near or in heritage sites play in their conservation, protection, and promotion? If a heritage site is supposedly meaningful to the whole of humanity, does it signify something special (or, perhaps, nothing at all) for the site's residents or neighbors? How might a small group of social actors stake a claim in what belongs, in a sense, to a nation or even the whole world? Here I will discuss the spatial practice of World Heritage as defined by the UNESCO and ascribed to by member states seeking to list the significant cultural properties within their national territories.

Thus far we have seen only elements of the territorial heritage assemblage as they operate across Mexican national space. Yet this view is far too restrictive, especially when we consider national landmarks as part of a "universal adventure." Since UNESCO's creation in 1945, the importance of Mexico's archaeological patrimony has extended far beyond its territorial borders. The nation has joined many others in drafting charters, declarations, and conventions to protect cultural properties deemed significant in one way or another—to science, the state, or public interest.[16]

World Heritage as organized by UNESCO presently encompasses more than 780 sites of natural, cultural, and "mixed" heritage in 124 countries. The Convention Concerning the Protection of the World Natural and Cultural Heritage, drafted in 1972, promotes international

cooperation between UNESCO and member states in "establishing an effective system of collective protection of the cultural and natural heritage
outstanding universal value, organized on a permanent basis and in accordance with modern scientific methods" (UNESCO 1972). In the
spirit of the United Nations organization, UNESCO World Heritage
works to complement the legislation and institutions of state parties regarding heritage matters while recognizing, respecting, and maintaining
state sovereignty. For example, Article 6 of the UNESCO (1972) Convention reads:

> Whilst fully respecting the sovereignty of the States in whose territory
> the cultural and natural heritage is situated, and without prejudice to
> property right provided by national legislation, the States Parties to the
> Convention recognize that such heritage constitutes a world heritage
> for whose protection it is the duty of the international community as a
> whole to cooperate.

While the international organization is positioned as a collaborator in the
conservation and preservation of heritage properties, Article 4 asserts
that it is the responsibility of each state to

> ensure the identification, protection, conservation, presentation, and
> transmission to future generations of the cultural and natural heri-
> tage . . . situated on its territory. . . . It will do all it can to this end, to
> the utmost of its own resources and, where appropriate, with any inter-
> national assistance and cooperation, in particular, financial, artistic, sci-
> entific, and technical, which it may be able to obtain.

Mexico signed the UNESCO World Heritage Convention in 1984
and has since played an active role through participation in the World
Heritage program.[17] "Indeed Mexico frequently serves as a model for
other Latin American countries" (Robles García and Corbett 2001: 4). As
of 2005 Mexico had succeeded in inscribing three natural sites and
twenty-two cultural sites on the World Heritage List, putting it in sixth
place in the world and first in North America in World Heritage sites declared by UNESCO.

Election of a site to the UNESCO's World Heritage list is significant
for most nations and reflects a great deal of promotion on the part of
multiple constituencies that participate and direct the nomination of candidate sites. The granting of World Heritage status simultaneously deter-
ritorializes and reterritorializes any given site of national heritage. Sites
are deterritorialized from the boundaries and borders of local, regional,

and national meanings—and in some cases, policies—as they become discursively attached to the UNESCO World Heritage program. Sites are reterritorialized as they are brought into accordance with the UNESCO's standard of "universal cultural value." These multiple processes of territorialization do not imply that one set of interpretations of a site is discarded or completely delegitimated in favor of another. Instead, the territorial heritage assemblage makes space for all.

Thus territorialization is not a zero-sum game. No single discursive embrace fully wraps itself around heritage practice, nor does a unitary rhetoric capture its range of meanings. World Heritage status may, however, tilt the territorial balance of power in any given site in unexpected ways. Take, for example, the fall 2004 controversy over the construction of the Bodega Aurrerá, part of the Wal-Mart chain, just outside of the World Heritage archaeological site of Teotihuacán. In this internationally publicized case, protestors utilized the renown of Mexico's most heavily visited archaeological site in an attempt to halt further construction of a superstore within eyeshot of the "Place Where Men Become Gods." The protests at Teotihuacán indeed serve as a now-familiar demonstration of local opposition to the encroachment of one of the most recognizable faces of multinational capitalism, Wal-Mart. What better stage to highlight the voraciousness of global capitalism than the towering Pyramids of the Sun and the Moon for which Teotihuacán is famous?

Yet the case of the Wal-Mart protests is instructive beyond a simple demonstration of local-global dynamics. In terms of analysis of the territorializing practices of heritage, both the global and the local consist of diverse, fractured consistencies. The transnational interests in the fray are seemingly unlikely bedfellows: the Wal-Mart corporation and UNESCO. At the local level we find at least two groups pitted against each other. Demonstrating against the Bodega Aurrerá were small business owners, vendors, and a coalition of heritage preservation activists organized as the Teotihuacán Valley Civil Defense Front (Vidal 2004). Meanwhile, another local constituency—residents of the nearby community of San Juan Teotihuacán—advocated in favor of the store's construction (Agence France Presse 2004). In grounding their positions, all parties stood to benefit from the "everybody's and nobody's" ambivalence of heritage. Yet the resulting complicity between the Mexican INAH (having officially approved the construction) and the International Council on Monuments and Sites (ICOMOS, a nongovernmental organization created by UNESCO) determined the construction project not to be a threat to the ruins and "denied claims that the store would ruin the view from the top of the pyramids" (Stevenson 2004). In the end, heritage's biggest protectors were precisely those who allowed for the construction to proceed. The territory of World Heritage was, ironically, not compromised, as UNESCO and ICOMOS were able to maintain a voice of authority in determining the integrity of cultural value at Teotihuacán. The Bodega Aurrerá opened in November 2004.

In various ways, UNESCO has reasserted the unassailable legitimacy of a "universal cultural value" transcendent of both time and space. In order to maintain a favorable position in the territorial balance of power played out in heritage sites across the globe, UNESCO must continually negotiate the ambivalence of heritage. Unlike what we saw in the Teotihuacán case, UNESCO and its partners are likely to, at least rhetorically, err on the side of caution when it comes to protecting cultural heritage. Evidenced by recent global promotional campaigns and the organization of an international response to heritage crises, UNESCO's maneuvers could be read as a strategic response to the perceived threat of heritage ambivalence.

The year 2002 marked the United Nations Year for Cultural Heritage, following on the heels of the new century's first major heritage crisis: the 2001 destruction of the Bamiyan Buddha statues in Afghanistan. The Taliban's act was answered with outrage to the monumental "crime against culture," in the words of UNESCO Director-General Koïchiro Matsuura. As reported by the organization's *New Courier* (UNESCO 2002: 48), Matsuura found it "abominable to witness the cold and calculated destruction of cultural properties that were the heritage, not only of the Afghan people, but the whole world." In her discussion of the destruction of the Bamiyan Buddhas, Lynn Meskell (2002: 558) points out, "we uncritically hold that heritage, specifically 'world heritage,' must necessarily be a good thing and thus find it difficult to comprehend groups who support counter-claims." While the case of the Buddha statues dramatically illustrates what is at stake when one group's exercise of power over a heritage site clashes with the universalized ideals promoted by World Heritage, other cases not so publicly contested abound.

International cultural and scientific organizations, private property owners, and usufruct land-grant holders have different stakes in the territories of archaeological sites. For UNESCO and its associated organizations, a World Heritage Site must be preserved and promoted according to a standard of universal cultural value, over and above particularities of cultural area and national boundaries. National agencies, in turn, appeal to and support abstract notions of a "cultural good," bolstering these with nationalist ideologies. Living communities surrounding or sometimes within archaeological sites negotiate these ideals and mandates according to the dynamics of everyday life at the sites. While it could be argued that these stakeholders negotiate contradictory state versus private interests, perhaps this does not adequately characterize the contemporary situation. While the neoliberal state contemplates the relinquishment of territorial control over national properties through privatization, my ethnographic and archival evidence clearly supports the claim that indeed the state has for at least a century merely assumed—through its laws, policies, and institutional management—that sites of monumental cultural patrimony were within its firm grasp all along.

Mexican laws as well as international accords, most of which derive from UNESCO and its associated organizations such as the International Council on Monuments and Sites (ICOMOS), have been written in an attempt to keep up with changing attitudes toward defining heritage, its significance in the contemporary world, and constantly changing social and political landscapes. This is most notable in the efforts to regulate intangible heritage and to protect heritage properties under conditions of military conflicts, modernization and development projects, and urbanization, as best exemplified through the UNESCO World Heritage in Danger list. But what about keeping up with transformations in global political economy?

As more nations are undertaking neoliberal agendas entailing the divestiture of state-owned enterprises and properties—including cultural heritage—it is an important moment to speculate on the structure and practices of the UNESCO World Heritage program as it relates to participating nations. If, for instance, a member nation such as Mexico were to "sell off" World heritage sites to the private sector, would UNESCO have to adjust any of its policies or practices? If, as voices of protest around the world suggest, privatization inherently poses a danger to cultural heritage, does UNESCO have some sort of responsibility in answering to activities of member states? These are fuzzy questions, to put it mildly.

Perhaps the greatest rub lies in the fact that UNESCO, as a subsidiary of the United Nations, holds the sovereignty of member-nations as a precondition for participation in the body. Thus, the United Nations would seem not to have the right to intervene in sovereign national territories. But as I have attempted to demonstrate, the heritage assemblage is a territorial machine that does not always recognize national borders. In 1945, the time of the UNESCO's establishment, or in 1972, with the resolution of the World Heritage Convention, the most recognized and significant cultural properties were held under custodianship of the nations in whose territories they were located. This may soon no longer be the case.

UNESCO's orchestration of World Heritage as juridical practice and ethos, then, is quite possibly on the brink of having to confront at least two problems. The first concerns the register of the national. If properties are not nationally owned, how are cultural properties promoted and adopted as World Heritage sites if not through national bodies? If properties already declared World Heritage Sites are transferred to the private sector, how do the rules and regulations, the duties and responsibilities that member states have agreed to uphold apply to private interests? What if these private interests are multinational in character? While UNESCO continues to treat heritage as an array of things in space, it is perhaps ignoring the more profound transformation in the production of space occurring around the globe. This is the transformation of the commons under neoliberalism, the new cartography of heritage constituted of and by spatial practices no longer confined to national borders.

A NEW CARTOGRAPHY OF HERITAGE

The other of the modern nation-state is the no-man's or contested land: the under- or over-definition, the demon of ambiguity. Since the sovereignty of the modern state is the power to define and to make definitions stick—everything that self-defines or eludes the power-assisted definition is subversive. The other of this sovereignty is no-go areas, unrest and disobedience, collapse of law and order. (Bauman 1991: 8)

Does the modernist cartography of heritage indicate the state's desire to resolve ambivalence? Or are heritage sites like Bauman's "no-man's lands," spaces that escape and thus challenge the precision of definition and, in turn, control? Perhaps the answers to these questions are "yes" and "yes." As we have seen, the Mexican state has taken great pains to identify, classify, and count its patrimonial resources. The creation of a complete knowledge of heritage resources within the nation's territory—in a word, mapping—serves to identify key points across the national landscape. These points—whether individual monuments, archaeological zones, or historic districts—appear to magically suspend the normal proceedings of space and time.

Next we will see how heritage sites are indeed contested spaces. What is more, this contestation is not always at odds with the state's strategy.

While the laws and institutions governing heritage in Mexico territorially define archaeological zones and restrict access to them, they also invite the world to participate in celebrating these national treasures as the common heritage of all of humankind.

This perfectly balanced ambivalence is threatened by privatization. The state and the citizenry have tacitly agreed upon strict parameters keeping monuments off limits to the private sector. Within these spaces, heritage is practiced by the state (with the help of its institutions and of fields such as anthropology) as a form of governance. The statist cartography of heritage is an attempt to render invisible the dynamics of inequality inherent in both defining and promoting heritage. Nestor García Canclini (1997: 61) comments on this disparity:

> Cultural patrimony functions as a resource for the reproduction of difference between social groups and the hegemony of who has preferential access to the production and distribution of heritage properties. The dominant sectors not only define which heritage properties are superior and deserve conservation, but also grant the economic and intellectual means to inscribe upon these properties a character of high quality and refinement.

Inscription, definition, distribution, and access are technical procedures that organize and deploy meaning across space. They are, in effect, mapping procedures in the statist cartography of heritage. Maps, always ideological, represent an attempt to impose order and make categorical classifications. They ambivalently illuminate and obfuscate abstract social, cultural, and political ideologies. Resource mapping is one stage in the process of the extraction of raw materials from nature. It is, following Lefebvre, a strategic logic followed by the state in the representation of space.

How do we, then, conceive of a new cartography of heritage that captures the dynamism and reach of the heritage assemblage? In a key passage outlining their concept of the rhizome,[18] Deleuze and Guattari (1987) call for "mapping," as opposed to "tracing," as a deterritorializing practice; one that would be useful is conceiving of a new cartography of heritage intended to identify and understand its statist counterpart yet not fall into its constant reproduction. I liken the heritage-as-practice approach to this sort of mapping: a performative, process-oriented enterprise, never teleological, always experimental. As such, it is a procedure, not a result. And by implication, it does not represent a resolution of the polysemic space of heritage. Rather, it promotes the sustenance of the ambivalence forming the core and feeding the pulse of the heritage assemblage.

As we have seen, monumentalization is a statist mapping procedure in the sense that it specifically marks territory as heritage. Black (1997: 17) finds that statist mapping is crucial, "as the cartographic propagation of nations depends on a clear-cut identification of peoples and territory." A national project of cultural resource mapping fits within a governmental rationality. To properly or effectively govern, the state needs to know the limits as well as the substantive contents of its territory, whether populations or resources. Mapping is one way of producing knowledge of the spatial disposition of these "things." Maps as data allow the state to see its strengths and weaknesses, its vulnerabilities and fault lines. Through delineation of economic regions and construction of areas based on a synthesis and ordering of cultural features (what anthropology calls "culture areas"), a map provides a universal perspective from which to link points through routes and circuits. In turn, the state strategically orchestrates these routes and circuits into "itineraries," which, rather than plans for travel, are instead agendas for transforming the value of heritage.

What I am suggesting is that in order to understand these itineraries, we must look at the relationships among various points of interest along a particular route, not just at the sites in and of themselves. One way of doing this is to pose archaeological zones as territories and proceed with an analysis of the practices through which they are constituted, managed, used, and represented. Given that these processes are intimately connected to an analytical perspective on the spatiality of the zones, I have suggested here that perhaps a spatialized methodology would be most appropriately employed in order to apprehend their complexities. If one were to attempt to ethnographically map the modern social, political, and economic histories of archaeological zones in Yucatán onto national and international cultural property law, regulatory institutions, and neoliberal privatization, how would this project differ in kind and scope from the Mexican national Cartography of Cultural Resources project?

The multiple territories of heritage require a map that is "open, connectable in all its dimensions, and capable of being dismantled; it is reversible, and susceptible to constant modification" (Deleuze and Guattari 1987: 21). To better grasp a politics of heritage beyond concerns for site management and tourism, it is necessary to map heritage, in the sense given here, to the overlapping territories of multiple discursive regimes: legal, economic, spatial, and so on. The gaping hole in the social scientific study of the local-level instantiations of the intensification and ever-widening reach of neoliberal economic programs, especially those manifest through privatization, in the cultural sphere opens a door for new, critical analyses to which I hope the following case studies contribute.

A question that haunts the first decades of archaeological and ethnological investigations in the Maya area is that of the relationship of the contemporary Maya people found living in Yucatán, highland Chiapas, Guatemala, Belize—the Modern Maya—to the Ancient Maya, those who built the great ceremonial centers of Chichén Itzá, Uxmal, Palenque, Mayapán, the ruins that cover the landscape of this region. Some of the most visceral representations of this relationship can be found in textual productions of the 1920s and 1930s, not coincidentally coming at the same time as the first systematic and sustained archaeological excavations at Chichén Itzá. Portrayed as pathos-inducing remnants of the "glorious past" of the Ancient Maya civilization, the Modern Maya present an anachronistic challenge to both archaeological interpretation and touristic development. Particularly compelling are three very different cultural texts: Sylvanus G. Morley's 1925 *National Geographic* article "Chichén Itzá, an Ancient American Mecca," Sergei Eisenstein's film *¡Que Viva México!*, and Robert Redfield's "Maya Archaeology as the Mayas See It," a presentation made to the American Anthropological Association in 1932. Though each substantially nourishes and nurtures the ideology of Modern Maya degeneration, the images they construct—in film, photography, or literary metaphor—are ambivalent.

It does not take a very keen eye to see that in the thirty-odd photos of "ruins" presented in Morley's *National Geographic* piece, nearly all have people in them. In these photos of ruins, Morley uses Maya people as human scale models to point out the architectural interests of buildings and artifacts. In one photo, a Maya man leans through the doughnut-hole center of "The Stone Ring of the Tlachtli Field" (Morley 1925: 70). His demeanor is both jaunty and somewhat seductive as he leans through the ring toward the camera, which squarely meets his gaze. The text below mentions a wheel of fate. Certainly the nameless Maya laborer is caught within this very wheel. Several pages later (86) we have another image of a Maya man or boy stiffly reclining against a stone column on the Colonnade of the yet-to-be reconstructed Temple of the Warriors. His left hand rests on the stone head of a serpent. The title of the photo reads "Past and Present," and the caption tells us:

> Two hundred thousand Maya toil for foreign masters today in the henequen fields of Yucatán, all memory of their former significance gone as completely as if it had never been. . . . With such a glorious past, it would seem as though his future might be made of greater promise than this. With proper educational facilities, with fair agricultural opportunities, and intelligent help over the rough places in the road, he must travel from his own simple past to the complicated world of today, and there is every reason to expect that he may again fashion for himself a destiny worthy of his splendid ancestry.

Suddenly, the pretext of using Mayas as human markers of scale is disrupted: no reference is made to the ruins in the background of the image's human subject. Indeed, the Modern Maya body is now explicitly made into the object of archaeological interest. Along with the caption text, this shot indeed suggests that the Modern Maya is anachronistic.

National Geographic is not the only place to find such texts. Sergei Eisenstein's *¡Que Viva México!*, filmed in 1931, features a series of shots taken at Chichén Itzá in the prologue sequence. In a fashion remarkably similar to Morley's "Past and Present" image, Eisenstein's sequence juxtaposes Modern Maya bodies with architectural ruins. The on-screen text accompanying the images reads:

> Time in the prologue is eternity.
> It might be today.
> It might well be twenty years ago.
> Might be a thousand.

> For the dwellers of Yucatán, land of ruins and huge pyramids, have still conserved, in feature and forms, the character of their ancestors, the great race of the ancient Mayas. . . . The people bear resemblance to the stone images, for those images represent the faces of their ancestors.

> Faces of stone. And faces of flesh. The man of Yucatán today. The same man who lived thousands of years ago. (Quoted in Karetnikova 1991: 39, 42)

Eisenstein's preoccupation with phenotypical semblance between living Maya and stone carvings suggests that unlike the previous examples, the living Maya have not degenerated per se. But the effect is the same: these living Maya are a more romanticized anachronism. The world has changed around them, but they are contained in a time warp, glaciated within the monuments that stand for Maya heritage.

Both Morley and Eisenstein construct contemporary Maya people—whether "conserving the character of their ancestors" or with a "vanished significance"—as a remnant, a trace. These kinds of images, which feed the popularized trope of the "Lost Maya," clearly present a problematic of temporality based on the terms "ancient" and "modern." What if one were to study Maya heritage without assuming to know the relationship between contemporary residents of Yucatán and representations of ancient Maya civilization? Or without presuming an ancestor-descendant relationship at all?

With these questions in mind, I move to our third example. In 1932, Robert Redfield presented a paper to the annual meeting of the American Anthropological Association entitled "Maya Archaeology as the Mayas See It," which appeared in the journal *Sociologus*. Redfield, a sociologist from the University of Chicago, was working in a multidisciplinary research milieu courtesy of the Carnegie Institution of Washington (CIW). By 1924, the CIW received permission from the federal government of Mexico to carry out excavation and restoration projects at the Maya-area archaeological site of Chichén Itzá. In addition to the archaeological work, the Carnegie sponsored geographic surveys, botany studies, physical anthropology investigations, and linguistic studies of the region, using Chichén Itzá as their base.

Redfield, like Eisenstein in film and Morley in *National Geographic*, juxtaposes Maya people and ruined buildings. He begins the piece (1932: 299–300):

> The Maya Indians of present-day Yucatán can be said to dwell in the ruined house of their ancestors. The walls of that house—more literally, the ancestral public buildings and roadways—obtrude themselves in shattered remnants upon the builders' lineal descendent.

In this piece Redfield asks a provocative question rife with countless overtones and undertones of race and civilization, of the relationships between the ancient and the traditional, the folkloric and the modern, and the archaeologist and the native. He initially frames his piece much as I have framed this inquiry—dwelling on the images of Maya people and buildings in ruins. According to Redfield, "It is the archaeologist, not the Indian, who sees the grandson living in the broken shell of his grandfather's mansion; certainly the Indian attributes to the situations no quality of pathos. The ruins are not, for him, a heritage" (300). Contemporary scholarship—whether studies of the social and political contexts of archaeology, the heritage industry, or cultural resource management—tells us that indeed the ruins are a heritage or, more accurately stated, are produced and consumed as heritage.

My reading of this passage has changed a bit since I initially encountered it well before my extended ethnographic fieldwork in Yucatán. Reading it over again, I am struck not only by its continued significance in direct relationship with my own research but also by its utter, almost blasphemous, irony. "The ruins are not . . . heritage." Here Redfield is admitting the territorializing interventions of archaeological science in the field of cultural heritage, pulling the veil off the role of archaeological science in the assemblage that both makes archaeological zones and makes them heritage sites. However, and I emphasize this important caveat, for Redfield, the ruins are not heritage for one key reason: the local Maya do not possess adequate historical or scientific knowledge of the ruins; for them, their knowledge is relegated to the category of an unsophisticated brand of folklore.

I distance my own interpretation of "The ruins are not . . . heritage" in this study for very different reasons. The primary among these is historical. At the time of Redfield's research and writing on Yucatán, in the 1930s and 1940s, the Mexican state was only beginning to systematically incorporate "ruins" into the nation's patrimony in a material and ideological sense. Therefore, it follows that for no one could the ruins really be heritage if the legal and institutional frameworks responsible for the transformation of ruins into heritage were not yet firmly in place. A second way in which my interpretation agrees and yet differs from Redfield's is tied to the specific genealogies of the archaeological zones of Chichén Itzá and Chunchucmil. My case studies of these two sites evidence other supporting reasons for which the ruins are not heritage. In the case of Chichén Itzá, patrimonial claims are based not upon the ruins themselves but on local family usufruct rights to the heritage site complex in which the ruins are only one, albeit important, feature. At Chunchucmil, local Maya assert patrimonial claims over the land upon which the ruins sit rather than on the structures in and of themselves.

Certainly—and here I agree with Redfield—"'ancient ruins' is not a single, organized idea in Maya culture" (1932: 300). But from a contemporary perspective (stemming from a series of institutional, societal, political, and economic developments) indeed the concept of ancient ruins has come to be organized in specific ways through claims by the Mexican state, by international organizations such as the UNESCO, and by local

Maya communities to create an array of "knowledges" intertwined with the polysemic idea of ancient ruins. This is the heritage assemblage as it works across Mexican national space and the landscape of ruins in Yucatán. As we have seen, a cartography of contemporary heritage practices in Mexico and across the globe reveals an uneven topography of patrimony. Some sites are marked by a greater intensification than others in the coalescence of built heritage and the overlapping discourses of nationalism, historical and scientific merit, and value as economic resources and aesthetic spaces.

While the built cultural heritage of Mexico includes more than 110,000 historical monuments and 29,000 archaeological zones, these seemingly large numbers fail to capture the reality that the entire national territory is a landscape of ruins: approximately 200,000 actual sites of archaeological vestiges are presently known (INAH 2004). In the present study I compare two of these archaeological zones that have very different modern histories but that now are facing similar dilemmas regarding the state's responsibilities toward the custodianship of Maya cultural patrimony. I will demonstrate that local-level heritage is understood and experienced differently between Maya communities according to their proximity to different archaeological zones with particular histories of excavation and positions within the regional economy.

In 1999 I conducted initial research, questioning the complex relationships between local Maya communities and state-administered archaeological zones. This pilot study demonstrated that people in Pisté and Chichén Itzá have personal ties to the archaeological zone based in a history of their or their families' participation in excavating the ruins. After the establishment of Chichén Itzá as a tourist site in the 1920s, archaeotourism displaced cattle ranching and intense agriculture from the immediate area. In contrast, the archaeological ruins of Chunchucmil have only begun to be excavated since 1998 and are located on former haciendas devoted to henequen production. These are now communal ejido lands devoted to agricultural production. Personal ties to the ruins were not evident, in terms of the discourse on cultural patrimony. Preliminary research in and around Chunchucmil demonstrated that local understandings of cultural heritage are connected to a different experience of the ruins as part of the natural forest world rather than part of the world of anthropology and tourism as in Pisté and Chichén Itzá. In both cases, the efforts made by archaeologists and others to rebuild Maya ruins into coherent structures may be read as attempts to create intelligible representations of space and thus, make heritage.

Chichén Itzá, in eastern Yucatán, is 125 kilometers southeast of Mérida, the Yucatán state capital, and 197 kilometers west-southwest of Cancún, a rather recently developed tourist playground on the Caribbean coast. Chichén is one node that triangulates these three destinations into a major tourism network. The archaeological zone, as a "Museum of Maya Culture" (Castañeda 1996), complements the sun and beach lure of Cancún with the cultural-historical appeal of the colonial city of Mérida. Thus these destinations are packaged for visitors as a combination of contemporary recreation with both ancient and historical cultural contextualization.

Cancún, targeted for tourism development by the Mexican government in the late 1960s, is not the only "invented" cultural tourism attraction on the Yucatán Peninsula. Nearly a half-century earlier, Chichén Itzá was invented as well, transformed through reconstructive efforts by U.S. and Mexican agencies. Once a colonial hacienda, the course of the twentieth century brought Chichén into the international spotlight, first as a site of curiosity for traveler-enthusiasts, then as a site of UNESCO World Heritage, and most recently into contention for a top spot in the Internet election of "the New Seven Wonders of the World."[1]

This series of transformations has been deeply felt in the Maya communities in and around Chichén Itzá, including the town of Pisté and the smaller communities of Xcalacoop, San Felipe, and San Francisco. Many residents surrounding the archaeological zone depend on the economic network based on the growth of the tourism industry in which the archaeological site serves as the regional center. Since the initiation of archaeological development in the mid-1920s, the archaeological site has served as a source of income for the local population. However, the "benefit stream" issuing forth from the zone is not unmitigated in its flow to the local communities. Private individuals as well as state and federal agencies have participated heavily in the production of Chichén Itzá as a renewable resource. As I survey the course of the past century, I will highlight the role of private sector interests in the archaeological site.

Ambivalence toward the ruins shapes the endeavors of various social actors who have been deeply involved in the historical production of Chichén Itzá as a premier site of both Maya and Mexican heritage and the ongoing reproduction of the ruins as a site of economic and political contestation. In the course of my research in Pisté and Chichén Itzá, I was hard-pressed to find anyone who denied the importance of the archaeological zone in their midst as both Maya cultural heritage and economic resource. In fact, acknowledgement of the international importance of Maya heritage (however ideologically slanted or watered down) as indicated by the hordes of annual visitors serves as a source of pride for many locals. But the ambivalent both-and character of this UNESCO World Heritage Site does not mean that Chichén Itzá can always be everything for everybody. Some among Chichén's various stakeholders hold firm beliefs regarding the extent to which Chichén is "everyone's" and "no one's." We will see that monumental ambivalence has its limits.

Chunchucmil is, in more than one sense, a world away from Chichén Itzá. With little archaeological investigation and practically no tourism infrastructural development accomplished to date, it is as if the ruins that cover a sixteen-square-kilometer stretch of otherwise flat, scrubby land are, as Redfield suggested, not quite heritage—at least not the heritage of tourism brochures. I was able to work as an ethnographer during some of the preliminary excavations at the site and thus have witnessed the becoming-heritage of Chunchucmil. I will describe the contexts and contestations that situate this seemingly new development at Chunchucmil, having found that the significance of the ruins for local Maya residents in the vicinity of Chunchucmil is not just a difference of degree, but of kind. Indeed, the farmers of these former haciendas locate a deep and meaningful heritage in their landscape, just not in the archaeological ruins.

Imagine yourself the sole owner of a plantation within which lies a
city more than twelve square miles in area; a city of palaces and
temples and mausoleums; a city of untold treasures, rich in sculp-
tures and paintings. Would you not feel shamefully wealthy? And
does it not seem strange that Don Eduardo, the master of such a
plantation, takes the fact of his ownership with apparent calmness?

T. A. WILLARD IN HIS 1926 ACCOUNT *THE CITY OF THE*
SACRED WELL (3), REFERRING TO THE REMARKABLE
CIRCUMSTANCE OF AMERICAN EDWARD THOMPSON'S
OWNERSHIP OF CHICHÉN ITZÁ

As a premier site of Maya, Mexican, and even World Heritage, Chichén Itzá is one of those places that most of us would like to think of as both "everybody's and nobody's." Yet this site stands as a most compelling monument to the ambivalence of common heritage, national patrimony, and public good. You see, Chichén Itzá has been privately owned for the entirety of its modern history. Perhaps this fact is of little significance to the thousands of visitors who stream through its famous ruins on any given day. In other words, is it possible that the private ownership of Chichén Itzá is publicly invisible? After all, how can privatization alter the grandeur of ancient pyramids? But the de facto private ownership of Chichén Itzá does matter—not only to the citizens at home and abroad who imagine and enact ownership claims to the heritage site, but in terms of the spatial arrangements and practices within the site and spilling over to local residential communities. The private sector has consistently intervened in the territory of this archaeological zone, significantly affecting how state officials and local residents shape their claims to this regional, national, and international cultural patrimony.

The fact that Chichén Itzá has been privately owned for most of its postcolonial history, remarkably enough, did not seem to contradict the fear on the part of site workers and local residents that "privatization" as proposed in 1999 signaled a new threat to this site of cultural patrimony. This case study of privatization at the archaeological site of Chichén Itzá focuses on nearly a century of transformation, from jungle-covered ruins to renowned international tourist destination. I demonstrate here that the site is and has been for more than a century privatized in other fashions and by other means.

The contemporary condition of the privatization of Chichén Itzá is expressed along two registers. The first is the historically documented involvement of private-sector actors in the ownership of Chichén Itzá as "ordinary" property, i.e., not as cultural heritage property. This form of privatization is found in the transfer of land and title to private individuals from the state and from other forms of collective or communal landholding systems. The second register of privatization finds expression in its supposedly new and more virulent form—neoliberal privatization. This is the privatization proposed in 1999 that has not come to pass. At different times, under different circumstances, and toward different ends, distinctively situated social actors and institutions have harnessed the polysemic, heterological character of the archaeological zone. This harnessing takes a multiplicity of forms including the buying and selling of land parcels, the demonstration of usufruct rights by local Maya, the opening and closing of roads, or the development of site infrastructure. From these two registers we might understand the privatization as an ambivalent intervention—not only in the field of heritage but also in the relationships between the public and the private more broadly construed.

FROM CATTLE HACIENDA TO TREASURE TROVE

Until the early decades of the twentieth century, the Yucatecan landscape did not reveal sharp distinctions between archaeological zones and the rest of the countryside. Instead, from the late sixteenth century for the next three hundred years, Yucatán was territorialized according to other ideologies and socioeconomic systems that concentrated extensive properties in the hands of a white elite, in some cases quite forcefully disrupting indigenous communal landholding.

A spatial genealogy of Chichén Itzá is concerned not only with the production of the archaeological site but also, and perhaps more importantly, with the patterns of occupation and land tenure in the context of its regional position and the peninsula as a whole. Spatial genealogy equally regards the historical dimensions of usufruct rights to the space. I rely here on the principle of usufruct rights to tie together space ands its "practitioners" or "users." While the next chapter focuses on one group—site custodians employed by the INAH over the past six decades—here we look at the spatial practices of multiple others. We will see how principles of usufruct are really different kinds of privatization. We will see how individuals with private landholdings (in the most straightforward sense) as well as explorers, archaeologists, foreign interests, and local farmers evaluate to the site's resource potential while negotiating and creatively interpreting the legal status of both land and monuments. Thus we will simultaneously examine the de jure and de facto practices of making and using heritage at Chichén Itzá.

Explorers, Proto-Archaeologists, and Early Custody Disputes

Until the first decades of the twentieth century, Chichén Itzá comprised an array of simultaneous territories. The first I will describe is Chichén Itzá, the cattle hacienda. From the earliest cited documentation on the ownership of the area of monument-bearing land known as Chichén Itzá, we find a space territorialized by private interests. As early as 1588, there are records of a cattle hacienda at Chichén Itzá from the accounts of a visit to Yucatán by one Father Alonso Ponce. A property title from 1729 indicates that Gerónimo de Ávila put up for sale the Estancia de Chichén (Olivé Negrete 1991: 121). The Títulos de Propiedad de la Hacienda Chichén document the owner of the hacienda between 1834 and 1845 as Juan Sosa Arce, likely one of several white Yucatec property owners through whose hands the hacienda passed until the late nineteenth century. Sosa Arce inherited the property upon the death of his father. The hacienda had cattle, horses, and mules valued at five to six thousand dollars (Olivé Negrete 1991: 121; Stephens 1843/1963: 183). The hacienda, typical of those of its time, most likely functioned as a mixed cattle and maize production center, with a small population of laborers who lived within the property.

The "discovery" of Chichén Itzá in the mid-nineteenth century by a handful of explorers and amateur archaeologists territorialized a piece of Yucatán's overgrown bush into a site ripe for the scientific and popular imaginations. This proto-archaeological site is the second territory of Chichén Itzá. It chronologically overlaps with the Hacienda Chichén Itzá. Sosa Arce held title to the hacienda when proto-archaeologist, writer, and explorer John Lloyd Stephens visited, accompanied by illustrator Frederick Catherwood. Having already distinguished his career through the "discovery" of Maya sites in Central America, most notably Copán in Honduras, Stephens continued his explorations into Yucatán with the objective of "finding who were the people who built these ruins" (Von Hagen 1947: 221).

The volumes of Stephens's writings, including *Incidents of Travel in Yucatán* (1843), give accounts of the ruins—accompanied by Catherwood's quasi–magical realist drawings of them—and the conditions of the peninsula at the time. Though the ruins of Chichén Itzá were much collapsed and overgrown, the site could hardly have been mistaken as lost or desolate. According to Stephens's account, the ruins of Chichén were not occupied by a resident population, though people from the surrounding settlements frequented the site.

Stephens portrays the residents at Pisté as bothersome, annoying, and unwelcome intruders at Chichén Itzá as they came to draw water for everyday use from the Sacred Cenote. The travelers were particularly bothered by the presence of the locals from Pisté during bathing hours, as Stephens recounts: "Upon one occasion we were so annoyed by the presence of two ladies of that village who seemed determined not to go away, that we were obliged to come to an amicable understanding by means of a preemptory notice that all persons must give us the benefit of their absence at that hour" (1843/1963: 185).

The explorers' predicament is, at least on its surface, humorous. Yet it carries a deep and even disturbing irony when we place this episode in a broader historical and ideological context. Here again, we have contemporary Maya appearing as an unruly and anachronistic intrusion on the foreigners' experience of the ruins. Especially interesting is how this narrative overlaps and fuses together two distinct acts of inappropriateness at the Sacred Cenote. In Stephens's brief, almost off-hand anecdote we have the bodily anachronism of the contemporary Maya with the act of exploitation of Chichén's resources (in this case, the water of the Sacred Cenote) bundled together into a singular problem: that of the maintenance of a proper relationship between exploration, intrusive local inhabitants (especially from Pisté), and the resources, both cultural and natural, of Chichén Itzá.

Maya access to resources does not, however, lurk only in the subtext of the *Incidents of Travel* narrative. While Stephens generally portrays the Maya as gregarious, nonthreatening opportunists, he does occasionally note the acute socioeconomic circumstances under which some appear as downtrodden and desperate. This impression is not surprising, given the social unrest exacerbated by agricultural hardships—failure of subsistence corn crops—of the decade preceding Stephens's visit.

The travelers' arrival at the Hacienda Chichén in 1842 makes local circumstances clear: the resident workers were about to pack up and leave in search of affordable corn to replace lost subsistence crops. The entrance of the cash-bearing foreigners halted the servants' exodus: "Our arrival . . . arrested this movement; instead of our being obliged to hunt them up, the poor Indians crowded round the door of our hut, begging employment" (187). Stephens conveys the plight of Maya at Chichén Itzá presciently: the crisis was far from isolated in either time or space. Famine was spreading throughout the peninsula, and it was not the first time. In fact, what Stephens and Catherwood observed at Chichén Itzá in 1842 was just a small glimpse of the social and economic unrest cited by historians and others as key factors contributing to Yucatán's Guerra de las Castas, or Caste War.

Beginning in 1847, the Caste War engulfed most of the Yucatán Peninsula. The struggle pitted indigenous Maya against the white Hispanic or hispanicized ruling class, though the conflict's causes reveal much more than ethnic strife. Indeed, the Caste War was fought over deep socioeconomic inequality. The Maya resistance called for the right to customary communal and public domain lands being lost to privatization, the reduction of obligatory tax contributions to church and state, and the forced condition of debt servitude as it was increasingly practiced on haciendas throughout the peninsula. In the early years of conflict, the Maya resistance met with sporadic success, though it did manage to territorialize whole portions of the peninsula out of state control.[1]

For the decades following the outbreak of the Caste War, Chichén Itzá mediated a de facto boundary between secure territory—that occupied by federal troops—and rebel territory. It should not be surprising, then, that mid- to late-nineteenth-century explorations of the ruins were affected by the politics and violence of the Caste War. Explorers Desiré Charnay, visiting in 1859 and 1887, and Augustus Le Plongeon in 1875 were supplied with armed escorts in their expeditions—Charnay to photograph the ruins and Le Plongeon to excavate them.

At the time of Le Plongeon's first visit, from November 1875 to January 1876, the area around Chichén Itzá was controlled by the Chan Santa Cruz (otherwise known as the Cruzob) Maya, one of the battling factions in Yucatán's Caste War. Before arriving with military escort at the ruins, Le Plongeon and his party, including his wife, Alice, passed through the town of Pisté. Desmond and Messenger (1988: 27) narrate the party's arrival scene:

> There, nestled around a cenote, they saw the remains of what had been a pretty village ten years earlier. On election Sunday 1865 the peaceful beauty of the village with its thatch-roofed houses, citrus trees, and kitchen gardens had been shaken by an attack of the Chan Santa Cruz Maya. They came to avenge anyone they thought had cooperated with their enemy, the government. The village was destroyed that day, and only a few of its residents, taking refuge in the bush, escaped the terrible machete blows.

Pisté's colonial church was handily converted into a military fortress to house government soldiers fighting the Cruzob Maya. Augustus and Alice used the church and Pisté as their headquarters, traveling daily back and forth to the ruins on foot. It appears that the hacienda was uninhabited at this time, most likely abandoned due to the continuing strife of the Caste War. Although *A Dream of Maya* (Desmond and Messenger 1988) mentions local Maya hired to clear paths to the ruins for Le Plongeon, this source does not indicate from where they came, although it is likely that they lived nearby.

The activities—or antics—of Le Plongeon at Chichén prompted an early custodial issue over the site and thus add a new legal dimension to Chichén as its second territory, a proto-archaeological site. In the course of his explorations at the site, Le Plongeon found the reclining statue—the Chacmool—a now-famous image of Chichén Itzá. This discovery initiated a series of events forming the first publicly documented dispute over the custodianship or stewardship of archaeological heritage at Chichén. Several months after finding the figure, Le Plongeon had it moved to the church in Pisté for safeguarding when he and Alice were forced to leave Pisté and Chichén following a local Maya revolt. Fearing uprisings from any armed Maya, the government ordered the disarmament of the soldiers who had belonged to the attachment protecting and assisting Le Plongeon at Chichén. Le Plongeon had the Chacmool transported on a wheeled platform a little more than two kilometers from the site to a hiding place closer to town.

Upon returning to Mérida, Le Plongeon solicited President Sebastian Lerdo de Tejada for permission to bring the statue to the American Centennial Exhibition in Philadelphia. This request initiated an interesting test case of the standing federal law on the nation's custodianship of cultural patrimony. Tejada cited an 1827 law, one of the earliest examples of post-Independence patrimony legislation, that specifically prohibited the export of artifacts from the country. The law did not apply, however, to collecting practices: the legislation provided no ban on the private ownership of archaeological materials. Desmond and Messenger (1988: 42) explain the legal complexities of the Chacmool case:

> Le Plongeon felt that he should at least receive some redress for the amount of money and labor it took to uncover the Chacmool. And, as he pointed out, they had found the piece in disputed territory. At the time, Chichén Itzá was not under control of the Mexican or Yucatecan governments, but in rebel territory. Furthermore, a law of Yucatan specifically stated that objects of value for the sciences and arts could be purchased at a just price from the finder, essentially acknowledging individual ownership of the object.

Le Plongeon did, however, export smaller artifacts to display at the exposition that were subsequently purchased in the United States by Stephen Salisbury III, director of the American Antiquarian Society. Le Plongeon and his wife returned to Chichén Itzá in 1883 to carry on further excavations, focusing their work on the Platform of Venus and the High Priest's Tomb.

Desmond and Messenger (1988) suggest that perhaps Salisbury's stumbling upon Le Plongeon's artifacts motivated the collector to send to Chichén Itzá an American amateur archaeological emissary, Edward H. Thompson. Thompson's involvement in Chichén Itzá marks a pivotal moment in a chain of events from the mid-nineteenth century through the twentieth that have shaped not only the specific ownership and custodianship arrangements of site itself, but national cultural heritage policy more generally.

Edward Thompson and the Scandal of Ownership

Without foreshadowing the infamy later to befall him, Edward H. Thompson (1857–1935) came to Yucatán in 1885 as the American consul to Mexico for the states of Yucatán and neighboring Campeche. Little more than an amateur enthusiast, Thompson was a self-proclaimed archaeologist, taking an active interest in the prehispanic resources of the region. Thompson's appointment was the result of a calculating collusion between Stephen Salisbury of the American Antiquarian Society, who had previously supported the explorations of Chichén Itzá by Augustus Le Plongeon, the Peabody Museum at Harvard University, and high-level politicians including Massachusetts Senator George F. Hoar and U.S. President Grover Cleveland.[2] Thompson (1932/1965: 18) recalls his surprise and delight when the consular appointment was offered to him at a dinner party:

> After dinner my host [Salisbury] . . . informed me that the American Antiquarian Society and the Peabody Museum of Cambridge desired to have certain ruined groups on the peninsula of Yucatan scientifically investigated and that they had chosen me to be the investigator. At the request of Senator Hoar, I was told, the President of the United States had agreed to appoint me an American consul to Mexico, my post being the states of Yucatan and Campeche, in order that my plans and my position might be on a surer basis. Mr. Salisbury then asked me if I would accept the appointment. It was an unnecessary question.

Upon Thompson's arrival in Yucatán with his wife and baby, he immediately took up his mandate for scientific exploration of ancient Maya ruins, though Chichén Itzá was not his first choice for investigation. He eschewed the two major known sites, Chichén Itzá and Uxmal, because "the latter had been worked over for a century and Chichén Itzá since the arrival of the Spaniards" (100). He instead chose Labná, "not only an important group of ruins, but virgin field" (ibid.).[3] Always on the lookout for lesser-known or unknown sites, Thompson followed up his Labná expedition with the exploration of nearby Xkichmook, dubbed by him "The Hidden City" (116). Following the rumors of native informants, Thompson made several failed attempts to locate Xkichmook before locating the group and carrying out a survey for the Field Museum in Chicago.[4]

In time, Thompson came to Chichén Itzá, which shortly became the scene of his crime. He narrates this decision:

> After I had visited and studied many of the ruined cities of Yucatan I concluded that Chichen Itzá was to be the scene of my life-work. In pursuance of this plan I later purchased a great abandoned plantation including within its boundaries that ancient capital and sacred city of the Mayas. (191)

Thompson purchased the Hacienda Chichén Itzá on July 29, 1895, from Delio Moreno Cantón, Emilio García Fajardo, and Leopoldo Cantón. The registered size of the property was eight hundred hectares, enough to include most of the large monumental structures tourists encounter when visiting Chichén Itzá today. Thompson purchased the nonfunctioning and barely habitable hacienda for three hundred pesos, an outrageously low price due to the instability in the region brought about by the Caste War.

Social unrest in and around Chichén Itzá played a role in the explorations of Le Plongeon two decades earlier and provide an important context to Thompson's as well. From the point of view of white Yucatecs and federal authorities, the southern and eastern parts of the peninsula were decidedly unsafe. Many portions of the peninsula including Chichén Itzá and its environs were not well within the perimeter marking the territory firmly under the control of Mexican federal troops even after several decades.[5] Thompson's book-length account of his time in Yucatán, *People of the Serpent* (1932/1965), is rife with references to the "Sublevados," or unpacified rebel Maya continuing to battle the Caste War. The references are so numerous as to lead a reader to wonder at the balance between real threat and, perhaps, paranoia. Thompson narrates to T. A. Willard (1926: 17), "A certain residue of Indians were never conquered by the Spaniards, nor have they ever been subdued by the government. . . . They are called Sublevados and I have been warned ever since I came to Chichén Itzá that some day the Sublevados would go on the war-path and wipe me and my hacienda clean off the map." In a retrospective piece entitled "Forty Years of Research in Yucatán," Thompson (1929: 42–43) narrates his early encounters with the Hacienda Chichén Itzá:

> [Upon arriving in Yucatán] I found that the old plantation of Chichén, founded in 1681, destroyed by the Sublevado Mayas in 1847 and since then abandoned, could be purchased. By the aid of Mr. Salisbury and Mr. [Allison V.] Armour I purchased the plantation, rebuilt the plantation, rebuilt the plantation house and outbuildings, adding modern improvements, peopled the plantation with servants, stocked it with fine cattle and then, not only made it my scientific home and that of my friends but from the sales of cattle and fine timber, commenced to materially aid in the financing of my archaeological undertakings.[6]

Thus Thompson was able to settle into the hacienda and the ruins, finding peace enough to carry out his investigation.

In 1891 Thompson was officially granted an indefinite leave of absence from his consular post so that he might take charge of "a scientific work of great importance" (*Worcester Daily Telegraph*, October 31, 1911). He was thus able to devote himself full-time to his archaeological work. However, a correspondence from Thompson to Stephen Salisbury Jr. of April 6, 1895,[7] indicates that he had not yet begun any excavation work at the site: "At present I am doing nothing directly in the way of research but am rather furthering the hacienda and getting everything ready for continuous accurate work when everything is ripe."

When Thompson's invasive exploration and excavation began in earnest following his period of preparation, questions arose regarding the legality of his activities. The most contentious of Thompson's activities at Chichén Itzá involved his exploration of the Sacred Cenote. The cenote had long been a draw for explorers and others at Chichén Itzá. Friar Diego de Landa reported in his Conquest-era *Relación de las cosas de Yucatán* (a text that enthralled Thompson), that the Maya would use the cenote as a repository for sacrificial objects, raising the hope that if gold were to be found in the peninsula, the deep, murky waters would be a likely resting place (Tozzer 1941). Charnay attempted to excavate the cenote in 1881, but the practical obstacles were too great for him to achieve any success.

Thompson describes how the Sacred Cenote became his "obsession":

> The thought of that grim old water pit and the wonderful objects that lay concealed within its depths became an obsession with me. . . . For days and weeks after I purchased the plantation, I was a frequent worshipper at the little shrine on the brink of the Sacred Well. I pondered, mused, and calculated. I made measurements and numberless soundings, until, not satisfied but patiently expectant, I put my notebook aside and awaited the accepted time. (1932/1965: 269)

But the proper time for Thompson's exploration of the cenote could not come until he had the funds and other support to realize this major undertaking. Backed by Stephen Salisbury and Charles Bowditch, another member of the board of the American Antiquarian Society, as well as Harvard University, Thompson was able to put his plans into action. In 1904 Thompson began the first in a series of attempts to dredge the Sacred Cenote. Another attempt was begun in 1905 and continued until 1909. When dredging proved unsatisfactory, Thompson donned a diving suit. Over the course of these attempts, Thompson recovered "objects of great scientific interest, earthen vessels, temple vases and incense burners . . . disks of beaten copper covered with symbolical elements and the conventionalized figures of the Maya deities, bells, and pendent figures of low-grade gold, beads . . . and fragments of jade," not to mention skeletal remains of "young women, [and] of thick-skulled, low-browed men" (1932/1965: 275). It is impossible to know either the quality or quantity of the objects Thompson recovered, as most were smuggled out of Mexico to institutions including the Peabody Museum or into private collections. Some of the artifacts recovered during this exploration are displayed at the on-site museum at Chichén Itzá, as is the dredge itself.[8]

According to standing Mexican law, the export of artifacts during the years of Thompson's cenote excavation was illegal. But this matter of legislative fact does little to shed light upon the complexities of perception and enforcement surrounding Thompson's activities at Chichén. What is more interesting than the law itself here is how different laws, justifications, and ethical understandings are brought to bear upon the Thompson case as the meaning and significance of national cultural patrimony shifts and takes new shape following the Mexican Revolution.

The cenote project was certainly not carried out under a veil of secrecy. Sponsors, colleagues, hired workers, visitors, and no doubt others knew about the cenote project. Why, then, would this not hit the regional newspapers for nearly two decades after the initiation of the cenote excavation? A look at the historical socioeconomic context of Thompson's ownership of Chichén Itzá gives us several clues as to why it was not until the early 1920s that a public outcry arose. In prerevolutionary days, as the hacendado of record, Thompson was quite protected in regard to his private-domain activities. At the time of his dredging projects, the white (though mostly Yucatec) hacendados formed the economic and political elite of Yucatán. Though most of the powerful hacienda owners were associated with the export-oriented henequen haciendas in the northwestern part of the state, the sway of these so-called Henequen Kings showed the untouchable status of private landowners across the region. With the adoption of the postrevolutionary 1917 Constitution, however, national patrimony—whether land, other natural resources, or even cultural heritage—became a more clearly defined issue. Specifically, Article 27 stipulates the eminent domain of the nation over national territories and waters, with a clause for direct domain over subsoil deposits, including artifacts. When put into effect this would later come to work in the favor of landless or land-poor Mayas across the peninsula; it also worked to provide a new discourse concerned with the preservation of the patrimony of the Mexican nation.

Reported in the Mexican press in the early 1920s, Thompson's excavation was publicly denounced as "looting." The outrage at the loss of Mexican cultural patrimony that ensued could not have been less concerned with the pedigree of Thompson's backing nor with the scientific merits of his work. A Mérida newspaper, *La Prensa*, on May 27, 1921, featured an article with the headline "Is Mr. Edward Thompson the legitimate owner of Chichén?". The charges made and issues raised in the piece boil down to the question that naturally arises from the curious legislative arrangement that treats monuments as distinct from the land upon which they sit: simply put, how can someone own archaeological ruins if they are the property of the nation?

The 1921 newspaper column points out the contradictions of ownership at Chichén: If anyone should have access to the land surrounding the monuments, the anonymous author points out, the legal usufruct rights should belong to the federal land-grant holders from Pisté.[9] Escalating the charges of impropriety at Chichén, the article further questions the legitimacy of the boundaries of the hacienda as expropriated under Article 27, finding it not likely, if at all possible, that Chichén's monuments would all fall within the perimeter of the *pequeña propiedad*, that parcel of land protected from distribution to ejido claims. It would seem, then, that Thompson was exploiting Chichén's resources without usufruct rights. Based on the limits imposed on the extent of property a hacienda owner might retain after ejido expropriation, there was simply no way that Thompson still legally held all of the monuments at Chichén Itzá.

In Thompson's defense, however, one might argue that his excavation work and the dredging of the Sacred Cenote gave fame to Chichén Itzá and attracted many visitors to the site in the early twentieth century, including Mexican President Porfirio Díaz in 1906,[10] as well as Inspector General de Monumentos Leopoldo Batres (Olivé Negrete 1991: 120). Thompson's arrangement with the Peabody Museum undoubtedly gave rise to Sylvanus G. Morley's early interest in the Maya during his years of study at Harvard University, possibly serving as the link between Chichén and the Carnegie Institution of Washington's subsequent major research project at the site. Thompson claimed that he was forced to abandon Chichén in 1921 due to a political situation in which local Maya led by the Socialist Party attempted to reclaim lands and set the Hacienda Chichén on fire in the process. Thompson (1932/1965: 298) offers his embittered perspective on the incident:

> During one of the revolutions which have ravaged the country within the last twenty years, the plantation was visited by emissaries of radically Socialist stripe who sought to teach the disgruntled spirits of the region that all things were theirs, that it was their right and privilege to seize for their own use whatever belonged to the ruling class. During this period my plantation house was burned with all it contained.

He and his family lost many valuable possessions, including items of historical significance, at the hands of "Mexican outlaws and bandits" (*New York Times* 1921).

As Olivé Negrete (1991: 120) argues, it is quite probable that this incident at Chichén did not in itself constitute a singular crisis to the Thompson estate. Indeed, Thompson was already embroiled in defending his rights to the exclusive proprietorship of Chichén's monuments against the Mexican national body governing archaeological activities, the Dirección de Antropología. The author further reports that Thompson offered to sell the land and the monuments to the Dirección de Antropología, which at the time was under the supervision of Manuel Gamio. The offer was of course refused by the government agency. A legal document (RPP Oficio número 541) details Mexico's legal position contra Thompson, who attempted to justify the work that he had done at Chichén Itzá as the property owner since 1894, prefiguring the Ley Especial of 1897.

Lucio Mendieta y Nuñez, a lawyer and student of Gamio, argued that the legislative precedents of the nation's claim to jurisdiction over archaeological ruins predated the nation itself. Mendieta y Nuñez began with the Spanish colonial Leyes de Indias, which formalized the Crown's dominion over the entirety of the territory of New Spain (Olivé Negrete 1991: 121). Through various forms of land distribution, the Crown ceded certain parcels of land:

> One might say that the archaeological ruins in the lands transformed from the patrimony of the Crown into private ownership were ceded by the royalty to the private property owners. However, this is not the case. Though the Crown distributed land . . . the royalty reserved their rights over ownership of the archaeological monuments. (Ibid.: 121–122)

While Thompson furnished a document of property title dated 1729, Mendieta y Nuñez argued that the law prohibiting the transfer of monuments to private hands dated back to 1575. Even from the time of the first owner of the hacienda, the archaeological monuments did not belong to this person: *no eran susceptibles de formar parte de dominio privado: estaban fuera de comercio* (they were not subject to incorporation into the private domain: they were outside of commerce) (122).

Thompson publicly disclosed his activities in smuggling the artifacts from the Sacred Cenote to the United States in an admission in a *New York Times* article in 1923. Yet an investigation by Mexican authorities into the matter was not begun until July 1926. Workers from Thompson's crew, hacienda workers, and residents from Pisté and Xcalacoop were asked to testify. A key witness was Juan Olalde, who had moved to Yucatán from San Miguel de Allende as a young man and found employment at Chichén as a foreman of Thompson's hacienda.

Officials questioned Olalde as to his possible role as an accomplice to Thompson's activities. He admitted his observations of the dredging and the packing of objects for transport but denied having any role in selling artifacts. He claimed, reported the *Diario de Yucatán* of September 18, 1926, that Thompson explained to him that the pieces from the Sacred Cenote were destined for two museums in Mexico. It was only later that Olalde, along with everyone else, came to discover that they left the country.

In a judicial inquiry, witnesses were asked to describe what they had seen during the Sacred Cenote exploration—how the dredging or diving suit methods worked (or did not) and what kinds of finds they witnessed. More than one person claimed to have witnessed nothing, but others, including a man who made his milpa nearby, got an eyeful. Pablo Tun was not permitted to get too close to the operation. He confirmed that many objects emerged from the cenote, although he was unable to distinguish the details of these objects due to the distance from his perspective. Faustino Tun observed Thompson and a group of assistants operating the dredge. He reported to investigating officials that in the initial stages of the extraction of artifacts from the cenote, they were placed around the opening's perimeter. After Thompson realized that his activities were under the observation of many locals, Tun reported, he began to conceal all finds inside bags. Faustino Tun reported having seen human skeletons and what looked like, though he was not sure, a large piece of gold.

Pending the settlement of charges of looting and illegally exporting artifacts removed from the Sacred Cenote, the Mexican government confiscated the hacienda. Looking for a sympathetic audience to his plight, Thompson humbled himself in a response published in the *Boston Globe* on October 25, 1926:

> If, as I am told, Mexico has seized my plantation, "Chichén," in reprisal for what I have done for science, so let it be. I am ready to make this sacrifice if need be . . . I should have been false in my duty as an archaeologist had I, believing that the scientific treasures were at the bottom of the sacred well, failed to improve the opportunity and attempt to bring them to light and thus make them available to scientific study instead of lying embedded in the mud and useless to the world. I hold it to be self-evident that these finds, taken from the Sacred Well, do not belong to any one Nation of this New World. They are part of prehistory and it may be that from them will come facts linking this New World with the old. It is unthinkable that these scientific objects be subjected to eventualities.[11]

Thompson's death in 1935 brought on a new phase to the penal action sought by Mexico that had remained unresolved until then: an extended legal argument that brought previous cultural patrimony legislation and the very Constitution itself into question. In 1943 the Mexican Supreme

Court ruled in favor of Thompson because of a curious omission in Article 27 of the 1917 Constitution that protected *subsoil* deposits as national patrimony yet did not take into account *subaquatic* materials such as the artifacts dredged from the Sacred Cenote.

Further complicating the Mexican case against Thompson was the question of the "monumentality" of the Sacred Cenote itself. At the time, legislation was directed toward monumental, built archaeological heritage. The Sacred Cenote is a natural topographical feature rather than a humanly built prehispanic monument. A memorandum issued by the INAH in 1943 to the Supreme Court argued that indeed the Sacred Cenote was monumental built heritage. The INAH justified this conclusion in the following manner: Although the formation of a cenote is a natural topographic feature, basically a sinkhole, the cenote at Chichén Itzá was altered by the site's ancient inhabitants through construction of a platform from which to make sacrifices. The memo went on to suggest that the presence of cultural materials below the waters of the cenote also indicates human alteration of the site. Thus, the cenote was a cultural feature rather than a strictly natural one. This argument is logical, compelling, and, by today's definitions of cultural heritage resources, sound. Nevertheless, the Supreme Court manifested its support for property laws over and above the less-anchored realm of heritage policy by eventually ruling in Thompson's favor.

Not since this court case played out more than sixty years ago have issues of ownership or usufruct at Chichén Itzá been so explicitly discussed, debated, or contested. As we move through the Thompson years into the next phase of private sector intervention in the site, it is important to keep this irony in mind. During Thompson's time at Chichén Itzá, the site was not highly developed and not systematically exploited in terms of the variety and extent of its cultural resource potential, and ownership of the nearly uninhabitable hacienda and barely accessible ruins frankly did not represent a great deal of either economic or cultural capital. We will see that as each of these circumstances dramatically moves in the reverse direction—in short, as Chichén becomes a more valuable resource whose economic potential is held in greater concentration by a single private concern—issues of both the ethics and economics of proprietorship become less, and less publicly, contested.

We could say that the Thompson scandal marks Chichén Itzá as a particular kind of representational space, in this case a space made representational of and for Mexican nationalism. This is the first significant step that the state took to embrace Chichén Itzá as national cultural heritage.

As food for thought, we might ask ourselves why the Thompson case stands as a singularly important battle over the private ownership of Chichén. Was it because his activities were so blatantly destructive to the architectural or scientific integrity of the site? Was it because someone realized the sheer economic value of Chichén's artifactual treasures? Or were Thompson's rights of ownership and usufruct called into question in the public arena of the media and judicial system because he was not Mexican?

The Edward Thompson scandal is still remembered around Pisté and Chichén Itzá, though his name is not widely reviled, and is, ironically enough, often confused with that of Sir J. Eric S. Thompson, famed and revered Maya archaeologist of the mid-twentieth century. The Sacred Cenote carries the scars of these projects, the most visible an imposing cement platform sitting directly in the line of the tourist approach to the cenote. And its treasures are scattered widely: in the Peabody Museum at Harvard University, in private collections, and in various museum displays as well as basements. Many of the objects bought originally as "stolen" property of the Mexican nation have since converted in status to donated materials (Ruz Lhullier 1970: 46–47). The Sacred Cenote dredging projects are immortalized in photographs that today hang, incidentally, just outside the restrooms in the tourist entrance hall of Chichén Itzá.

EXPROPRIATION, REPRIVATIZATION, AND THE MAKING OF A MODERN ARCHAEOLOGICAL SITE

The period of Thompson's ownership of Chichén Itzá signals a more intense convergence of the three overlapping territories I have already described: as a privately owned land tract, a hacienda; as a proto-archaeological site; and as a land and water resource for the local Maya population. In the first decades of the twentieth century, the archaeological riches of Chichén Itzá became better known; the cattle hacienda changed private hands and became a new economic unit (an "archaeological hacienda," if you will); and local Maya populations begin to be converted into a workforce used to exploit the site as an archaeological and touristic resource. As the century unfolds, these territories become more fused and confused, yet I think it is important to keep their genealogies distinct as we move toward assessing privatization at Chichén Itzá in the present period. Here I focus more on the land of the site than on the ruins. Later I will do the same in my spatial analysis of heritage practice at the site of Chunchucmil. This somewhat counterintuitive approach to the analysis of heritage per se shifts our focus from one concerned with things in space to an analysis of the production of space of the site itself.

Beginning in the 1920s, great postrevolutionary land-reform movements swept Mexico and in the latter part of the decade reached southern and eastern Yucatán. Bit by bit over the course of several decades, pieces of the Hacienda Chichén Itzá were expropriated from private ownership to create ejidos for the surrounding Maya settlements.[12] Expropriation was a long, legally complicated, and contestable process, particularly when a private landowner had considerable economic resources for hiring of legal representation and ties to the political elite.

The expropriation of the Hacienda Chichén Itzá is at least as complicated as most, if not more so. Edward H. Thompson remained the hacienda's owner of record until the mid-1930s, though it is evident from public archives that Thompson was physically absent. He appears to have been the owner of the hacienda until his death in 1935 and even beyond, as a document dated 1947 still lists Thompson as the proprietor of the Hacienda Chichén Itzá (CAM-RAN, Exp. 726 San Felipe extension). From the mid-1920s until that time, José Casares Martínez de Arredondo, an attorney for Thompson, repeatedly protested the expropriation of the hacienda property. In a letter of November 21, 1928, Casares Martínez, on behalf of his client, the "exiled" owner of record, argued against the expropriation of a parcel of land belonging to the hacienda:

> The ejido grant which purports to affect the lands which belong to the hacienda Chichén Itzá and annexes under the ownership of my client Edward H. Thompson, in extension of 1,521 hectares, 48 ares. As this land grant is completely illegal, I plan to challenge it by means of this memorandum before the local Agrarian Commission, in order to resolve that this affectation shall not proceed. (CAM-RAN Exp. 205)[13]

The lawyer went on to argue that the amount of land requested by the residents of Ticimul is excessive and that his client's property rights were in danger of being violated. Why, he asked, was the hacienda property a target for expropriation when there were abundant *terrenos nacionales*, federal lands, in the area? Agrarian authorities from Ticimul had previously requested enough land to create fifty-two-hectare land parcels for each of fifty-five eligible farmers from their community.

The records of the ejido grants for a number of communities as well as those on file with the Registro Público de Propiedad demonstrate considerable confusion regarding the amount of property that Thompson actually held under the title to Hacienda Chichén Itzá and Annexes. A report dated November 21, 1934, concerning the grant to create the ejido of Xkatun states that:

in itself the hacienda has a far greater size, as its American owner Edward H. Thompson was acquiring lands, purchasing them at laughable prices or denouncing them as abandoned or uncultivated. These lands were then annexed to the main hacienda, without reporting to the Public Property Records office. (CAM-RAN Exp. Xkatun)[14]

The confusion over the size of the property, exacerbated by the dubious ownership status of the lands of the Hacienda Chichén Itzá—i.e., did it still belong to Edward Thompson?—was of great advantage to one Yucatec businessman. Fernando Barbachano Peón, a wealthy entrepreneur of the Mérida elite, had an eye for the touristic possibilities of the peninsula as early as the 1920s. In 1932 Barbachano Peón purchased two hectares of the hacienda from Thompson's estate for the price of two hundred pesos (RPP Folio 385, Tomo 2B). Upon this small parcel of land, Barbachano, in the absence of Thompson or apparently anyone else who was going to stop him, had already begun construction on the Mayaland Hotel in 1930. This was the first in a series of purchases by Barbachano and his descendants, family members, and associates of various lots comprising a large portion of Chichén Itzá.[15]

By the mid-1930s—and not insignificantly coinciding with Barbachano's interest in purchasing land—a particular part of the Hacienda Chichén Itzá began to be identified in the ejido records and maps as an archaeological zone. From this time on, the areas of monument concentration took on a special status, and efforts were made to identify these areas as needing protective measures. Perhaps the most explicit statement of the early importance of the ownership of the land containing the archaeological ruins, an area defined as a 48-hectare nucleus, is found in the request for a second extension to be granted to the ejido of Xcalacoop in 1954. Xcalacoop had already received 643 hectares in the original ejido grant on March 26, 1935, to which were added 432 hectares as a first extension on August 26, 1942. With an increasing population and lack of land resources, the ejido community filed a request for the second extension, a typical procedure for growing ejido communities, especially in this area of the peninsula.

Barbachano strongly protested the extension, arguing that it would invade the monument zone of the property. Exactly what part of Chichén would be affected by the Xcalacoop ejido extension? Portions to the east and south of the former Casa Principal of the hacienda on which are found "key monuments of national and international importance, among them those which form Chichén Viejo and the Three Lintels," areas he said must remain "absolutely clean . . . inasmuch as it interests their conservation for tourism and so that these archaeologically valuable things not be destroyed" (CAM-RAN Exp. 797, October 21, 1954). The same document expresses Barbachano's "desire to cooperate in the conservation and maintenance in the best conditions of the zones of Yucatán in which archaeological monuments are found, for the interests of the nation and the state in the archaeological monuments that attract both the scientific world as well as national and foreign tourism."

A memorandum of April 14, 1954, to the Comisión Agraria Mixta in Mérida from the commission's own surveyor leans toward supporting Barbachano for the sake of protecting the archaeological monuments. The memo supports the designation of the 48-hectare site nucleus, stating that even the surrounding land is covered with monuments, all of which were being damaged by agricultural practices. Arguing in favor of the hotel owner, the memo stated that well before Xcalacoop's request for the second ejido extension, Barbachano had filed for a *solicitud de inafectabilidad ganadera*—a petition for a twenty-five-year concession on a larger piece of property for the purpose of raising cattle. Barbachano requested the concession with the principal objective of saving the archaeological monuments (CAM-RAN Exp. 719).

Concessions were granted if the property owner met the following requirements: he had at least two hundred head of cattle; the cattle-raising was for business purposes; and the land in question was in an area where the agrarian needs of nearby population centers were already satisfied or if other lands were available for grants within a seven-kilometer radius. The benefits of this kind of concession are obvious: once the concession was granted, the land could not be expropriated; and further, the land concessions were much larger than the limits set on pequeñas propiedades that landholders were allowed to keep upon expropriation.

Barbachano came into some luck when land reform moved away from granting large, collective ejidos to encouraging the establishment and growth of small private landholdings. The Agrarian Code of 1942 came just in time for Barbachano to legally increase the size of his pequeña propiedad. The Agrarian Code set the maximum size of such concessions between three hundred hectares for the highest-quality land and five thousand hectares for the lowest-quality land.[16] This rule allowed for some flexibility. The judgments as to the quality of the land (which, in ratio with number of head of cattle, determined the legal size of the land concession) were most likely made on an ad hoc basis, the results of which were easily manipulated.

Adding to this fluidity in determining concession size was the clause in the 1942 Agrarian Code stating that a petitioner could request twice as much land as necessary for the cattle held at the time of the original request. Clearly, the amounts of land that could be controlled through this concession system were much greater than the more rigid national restrictions on the small property holdings retained by hacienda owners after expropriations, as per the constitution. Before the 1942 reform, an expropriated hacienda transformed into a small private holding could not legally exceed 150 hectares of irrigated land (*riego*) or 300 hectares of rain-fed land (*temporal*).[17] Barbachano's application for a concession of inafectabilidad ganadera effectively allowed him to increase the size of his landholding, though precisely how much is difficult to say.

The same memorandum concerning Barbachano Peón's control of Chichén's site center posed the wealthy businessman as a steward of cultural patrimony: "Señor Barbachano Peón with the objective of avoiding as much as possible the disappearance and destruction of the meritorious monuments, has acquired, at high cost, the property of the *finca* [ranch] Halakal in exchange." Barbachano, circumventing state or national agrarian officials, had proposed a deal to the local farmers. Barbachano offered a land swap deal to Xcalacoop that the ejidatarios eventually accepted: he purchased 158 hectares of land known as Halakal, five kilometers northeast of Xcalacoop, and gave it to Xcalacoop in exchange for the ejido's concession of any lands within the 48-hectare monument zone.[18] Ejidatarios of Xcalacoop, savvy about looking out for their own interests, initially protested. Halakal was an inconvenient distance from town and the land was *monte bajo*, low scrubland of poor quality. Much to his own benefit, Barbachano finally did reach an agreement with the ejidatarios of Xcalacoop "that of the Hacienda Chichén Itzá only 410 hectares were to be affected, only in the area indicated through mutual agreement" (CAM-RAN Exp. 719). The arrangement and the ejido extension were officially approved on May 14, 1955 (CAM-RAN Exp. 797).

Despite the astonishing amount of archaeological, touristic, and economic development at Chichén, this land swap is one example of how, just decades ago, the presence of archaeological monuments did not factor significantly for all parties in the negotiation of landholding or value. Through a well-executed legal maneuver, the site has remained in the Barbachano family for more than fifty years. It is difficult to say precisely how much land came into the hands of the Barbachano family and remained after several decades of expropriation of the Hacienda Chichén Itzá. Not only is the archival trail itself muddy, but so is the large size of the original hacienda property, the deliberate falsification of this size, and the number of interests (mostly family members and heirs) in getting a piece of the hacienda, all of which complicate the case dramatically.

An additional complicating factor is Thompson's ownership and the claims of his heirs. It was not until 1951 (RPP, Folio 167, Libro 1, Tomo 10-B) that a document cited the names of Thompson's descendants as heirs of a portion of the former hacienda property. This document relates to the sale and transfer of eight hundred hectares to Fernando Barbachano Peón for US$10,000 from Edward J. Thompson, Ernest H. Thompson, Alice T. Fischer, and Margarita F. Diddel.[19] This document identifies the sale of "Chichén Itzá and annexes Yula, Xcatun, Xicatuna, totaling 800 hectares" to Fernando Barbachano Peón. This transaction initiated what is now a Barbachano family tourism empire stretching across the peninsula.

While considering the details of the hacienda expropriation is somewhat painstaking and laborious, they are important evidence of the legal, political, economic, and social registers inflecting the territory of the archaeological zone since the 1930s. Thus I found ejido records to be crucial sources in mapping the spatial genealogy of Chichén Itzá. This case study of hacienda expropriation, rather than an isolated process, is one that echoed and was repeated over several decades throughout Mexico. Ejido communities continue to battle land disputes among neighbors, often in very fraught contention. Detailed study of archival records thus becomes imminent critique. Second, in this case we see, perhaps for the first time, the presence of monuments articulated specifically to the character of a land parcel's "quality." Barbachano's land-swap deal to retain the monumental center of Chichén is a crucial moment in the commodifying of Maya monuments. Closely related to this is the third vital point: the calculating efforts of the elder Barbachano, whom we might justifiably call the first tourism entrepreneur of Yucatán, resulted in a new distinction between private and national property, and an infrastructure began to form that enabled other kinds of development, even the scientific development accomplished through archaeology, to follow. The effects of the hacienda expropriation resonate until today, and resonate deeply.

The Carnegie Institution Presence at Chichén

The purchase of Chichén Itzá by Fernando Barbachano Peón, the construction of the Hotel Mayaland and the Hotel Hacienda Chichén Itzá, and other tourism development efforts would have been relatively insignificant without the opening of Chichén Itzá to the possibilities of mass tourism through the reconstruction and restoration of large portions of the archaeological zone. The institution responsible for much of this is the Carnegie Institution of Washington. A scientific philanthropic organization, the CIW negotiated a concession contract with the Mexican federal government and initiated Project Chichén Itzá in 1924. According to Clause 1 of the contract between the Mexican government and the CIW:

> Permission is hereby granted to the Carnegie Institution of Washington—hereinafter designated the concessionaire—for carrying out archaeological explorations and excavations, as well as works necessary for reparation and reconstruction in the archaeological zone of Chichén Itzá, State of the Yucatán. In addition to the archaeological works, the concessionaire may effect in the State of Yucatan complementary studies of engineering, architecture, art, stratigraphy, physical anthropology, linguistic studies, history and in general any other studies relating to Maya civilization.

With "Father of Maya Archaeology" Sylvanus G. Morley at the helm, the CIW's Project Chichén Itzá thus began two decades of work based in Chichén. The project mapped, excavated, and reconstructed the ruins and interpreted and organized the entire landscape into a new representation of space, the product of a vision that combined the best science of the day with an aesthetic designed to highlight both the mystery and intelligibility of the ruins. In other words, alongside the desire to expand scientific knowledge of Chichén was the twin goal of "increasing area for the archaeological zone . . . with a view of making the region a very beautiful place" (CIW 1933: 1). The CIW and Morley carried out work at Chichén Itzá for more than twenty years.[20]

The CIW negotiated with the Mexican state to gain legal access to the site for the excavation and reconstruction work. But how did this scientific, nongovernmental agency negotiate the private-sector presence at Chichén? The CIW, well aware of its politically sensitive and delicate position in the Mexican national territory, did not neglect Thompson's ownership rights to the site at the outset of their project. The core members and constant stream of visitors stayed in the hacienda's Casa Principal, rented from Edward Thompson. The Carnegie project also battled with Edward Thompson over both the Casa Principal and the extensive hacienda property including Chichén's principal monuments.

Brunhouse (1971: 210) details the situation during the CIW's first years at the site as one of Thompson continually causing "headaches" for the project; the CIW agreed to pay Thompson a generous $1,200 a year rent for the use of the hacienda buildings and one hundred acres of land.

Upon receiving notice of an encumbrance on the property, the CIW went ahead and paid Thompson's delinquent taxes, all of this in efforts to not lose its presence in the archaeological zone.

This evidence prompts a couple of interpretations. First, it strongly suggests that the CIW relied upon Thompson's ownership to ensure its own physical presence within the site. After all, there was nowhere nearby for a whole crew to live, and the shade, comfort, and protection of indoor space was necessary for many of the activities of archaeological investigation. To put it simply, the only available buildings on or near the ruins were owned by Thompson. An alternative interpretation of the CIW's actions in relation to Thompson is a bit less obvious and perhaps less innocent when it comes to the question of private-sector intervention at Chichén Itzá.

In the description of the CIW's rental arrangement we can see that the CIW paid Thompson not only for the use of the buildings, but for the access and use of one hundred acres of land. This arrangement shows clear evidence that the juridical distinction between horizontal and vertical ownership, between the land and the monuments, did indeed play out. The CIW had permission to intervene in the monuments through the Mexican government; it had permission to access and move among the monuments through its rental agreement with Thompson. In effect, as a renting party, the CIW participated in the de facto privatization of Chichén Itzá.

After Fernando Barbachano began to purchase parcels of land pertaining to the Hacienda Chichén, it seems that archaeology worked comfortably hand in hand with private-sector entrepreneurship. This new landowner was, contrary to Thompson by this point, far richer in capital and soon improved the hacienda's buildings, converting them into the core of the Hotel Hacienda Chichén Itzá, and constructing new accommodations close by—the Mayaland Hotel. The CIW staff members are immortalized at contemporary Chichén. During the years of the CIW project, its staff lived in bungalows near the main house of the hacienda that were part of hacienda property, improved by CIW, and maintained by the Barbachano family since the 1930s. The pricey Hotel Hacienda Chichén now features the bungalows as individual villas, each named after an archaeologist or other figure associated with the excavations and reconstructions at the site. Guests may stay in, for example, the Earl Morris memorial bungalow.

Public Monuments, Private Land

As early as 1940, the state government of Yucatán planned the development of the zone with the cooperation of the SEP. Through the first

FIGURE 3.1. *Hacienda Chichén: The modern signage marking the cattle ranch turned luxury hotel adjacent to the archaeological zone. Photograph by author.*

decades of excavation and reconstruction, approximately 1926 to 1936, the Mexican agency Monumentos Prehispánicos, under the auspices of SEP, worked alongside the archaeologists of the CIW. While the CIW archaeologists worked to explore structures such as the Temple of the Warriors and the Caracol (the Observatory), Mexican archaeologists with the Prehispanic Monuments Department carried out work on the Castillo and the Ball Court. In 1936 the INAH was founded and subsequently took charge of administrating all work within the site.

Once reestablished as the sole purveyors of the site, how was the Mexican state going to negotiate the interests, plans, and demands of Chichén's private owner? Let's look more closely at the conditions of private ownership of archaeological sites. The archaeological sites of Uxmal, in the Puuc region of western Yucatán, and Chichén Itzá contain ruins and are owned by the Barbachano family. Legally, this form of ownership works in the following way: an archaeological zone may be situated on national lands, ejido lands, or privately owned property; surrounding land is distinguished from the monuments, and only the monuments themselves figure as national property housed under federal jurisdiction. Around each monument in a defined zone is a twenty-meter boundary marking the monument's buffer zone, which delimits the monument's primary sphere of influence. In certain heritage parlance this kind of a buffer zone is referred to as a "curtilage," the immediate area around a structure acting as an "envelope around the main item" (Aplin 2002: 122).

The curtilage is particularly important in archaeological heritage for two reasons. First, the notion that archaeological or historic monuments are part of an integrated cultural landscape has become more prevalent in recent decades. The second reason is that for archaeological investigation and site interpretation, it is important to protect areas surrounding monuments to help maintain their context and integrity. Beyond this twenty-meter perimeter, a private owner has control of the land. Thus, under current Mexican cultural patrimony legislation, private owners are not free to do whatever they please with land up to the monuments' buffer zones.

INAH regulations distinguish boundaries around a monument into two types of zones. Zone A refers to the monument's immediate perimeter; its exact width may vary. Inside Zone A, the near perimeter, land use is fully restricted to scientific investigations and other activities directly linked to maintenance and conservation. However, a provision allows for activities directly related to supplying basic services necessary to improving the monument zone (Sánchez Caero 1995: 195). In Zone B, the secondary perimeter, partial restrictions on land use are put into place. These internal zoning differentiations act as jurisdictional divisions as well, designating where private property lines end and federal zones begin.

What are private owners' responsibilities to monuments? Article 6 of the 1972 Ley Federal Sobre Monumentos y Zonas Arqueológicos, Artísticos e Históricos, as revised in 1995, states that the owner of an artistic or historic monument is obligated to conserve the monument; when an owner wants to restore a monument, the restoration must be carried out under INAH authority. Further, the owner of a property bordering a monument must have INAH permission to perform any excavation, consolidation, demolition, or construction projects in the area immediately surrounding the monument that might affect its "character."

Article 10 dictates that if a property owner is not properly carrying out conservation or restoration measures, the tasks may be taken over by INAH. Article 11 provides tax deductions and certain exemptions to property owners who undertake these responsibilities. Workers at Chichén Itzá have reported that the Barbachano family consistently maintains a cordial and cooperative relationship with the INAH, and very few locals were willing to criticize the Barbachano family, save the occasional reference to their wealth and power.

Through the middle decades of the twentieth century, the Mexican state deployed its multiple means of taking Chichén Itzá back, so to speak, from its occupation by foreigners. Most significant in establishing state authority at Chichén Itzá was a declaration of the site boundaries when it became an officially delimited archaeological zone in 1950.[21]

Through delimitation, cultural properties—artifacts and monuments—are marked and brought more visibly under the protection of federal cultural property laws. Delimitation under INAH auspices not only decides the boundaries of the archaeological zone but profoundly affects what the zone will contain and thus what gets marked or not marked for heritage status. In practical terms, "delimitation of an archaeological zone is the act of measuring what will be protected as evidence of prehispanic cultures" (Sánchez Caero 1995: 187). In our analysis, this change in legal status marks the coincidence of two kinds of representational space: Chichén as space representing Mexican nationalism, codified and territorialized by constitutional law governing the nation's patrimony, and Chichén as a political-economic space receptive to tourism. As these two representational spaces mapped onto each other, the newly established archaeological zone became a site for the emergence of new kinds of social relationships. I next turn to these.

LIVING IN RUINS

I have chronicled a series of different forms of ownership and development at Chichén Itzá and have noted that these varying interventions represent transformations in the production of space of the site and its environs. If the production of space is intimately tied to the field of social relations, as Lefebvre (1974/1991) suggests, then it is important to turn toward a closer examination of how the establishment of the archaeological zone in its present form affects local residential communities.

If the archaeological zone of Chichén Itzá were solely in the control of private interests, a range of potential effects at the local level might come into play: local residents' physical access to the site could be restricted; formal employment arrangements for federal INAH and state CULTUR employees could be disrupted; and the livelihoods of informal-sector workers who rely on the attraction of the archaeological zone could suffer.

At the present time, local people can fairly easily enter the archaeological zone without paying. Some cross the zone on bicycles each day going to and from jobs at the Mayaland Hotel. For residents of Pisté who work at Mayaland, transportation has to be carefully considered, as the Mérida-Cancún highway that connects the town and the hotel has no sidewalk or even shoulder and has dangerous blind curves that have claimed several bicyclists' lives over the years. While the Mayaland Hotel provides a shuttle bus to pick up employees in front of the *comisaria* (town hall) in the *centro* (business district) of Pisté at certain times each day, many other Mayaland employees travel by bicycle, and a few by taxi.[22]

Bicyclists often cut through the archaeological zone for reasons of safety as well as distance. The shortcut through the zone cuts a full kilometer from the trip from Pisté to the Mayaland. No formal permission system or permits accompany this right of passage through the zone. It relies on local practice and custom, and anyone who cuts through the zone on a bicycle had better be easily recognizable as a local to site wardens working inside the zone and at the Mayaland entrance ticket booth. Coming from Pisté, those who pass through avoid the main guest entrance, the *parador turístico*, and enter instead at the INAH *campamento*, an alternative entrance outside the property controlled by CULTUR (Patronato de las Unidades de Servicios Culturales y Turísticos del Estado de Yucatán, the Yucatán state agency devoted to the development of tourism infrastructure and services). Commuters proceed through the zone on the Old Road, now converted into a tourist pedestrian path within the zone. On the Mayaland side, a narrow path swings around the ticket booth and out of the zone to the hotel parking lot and entrance, thereby facilitating bicyclists who need not dismount to pass through the entrance gates.

Observing the activities of state and private-sector employees moving casually and conveniently through what is otherwise a carefully controlled and regulated site gives some pause for thought regarding Chichén Itzá as a site that is both everyone's and no one's. The hum of everyday business cutting through this landscape of Chichén Itzá obscures more than it reveals about the contentious history of the site's ownership. Nor does the workaday activity of Chichén Itzá expose the tensions between federal jurisdiction and private landholding. The fact that the ruins sit on private land is not a rallying point that coalesces public sentiment against Chichén's owners. Instead, it is something simply not discussed. I have chosen to explicitly address the issue here because it sets the stage for getting to a deeper matter—how the ownership of cultural patrimony cannot be divorced, in the case of archaeology heritage, from questions of landownership, use, and tenure.

The case of Chichén Itzá reveals that the historical trajectory of cultural heritage legislation in Mexico has to be read alongside that of land privatization. The nineteenth century was marked by the expropriation of terrenos baldíos and community lands. This forced breakdown of indigenous communal land tenure was supported by the institutionalization of a liberal vision of the economy based in the ideal of private property. Owned privately, land could be used more rationally and thus more profitably. Under communal tenure, lands were not seen as fulfilling their resource potential. The twentieth century recapitulates these arguments through a neoliberal ideology. Once again, land privatization becomes a central issue. Only in 1992 did the privatization of ejidos gain juridical status through a constitutional amendment to Article 27. However, in the case of heritage properties, the effects remain to be seen.

Privatization is not new in the history of the territories of archaeological ruins. I have demonstrated how for one hundred years private-sector interests and the nation's cultural patrimony have deeply intertwined. In fact, the public-private coexistence is virtually impossible to avoid or ignore, given that the territorializing practices of the state have failed, in a certain sense, to fully contain archaeological properties.

The problem of containing archaeological sites may be demonstrated on several counts; to begin with, not all ruins are within juridically defined zones. Ruins and artifacts dominate the landscape of the Yucatán Peninsula. Limited in funds and personnel, the government cannot ensure that all of these will be explored, consolidated, and protected under law. It is often said that there are nearly 2,000 archaeological zones in the state (not the entire peninsula) of Yucatán. Though the figure seems enormous, it represents less than 1 percent of the estimated 250,000 archaeological sites in Mexico (Sánchez Caero 1995: 195). One might be tempted to affirm, and it would be hard to argue against, the notion that the whole region is, indeed, an archaeological zone itself.

Many people throughout Yucatán have located significant building foundations, carved stones, and other structures within the limits of their own properties. Artifacts litter the landscapes, whether pieces of ceramic, whole pottery vessels, or carved stones. Some pieces are tossed aside, some are put to convenient uses, and others are displayed. It is commonly understood by scholars and local people that cut stone from nearby archaeological mounds were used in the construction of colonial structures—for the most part, churches—as well as eighteenth- and nineteenth-century hacienda structures.

The distinct presence of artifacts in a modern community significantly affects residents' everyday lives. Take the following case in point. The community of San Felipe is the closest contemporary settlement to the ruins of Chichén Itzá, separated from the zone's federal boundaries by the

Mayaland Hotel. San Felipe is just across the street from Chichén Itzá. With a population of several hundred, most of San Felipe's residents are employed in agricultural work combined with some form of income-generating activity associated with the archaeological zone. Though only meters from one of the oldest and most luxurious hotels in Yucatán, San Felipe represents the underside of tourism development: only in the 1990s were electric power lines extended to the houses of San Felipe residents.

San Felipe has merited the close scrutiny of INAH archaeologists, one of whom reported to me his dismay that people are even living in this federally granted ejido community at all. The archaeologist worries about the further destruction of artifacts and monuments under the stress of a living and growing community. He told me, "We do what we can to limit the growth of San Felipe. The residents have been instructed of the value of the ruins in which they are living, and what they can and cannot do."

Exactly what can and cannot be done in this ejido community is not expressly stated, however. In the course of my research, I was not able to locate any "rules" for living within the border area of Chichén Itzá from either INAH officials or community leaders, although they do agree on certain ground rules against planting crops or constructing new dwellings or outbuildings. Many residents of San Felipe are reluctant to notify authorities, not for fear of legal sanctions if illicit practices are exposed but rather for the inconvenience that would arise should INAH archaeologists want to excavate architectural features found in a milpa or a *solar* (house garden) or near a dwelling in current use. Along with this reluctance to report structures or artifacts is a sense of pride in having ancient cut-stone foundations, column fragments, or *metates* on one's own property, as many readily and even boastfully revealed to me. At the same time, the presence of artifactual materials on "one's own property"—particularly within a federally granted ejido community—is a dangerous irony. Although one's backyard is de facto private space, it is de jure property of the nation. The residents of San Felipe have thus far seen the benefits of a certain degree of archaeological/tourism development at Chichén Itzá but stand to lose out with any change in the status quo, whether it be further concessions to the private sector or further financial resources designated for archaeological excavation.

The juridical frameworks for defining and regulating cultural heritage in Mexico carve out zones and mark them for special attention by scientists, tourists, or the state. As marked areas, these archaeological zones pass from being the ordinary public space of everyday life to regulated spaces of special distinction and importance. From this baseline arises a particular kind of tension for people who live within ruins, especially residents of the border regions of officially delimited federal archaeological zones.

After visiting San Felipe one afternoon for a tour of numerous backyard ruins by a founding member of the community, I announced my plan to head over to the archaeological zone. Don Efraín, my tour guide, pointed out the quickest way inside the zone. We crossed the two-lane Mérida-Cancún highway, entered the scrubby bush, and proceeded along a clearly marked footpath. A bit disoriented, I was surprised when we emerged—after only five minutes of walking and then climbing over the remains of a nominal fence—directly behind the Temple of the Warriors, immediately within the archaeological site center. I use this anecdote to illustrate that even within the highly striated space of the archaeological zone, territorialized as it is by private, state, and federal interests, there are still hidden entrances, secret passages that form networks representing the history and local use of the site and that continually modify and exceed the zone's official boundaries.

As we can see from the daily lived experiences of the Maya community of San Felipe, the spatial uncontainability of Chichén Itzá is yet another occasion of monumental ambivalence. This ambivalence is shared by residents and site officials alike. While residents of San Felipe are hyperconscious of the ruins in their midst, they also know that the multitude of activities that make up contemporary life do not stop at the arbitrary borders intended to define a space of ancient civilization. Nor do archaeologists, for that matter. The rhetoric of conservation and protection of cultural patrimony gives archaeologists the mandate to sanction these activities, while a farmer perhaps feels a mandate just as powerful to cultivate his land. Certainly, legal instruments may intervene in the near future in an attempt to resolve this ambivalence. But as this case shows, the present always trespasses on the privileged site of ancient heritage.

CONCLUSION

For some, the notion is downright inconceivable that a premier site of ancient Maya culture, Mexican national patrimony, and UNESCO World Heritage and a top candidate as one of the New Seven Wonders of the World is on privately held land. But not inconceivable for everyone. Big-business tourism interests, entrepreneurs, state officials, and the INAH—including both bureaucrats and archaeologists—have for decades negotiated the strong private-sector presence at Chichén. Especially for local residents in and around the archaeological site, the curious circumstance of Chichén Itzá holds little irony. Bearing witness to more than a century of private sector intervention in the patrimonial site has certainly left many with decidedly ambivalent positions in regard to their own relationships to the site, not only as Maya people but as a local residential population socially and spatially marginalized from the site via its colonization of Chichén Itzá by both archaeological science and the Mexican state. A spatial genealogy of Chichén Itzá would seem, at first, an attempt to answer the question of how the archaeological zone stood to be transformed by the threat of neoliberal privatization. However, the evidence from Chichén Itzá tells us instead how the heritage site has long been private property, at least, as we have seen so far, since the sixteenth century! The events and persons detailed in this chapter do not all seek to formally privatize Chichén Itzá. What I chose to highlight here are the multiple social actors and institutions—from nineteenth-century explorers to Edward Thompson, then Morley and the CIW, to the Barbachano family—who have participated in conditioning the possibility for Chichén to become a world-renowned heritage site.

Dating back at least to the time of the purchase of the Hacienda Chichén Itzá by Edward H. Thompson in 1894, there has been a continuing living presence within the archaeological zone and its immediate surrounding area. Mayas, Mexicans, and foreigners lived within the main part of the hacienda since before Thompson's times, and though the property has changed quite a bit, the area, now a hotel, continues to be inhabited by different groups of residents and guests. Mayaland and Hacienda Chichen hotel workers through the 1970s lived in small houses on the hacienda property. During the Carnegie and Mexican excavation and restoration project years, the site was continually occupied by different groups—though most of the contracted Maya laborers actually resided in Pisté or another close-by community. Within the ruins themselves, not more than several hundred meters from the hacienda main house, the archaeological site's custodians and their families lived from the late 1930s through 1983. It is this group that lived most fully and for the longest sustained period directly within the ruins. These "INAH families" acted as a different kind of private interest in the site as they became entrepreneurs in providing services for the slowly increasing number of visitors to the archaeological zone at a time of relatively little presence of the state in the archaeological zone. In Chapter Four we will explore more fully the role of these workers, their families, and the ways in which they have invested their patrimonial claims in Chichén Itzá.

FIGURE 4.1. *An INAH guard stands near the top of Chichén Itzá's most famous monument, the Castillo, observing the morning's first visitors. Photograph by author.*

Given the long and complicated history of private-sector intervention within the archaeological zone at Chichén Itzá, how could the privatization signaled by the 1999 constitutional amendment initiative present a new threat to the ownership and custodianship of these monuments to ancient Maya civilization and the Mexican nation? Some time after watching the protestors at Chichén Itzá in 1999 I understood what they were really protesting. While public concern centered on the integrity of the nation's tangible cultural patrimony, local INAH site guards and custodios at Chichén Itzá trained their anxious attention in another direction: toward the intangible institutional structure of heritage management in Mexico. If privatization promised to relieve the state's responsibility for managing, protecting, and investigating the tens of thousands of archaeological sites across the national territory, what would become of the federal INAH employees: the thousands of academics, managers, and site guards who staff the workaday production and reproduction of heritage across the national territory?

Privatization signaled the potential for Chichén's workers to lose not only their federal employment under the auspices of the INAH but perhaps even more significantly, all the perks—some legally sanctioned and some not—that accompany working inside the archaeological zone. Focusing here on the INAH employees at Chichén Itzá, we will explore this issue of job security. Over and above any reference to the ancient Maya past, the three generations of caretakers at the site view the ruins as a modern workplace and understand their employment itself to be a kind of patrimony.

While the 1999 protests mark a moment of crystallization and intensification of ambivalence toward cultural patrimony, this moment is neither isolated nor without antecedents. The heartfelt sentiment of "Our culture is not for sale" has long simmered among workers and local residents in and around Chichén Itzá. Countless residents of Pisté and the smaller communities surrounding the archaeological zone express worry and even anger over the increasing loss of the site to big-business tourism developers and the state.

The notion that the site is slipping away from the hands of the local Maya residents into the grip of the powerful *mercadotecnia* (market force) is only relatively recent, coming with the major infrastructural development projects beginning in the mid-1980s. If the 1999 privatization initiative spurred protest by the extended Chichén community, why, then, would I look at this moment as one marking an intensification of ambivalence? To answer this question, I document the actions and reactions on the part of INAH employees at Chichén Itzá for whom privatization of cultural patrimony first and foremost signals the restructuring of the cultural labor market of which they are a part. For these archaeological site custodians, privatization does not undermine their cultural identity as indigenous Maya as much as it threatens their job benefits as federal employees.

MODERN ANCIENTS

Just about everyone who lives near the world-renowned Maya archaeological site Chichén Itzá knows that the *antiguos*, the ancient ones, still haunt the ruins.[1] While an occasional tourist among the thousands who arrive daily might hope for some kind of spiritual or mystical connection with an antiguo, they are likely to be quite surprised—and more than a little disappointed—upon seeing Chichén's antiguos wearing blue uniforms and carrying walkie-talkies. No, these "ancient ones" are not some sort of doppelganger. They are INAH employees.

Though Maya residents in and around Chichén Itzá have been employed in the sites' excavation and restoration, maintenance, and protection on a regular basis since the 1920s, only with the establishment of the INAH in 1938 did a small number of these Maya workers became official custodians of the site. It followed for the next six decades that the everyday care of Chichén Itzá became a dynastic enterprise as work positions have passed from father to son until today. Thus, the contemporary caretaking of this World Heritage Site is a sort of family business. And the modern antiguos remain among the ruins—not as ghosts of the ancient past, but as none-too-distant descendants of the very first Maya workers at Chichén to rebuild and reconstruct the monuments and plazas one sees now upon visiting the site.

Chichén's modern antiguos do not hide in a shadow of mystery, as the popular discourse on Maya civilization suggests. Much to the contrary, they occupy the archaeological zone with loud silver whistles and unmistakable swaggers. One even rides a shiny red scooter up and down the tourist paths. They guard Chichén, they protect the monuments, and they say they love these ruins. Here they work. Here, until the early 1980s, they actually lived. From Chichén Itzá, all have earned their livelihoods.

In this chapter I trace the contemporary history of Maya labor at Chichén Itzá, recreating through remembering the meanings of a key site of ancient Maya culture through the perspective of those who spend their workdays inside the zone as federal and state employees. This analysis focuses on thirty-four men and two women who work at the site for the INAH. Due to its extensive area and high-volume tourism, Chichén Itzá has more than double the custodial staff of any other site open to the public in Yucatán. These custodios carry out the day-to-day functions of the archaeological zone—selling tickets, groundskeeping, patrolling tourist activities on the pyramids and other structures. While doing so is not technically among their official duties, custodios also answer visitors' questions on a variety of topics, help them plan their tours of the zone, take photos, and even pose for some, too.

When considering the field of cultural patrimony, privatization is more than simply a symptom or indicator of the implementation of neoliberal economic theory into policy. It is, perhaps more compellingly, a very local phenomenon tied to space-claiming techniques practiced by a community of daily users of the archaeological zone—those who have personal and family history attached to a heritage site. I previously created a provenance—or spatial genealogy—of Chichén Itzá, tracing the various hands through which it has passed. In doing so, I demonstrated that the archaeological zone is a produced space representing multiple interests, most notably those of the state and the private sector. Here we will look at another group of social actors who represent a different spatial genealogy of Chichén and who possess it as another form of privatization.

The antiguo custodios, using their advantageous presence in the archaeological zone, assemble and enact a system of what I call "patrifruct"-based rights. In principle and so far in practice, patrifruct rights guarantee *users* of heritage access to it. In another demonstration of territorialization, the claiming of patrifruct rights extracts certain aspects of the meaning of Chichén Itzá from the public realm to maintain it in a privatized realm—that of their families. We might call this kind of privatization a territorialization of meaning. Not always a unidirectional process, initiated top-down by the state, this ambivalent territorialization of meaning is enacted by an unexpected group of major players in the privatization of Chichén Itzá: the Maya laborers who participated in the initial phases of development whose descendants now work as site guards and caretakers. As Chichén's antiguo custodios creatively claim the archaeological site as their patrimony, they demonstrate yet another form of monumental ambivalence. As a site of national and World Heritage, Chichén belongs to everyone, and therefore the workers have the right to claim this renewable cultural resource as theirs.

CARING FOR THE RUINS

> The natives were energetic and willing to carry out their tasks. . . . Small in build but with strong bodies, these Indians sometimes labored in oppressive heat and stifling interiors, always without complaint. They resisted only when they were faced with unfamiliar techniques. (A description of Maya laborers at Chichén, circa 1930, cited in Brunhouse 1971: 209)

> Nor should there be forgotten the native workmen whose toil transformed a shapeless hill into a thing of enduring beauty. As a whole, they were as efficient, as dependable, and as agreeable as any group one could hope to find in any land. (Archaeologist Earl Morris 1931: 9)

Each morning at around seven o'clock there is a changing of the guard at Chichén Itzá. With no pomp and even less ceremony, the night watchman leaves the sun to rise from behind the Temple of the Warriors and the day shift enters the archaeological zone. Of the custodios arriving early in the morning, just a few are uniformed for patrolling the site's public areas. Most are outfitted in outdoor work clothes. They head off in a group of eight to begin clearing the dense undergrowth that threatens to overtake the tourist paths around the Cenote Xtoloc. By eight o'clock more blue-uniformed guards enter, the gates are unlocked, and the first visitors trickle in. Another typical day at Chichén Itzá begins to unfold.

Perhaps the following illuminations of "backstage" Chichén Itzá—or any tourist site for that matter—spoil the semiotic pleasures of touristic or imaginative consumption. Indeed, the *jouissance* of a site of ancient Maya civilization, for tourists that is, requires an experience of the site as discrete in time and place. For a place to be produced for tourist consumption, it must first be marked out, or defined, and then commodified so that it can be consumed by the tourist as either a discrete experience or as an image (MacCannell 1989; Urry 1990). The pleasure that tourists take in exploring Chichén Itzá arises—perhaps only in part—from the circumstance of its hermetic containment from the everyday lives of contemporary Maya. The mystery machine of the heritage assemblage properly commodifies Chichén Itzá, hiding the anachronistic conditions of its production.

The heritage assemblage territorializes the archaeological site both spatially and temporally to subvert the historical reality of "Mayas (re)building Maya ruins" in service to archaeological science and the state. To put it simply, the commodification of Chichén Itzá as a tourist site masks the labor of the site's production. I am not speaking of a singular, originary moment of production, such as the reconstruction projects of the 1920s through 1940s, but rather the ongoing, everyday presentation, maintenance, and protection of Maya Culture. For the thousands of men and women who work at Mexico's archaeological zones as archaeologists, administrators, tour guides, guards, or vendors, what is perceived by the "tourist gaze" (Urry 1990) is a carefully constructed vision that promotes the ancient mystery of the monuments and obscures the labor of its every production and reproduction. Yet we will see workers reflecting on the commodification of Chichén Itzá, defining their own relationships to the zone and its genealogy. We will see that Chichén's custodios are not so much subverting the tourist gaze, supported as it is by archaeology and the state, as they are deflecting its hegemony of vision, giving rise to yet another form of monumental ambivalence.

MAYAS REBUILDING MAYA RUINS

> Who built the temples of Chichén Itzá? Who knows? I have heard the old people say it was the Itzá who built them. They were people like us, but they knew things we do not know. (Eleuterio Pat, cited in Redfield and Villa Rojas 1934: 330)

How have Maya people worked to create and recreate Maya heritage sites? How might we understand their participation in the "archaeologization" of the Yucatecan landscape? Since the early days of Maya archaeology, researchers in the field rely on local communities to provide the labor required in large- and small-scale excavation projects. These practices continue today. Maya laborers may be skilled in the masonry of architectural consolidation or the drawing of architectural profiles. Unskilled workers haul stones, clear vegetation, and excavate. Male workers may perform heavy digging and lifting at the excavation site, while women and young people wash and label ceramics at an off-site lab or base camp. Women also work in tasks that are supportive of the investigation, such as cooking, housekeeping, and doing laundry for the project staff.

The early excavation and reconstruction projects at Chichén Itzá carried out by the CIW and the Mexican agency Monumentos Prehispánicos, precursor to the INAH, required dozens of on-site laborers. Maya workers cleared overgrown structures, disassembled them, organized the pieces, fired new stones from an on-site lime kiln, and rebuilt portions of the structures. Some skilled workers with experience in reconstruction projects were brought by archaeologists from other sites in Campeche and Yucatán. However, most of the workers were recruited locally from the town of Pisté, just two kilometers from the site.

Proto-archaeological amateur explorers and later professional scientific investigators describe a particular relationship to their projects, the archaeological site, and the inhabitants of Pisté. In this manner, archaeology, broadly construed, has provided the occasion for informal analyses of living Maya communities. Rather than scientific results, these analyses are relegated to commentary, asides, or acknowledgments marginal to the official reporting activities of the discipline. For the most part, they are economic in substance and framed in colonialist terms. In particular, Pisté is presented as an exploitable labor resource that would, in turn, make possible the exploitation of the ruins-as-resource.

Austrian photographer and archaeological explorer Teobert Maler described his perspective on labor relations between himself and workers from Pisté while working at Chichén Itzá in 1891:

> Pisté is a sad village in which some dozen native families gain a living from their small maize farms, spending on a vile *aguardiente* [grain alcohol] the entire product of their labor. . . . Money has little attraction for these native people, and at Pisté, no one works when he has earned four *reales* or a peso. . . . Only when the last centavo has been spent will they again resolve to work for a day or two. (Maler 1932 quoted in Steggerda 1941: 8)

In the 1920s, as the CIW's Project Chichén Itzá directed by Sylvanus G. Morley was getting under way, a clause in the concession contract between the CIW and the Mexican government set the first institutionalized parameters of modern labor relations at Chichén. This labor clause stipulated that the CIW had to hire Mexican workers except for the technical directors and specialists. Rather than shift the dynamics of the de facto labor relations that had existed for decades, the provision affirmed a paternalistic role for both the state and foreign researchers in the custodianship of national cultural patrimony.

The U.S. and Mexican reconstruction projects from the mid-1920s through the end of the 1940s represent a level of site development unsurpassed at Chichén Itzá until the "megaprojects" of the 1980s. Morley's biographer, Brunhouse (1971: 208–209) gives a glimpse of the scope and intensity of labor required for excavating and rebuilding some of the site's best-known structures—the Great Ball Court, the Temple of the Warriors, the Nunnery, and, of course, the Castillo, or Pyramid of Kukulkan:

> Just after the season began in 1925 with sixty-nine workers, the number jumped to eighty-two. . . . [When Morley] returned after a brief absence he discovered to his consternation that the [Maya] foreman had gone on hiring natives until 215 were on the payroll. . . . The next day he called 133 of them into the yard of the Casa Principal [Hacienda Chichén Itzá], explained that they had been taken on by mistake, paid them off and added a gratuity, and sent them away in good humor. He realized that he might need them in the future.

The colorful details presented in biographical material, particularly of Morley, match those that most vividly remain in the living memory of Chichén's current workers, including CIW cook Tarsisio "Jimmy" Chang, of Maya-Korean mixed ancestry; Eugenio May, a Maya worker whose photo now hangs on the wall of a small museum at the entrance of the archaeological zone of Chichén Itzá; and Isauro Olalde, whose circa-1930 portrait hangs inside a sitting room off the lobby of the Hotel Hacienda Chichén, the former headquarters for Edward H. Thompson and the Carnegie staff, adjacent to the archaeological zone.

Notable exceptions to such representations may be found, among other places, in the front matter of archaeological monographs. A good example is a note in the preface to Earl Morris's (1931: 9) publication of the results of the excavation and reconstruction of the Temple of the Warriors:

> Juan Olalde, Mayordomo, and his son and first lieutenant, Isauro, served faithfully and intelligently.[2] Because of their understanding of local conditions and their intimate familiarity with the material environment, they were able to give assistance which it would have been difficult in the extreme to do without. . . . Angelino Pat, master mason, courteous, faithful, and intelligent to a rare degree, brought to bear

upon his work a resourcefulness that I have not seen equaled. To him is due the credit for difficult pieces of construction, far more than to those to whom, in the natural course of events, it would be given.

Morris's naming of specific workers and their contributions to the project stands in contrast to Maler's and Steggerda's commentaries. And although Morris's salute to the workers denotes more a view of them as Noble Savage than trusted colleague, the acuity of Morris's last statement is remarkable. In the natural course of events, credit to Maya workers is erased from the projects in which they have reconstructed their cultural patrimony, and they risk losing claims on it that they never even knew they could make. After all, Chichén was a site of ruins but not a heritage site until it was rebuilt in the 1920s and 1930s.

Though I want to focus the rest of this chapter on contemporary Chichén, I include these references to repopulate, so the speak, the history of Chichén Itzá. So much of the discourse on Maya archaeological sites focuses on abandonment, lost civilizations, and European discovery. Even the archaeological zone's history in the twentieth century adds to popular misconceptions that the Maya no longer exist or that the living communities are mere remnants of a former great civilization.

CONTEMPORARY CUSTODIANSHIP

The labor regime governing Chichén Itzá has shifted from the colonial-style paternalism of early archaeological development (1920s–1940s) to one more characteristic of a modern bureaucratic state. Custodios are salaried federal employees who receive health care and pension benefits, uniform allowances, and generous paid vacation. Chichén's thirty-six custodios—most of whom speak Yucatec Maya as well as Spanish—sell tickets, guard the entrance gates, keep the monuments free of weeds and debris, and frantically blow their whistles when young tourists get too rowdy while climbing the precarious steps of a pyramid.

Custodianship at Chichén Itzá is more than keeping the grounds clean and ensuring visitor safety. These formal duties only partially fulfill what many site employees sense and enact as their larger responsibility in caring for the archaeological zone. Custodios stand guard at various points throughout the site, inside the small museum, and at the two entrance gates. One custodio per shift patrols Chichén Viejo (Old Chichén), another part of the zone two kilometers from the main tourist area currently closed to the public due to ongoing excavation and restoration.

FIGURE 4.2. *INAH custodio Javier Pat checks tickets at Chichén's main entrance. Photograph by author.*

While guarding Chichén may appear to be a rather passive activity, custodios actively engage in constructing a possessive relationship with the site, as when they speak of the ruins as "My Chichén." Their intimacy with the zone cannot be accounted for in the dominant discursive arenas of either archaeology or the state. Nor does it find a venue of expression in the tourism industrial complex, rigid as it is in both creating and disseminating proper interpretations of ancient history. Instead, the intimacy of

FIGURE 4.3.   *INAH employees Felipe Yam Pat and Julio Salazar pose for a photo in a shaded area between the Castillo and the Ball Court. Photograph by author.*

Chichén Itzá emanates from experiences of the night watchman who has spent twenty years of long and very dark nights protecting the archaeological zone. It arises out of the banter between older workers as they seek the shade of a ceiba tree during a slow afternoon shift; for those who walk across the site's main plaza remembering the baseball games or futból (soccer) matches played there in their youth. Indeed, the everyday life of the archaeological zone is a pastiche of memories and overlapping images, of what the site used to be, what it has now become, and how their own lives have intertwined with the monuments. There seems to be something about working at a famous archaeological site that exceeds the reach of official mandates, rules, policies, and procedures.

The administrative hierarchy at the site is fairly simple and is exclusive to Chichén Itzá as the most heavily staffed site in Yucatán. At the top is the *encargado*, the administrative site manager. Chichén and one other site have encargados who are not custodios; the rest have senior custodios in charge. Chichén's encargado does not patrol the zone regularly, nor does he wear a uniform, but he does generally accompany important visitors in their tours of the archaeological site. The encargado at Chichén Itzá during the period of my fieldwork had held his job for nine years and has since been replaced. Significant in terms of the internal dynamics of the working atmosphere at Chichén Itzá, the encargado was not from Pisté, nor did he speak Maya. Rather than choose to live locally, the encargado preferred to commute daily from Mérida. A lawyer with no notable professional experience in the field of cultural heritage, the *licenciado* was quite successful in his private legal practice maintained throughout his tenure at Chichén.[3] The encargado used his position of authority at the site as a local base from which he could extend his network of private clients.

The thirty-six custodios at Chichén are organized from within and without in both a de jure and de facto hierarchy. The workers are officially divided into two groups, *grupo norte* (north) and *grupo sur* (south), who rotate weekly work schedules. On a typical day, only one group patrols the zone. Meanwhile, the other group works behind the scenes in site maintenance (weeding, clearing footpaths, erecting or repairing protective fencing, etc.). The group on maintenance finishes its week early with a long weekend off.

The north and south labels, then, do not correspond to distinct areas of responsibility inside the archaeological zone. Instead, they are arbitrary names that are rarely used. Custodios prefer to identify their group using the first name (or even nickname) of their group leader. The two group leaders are administrative coordinators, both second-generation INAH employees and both with fathers who are still full-time custodios on site. The coordinators, though younger than many of the other custodios, are generally respected among the workers, most likely because they tend not to engage in public displays of authority over their groups.

Perhaps this is because the group leaders do not, in fact, hold the authority that the official administrative structure at the zone gives them.

While the official designation of the two work groups decides the logistics of covering shifts and tasks, there also exists a hierarchy of de facto organization based on kinship, place of birth, and place of residence. Among the custodios, it is clear that a third-generation custodio born in Pisté—regardless of work skills and often even of personal temperament—is of a higher caste than a first-generation employee whose family comes from another Maya town, even one only thirty to forty kilometers away. Place of residence factors more complexly and more ambiguously. Owning a home in Mérida offers significant cultural capital to a custodio, yet owning a large, ostentatious home in Pisté can factor similarly. These weighted and measured distinctions both shape and reflect how the custodios express and justify their rights to claim "My Chichén."

Maintaining Security

One of the primary responsibilities of custodianship is maintaining security and order among the monuments. Security concerns have two facets: first for the concern for the material patrimony itself, including artifacts on display or stored in a museum, monuments, and archaeological materials yet to be unearthed; and also for the safety and comfort of the visitors. Preventive measures at Chichén Itzá have included the installation of ropes or chains to aid in climbing certain structures and to prohibit public access to others. For many years, a heavy chain hung down one of the two reconstructed staircases of the Castillo. The chain eventually wore a deep groove down the center of the pyramid's staircase and was subsequently replaced with a thick rope. The stairs of the structure, with their narrow footholds and uneven heights, are difficult for some visitors to navigate even under dry conditions. It is not an official policy for custodios to warn visitors against climbing, even when the lightest rains turn climbing into a slippery and dangerous undertaking.

Custodios report that many visitors view climbing the Castillo's 365 steps as the main goal of their visit to Chichén Itzá, and staff members have little chance of dissuading visitors from this goal. Deaths of both tourists and locals from falling and lightning strikes have not received wide publicity, but lightning rods were installed on top of the Castillo to deflect future lightning strikes during the frequent storms of summer and fall. During extreme weather conditions such as hurricanes, the entire zone may be closed to visitors.

I observed several incidents and accidents at Chichén Itzá during the spring and summer of 2001 that appear to be representative of those that normally, though infrequently, occur at the archaeological zone. Some, such as heat stroke or exhaustion, can be attributed to the extremely hot and humid weather. Other safety-related problems involve falling from structures. Two incidents live on in custodios' memory. One occurred when a twenty-five-year-old man from Guadalajara unsuccessfully attempted to slide down the balustrade of the Castillo instead of climbing down the steps. Custodios who witnessed the event found it "so stupid" they did not know if it was suicidal or just foolish. He left the zone by ambulance in critical condition. The other incident belongs to a third category of mishaps at the zone involving visitors deliberately damaging structures. Custodians tell of a man who claimed to be competing in the "Super Champion of the World" contest after moving one of the Thousand Columns beside the Temple of the Warriors. This modern-day warrior ended up paying a fine of several thousand pesos.

Containment, Control, and Boundaries

The expansive size and outdoor setting of the zone together produce an environment that cannot always be controlled. While in decades past the site had abundant flora and fauna, visitors today are more likely to confront a roaming dog, of which there are many, than a jaguar. On one occasion, I accompanied the INAH site manager in a search through the bush around the monuments for a dog that had reportedly committed an unmotivated act of aggression on a tourist. The tourist was bitten on the finger, which was, moments after the incident, bleeding slightly. The dog in question had to be found in order to assess its state of well-being and what sorts of dangers it posed to the bite victim.[4]

The search for the dog along the back paths of the zone provided an occasion for the encargado to comment upon such problems of daily occurrence at Chichén and his role in handling these issues, and in a more generalized sense, he commented upon what I would call the "problem of containment" concerning the zone's boundaries. Rather than directing and managing all of the INAH activities at the archaeological zone, the encargado's daily routine was more directed toward acting as the public face of the INAH at the archaeological site. As such, custodios called on him to resolve visitor problems of a routine nature, whether disputes over the payment of entrance fees, the adequacy of services, or justification of the rules and regulations under which the site operated. Visitors are surprisingly likely to advocate for less-restricted access to the site: wanting to enter the zone before opening hours and stay beyond closing time, desiring to climb or enter prohibited areas or take unsanctioned photographs.[5] In sum, many of the everyday problems at Chichén revolve around one central theme: the freedoms and restrictions of visitors in interactions with material embodiments of national and world heritage.

While the above are spatially articulated to the area within the officially delimited boundaries of the archaeological zone, we can see how these borders are both permeable and negotiable. The instability of the line distinguishing the zone from its outside confounds the territorial limits. This takes multiple forms. First, it is an issue of physical access to the zone. There are two official entrances to the archaeological zone. One is through the *parador turístico* (the public entrance hall), and the other is near the Mayaland Hotel. Another entrance, used by locals but not the public at large, is at the INAH *campamento*. Because several contemporary living communities surround the archaeological zone, there are, as I indicated previously, numerous paths and trails skirting the perimeter of the zone and even permitting direct entrance to the site center. The zone is enclosed, except in the most public areas, by a haphazard fence of wooden posts and wire.

It was not until a crisis of containment emerged in the late 1980s—the initiation of an ongoing series of artisan "invasions" at Chichén—that some of the site's perimeter was enclosed at all. In successive waves throughout the past twenty or so years, local artisans and handicraft vendors have illegally entered (or "invaded") the archaeological zone to sell souvenirs to tourists. Armed only with bundles of hand-carved wooden statues or small molded-cement figures, dozens of vendors including women and children have taken advantage of Chichén's porous and permeable boundaries, to the consternation of INAH officials.[6] Indeed, one does not have to be particularly sneaky or adept to enter the zone. However, upon occasion custodios themselves have turned a blind eye to the ambulant vendors who might well be friends, neighbors, or even kin from Pisté. I have myself witnessed occasions when this has clearly been the case. Chichén's active rumor mill charges certain custodios with direct (financial) complicity with the vendors. Though posed as hypothetical, the following scenario described to me by custodio Don Sebas in the spring of 2001 (a time when, incidentally, no ambulant vendors were to be found in the zone) is highly probable:

> INAH employment pays a good salary and has good benefits. It allows for a custodio to accumulate capital. With this capital, one can invest in a business such as artisanry, T-shirts, whatever you like. When the tour-

ism market is low, it is difficult to sell things in a shop or on the street in Pisté. [Therefore] the vendor must enter the archaeological zone to sell.

In such a situation, the custodio is complicit with the "invading" ambulant vendor as the vendor works to sell the merchandise belonging to the custodio. This type of arrangement is not unusual, and I see it as an integral part of the issue of containing and controlling a zone. The case of the artisan invasions presents at once the transgression of physical borders and the manipulation of the boundaries set upon the official duty or responsibility of a custodio. We see here that Chichén cannot be contained. Not only is this failure located along the site's extensive, unattended perimeter but also in the ambivalent role played by the zone's front-line defense: the custodios.

Custodianship is an attempt to contain not only the physical limits of the archaeological zone but also social and even moral limits. Part of a custodian's duty is to maintain order at the multiple intersections of these various kinds of boundaries. These efforts play out on a daily basis, even in the most routine of custodial activities. While no book of rules delineates the proper etiquette of either custodians or site visitors, it is as if both parties enter into a tacit agreement to respect the site and its authority figures once the visitors enter the zone's territory.

When the agreement is violated, a shrill whistle sounds—literally. Most custodios wear a whistle on a cord around their necks, the only "weapon," as one junior worker called them, with which they are armed. Some custodios are known for using their whistles too much, while others rarely use it. Don Ceso is known among his cohorts for overusing his whistle, a practice embedded within his complex and often contradictory opinions regarding his work and the tourists he observes and often interacts with at the archaeological zone. He coined the term *turismo agresivo*, aggressive tourism, to describe visitors who actively and blatantly disregard the zone's regulations.

Don Ceso and other site guards rank different national groups based on their tendency toward turismo agresivo and their behavior in general. Custodios report that they find Argentinians to be the rudest and most likely to break the rules. Italians rank high as well. In Argentinians and Italians many guards perceive a generalized aggressive, noncompliant behavior often stemming from visitors' previous experiences in archaeological sites in their home countries. A disparity in the manner of protecting archaeological monuments around the world seems to promote disagreement on how the public may interact with a site. Custodios are quite vocal and articulate about the problems they encounter with Mexican nationals—nonlocal, non-Yucatec citizens—whom they ultimately define as the most unruly of all visitors to the site. According to one frustrated custodian, Mexican tourists "assume the rules don't apply to them. They ignore the 'No Trespassing' signs and walk around and climb wherever they want. More than once, I have stopped someone by shouting or blowing my whistle, only to have the visitor shout back at me, arguing that it is his patrimony, too, and he can do what he pleases."

Recently, custodios have half-seriously requested badges, something like police shields, and T-shirts with "INAH" printed in block letters across the chest, like FBI T-shirts in American movies. These would not be for everyday wear but for special events that draw large crowds, such as the fall and spring equinox. Each March and increasingly in September as well, tens of thousands of visitors come to the zone to see the Feathered Serpent "descend" the balustrade of the Castillo through a play of light and shadow.[7]

Even on the most heavily visited days at Chichén, custodios are armed with the same basic equipment: a uniform, a whistle, maybe a two-way radio, and nothing else. To my knowledge, no daytime custodio at Chichén carries a weapon inside the zone. In the more remote archaeological zones of the Yucatán Peninsula's Ruta Puuc, guns or machetes are kept in the ticket booth areas. In the past, it would not be unusual for a custodian to patrol Chichén Itzá with the long-barreled rifle he used for hunting. For this was when the two activities were easily and naturally combined, as the job of a custodio was a job of the *campo* (the rural outdoors), not of a site in the highly developed international tourism-industrial complex.

Over the past several decades, the work of custodianship has transformed, in a sense, from taming nature to containing culture. In other words, contemporary custodianship requires that the "nature skills" of the Maya campesino are kept offstage at Chichén Itzá. In their stead, as we will see, custodianship demands "culture skills," understood here as the ability to police the boundaries of appropriateness in the activities or behaviors of tourists.

IDEOLOGICAL CRISES OF CUSTODIANSHIP

It was a particularly hot and slow afternoon. But the sun had slipped behind deep blue clouds threatening a rainstorm still hours, even days, away. I entered the zone and immediately headed for the Observatory, or

Caracol, where I knew I could usually find Don Hugo waiting away the afternoon. Don Hugo was only a few months from his retirement, having worked for the INAH as a custodio for nearly thirty years, first in the Puuc-area sites, then at Chichén Itzá. His was one of fifteen families that until 1983 lived inside the archaeological zone.

A grandfather in his late sixties, Don Hugo had little formal education but was an avid reader, with tastes ranging from the daily newspaper to popular magazines to historical and anthropological texts about Yucatán and the Maya. He is an attentive television viewer, and the introduction of Sky TV to the pueblo of Pisté, where he lives, offered the Discovery Channel and A&E. He rarely missed a documentary or investigative journalism piece. Don Hugo is also a fan of the program *Wild On*, broadcast on the E! entertainment channel. *Wild On* takes its viewers around the world to show partying and nightlife, replete with images of barely clad women and excessively carefree behaviors. The Cancún episode is typical of the genre, showing drunken and sunburned spring breakers moving their partying from the beach to Chichén Itzá, following a pattern common among tourists visiting Yucatán.

On this particular day that I met up with Don Hugo, he had with him in addition to his ever-present copy of that day's *Diario de Yucatán* newspaper a several-month-old copy of a popular culture and entertainment magazine for teenagers. He waved it at me and called, "Come over here and look at Britney Spears!" I, as one of the few familiar nontourists at the site, often found myself as the unwilling bearer of U.S. culture, somehow deeply intertwined with, if not responsible for, the profusion of signifiers from the United States.

"What do you think about this: is she really a virgin?" he asked me with just a hint of a smile. "I don't know, but she sure likes to show it off!" I replied. "Just like a lot of the tourists here," he observed. "They walk around looking at Chichén Itzá in their short shorts and miniskirts and bikinis. I guess they forgot they left the beach when they got on the bus in Cancun." He continued, "If someone told me thirty years ago that the zone would be like this today, I would have told him he was drinking too much."

I was surprised at his statement, revealing as it did an unusual hint of lament. After all, Don Hugo was more often than not highly ambivalent toward the politics of the zone. So I asked, "But do you think it is OK for women to walk around the zone in their bathing suits?" He replied, "It depends on who you ask. For some of my co-workers, it is perfectly fine. They want to see people enjoy themselves, and they also want to enjoy themselves. For others, they want them to cover up, at least on the bottom. This is an important place. People should have some respect."

Though Hugo had worked at Chichén for thirty years, it was not through this entire course of time that the zone has changed so dramatically. Archaeological and infrastructural plans dating back to the 1920s consistently had the increase in tourism as a goal, but it was not until the late 1970s and the establishment of Cancún as an international tourism center that the everyday scenery of Chichén was affected. One marker of this change is the presence of large numbers of international tourists who visit the archaeological site on chartered day trips.

Girls in bikinis present a crisis in the custodianship of the archaeological zones in a logistical sense as well as in terms of representation. This crisis, alternatively described as a symbolic reversal of the tourist gaze, constitutes a transformative moment in the genealogy of labor at Chichén. In this transformation, custodios move from being campesinos to imagining themselves as cosmopolitan, at home in the archaeological zone as an international space of multiple signifiers. In this space a discussion of Britney Spears' virginity and the difference between showing off breasts or bottoms is part of the everyday language of working at Chichén. As a logistical crisis that is also a crisis of vision, custodios have to negotiate the appearances and practices of visitors that are not necessarily defined by the rules of the zone but that they might find inappropriate. Next to the monuments of national cultural patrimony, girls in bikinis are signs of the success of tourism development and symbols of decadence within the ruins.

CHICHÉN'S ANTIGUOS

In a fashion that cannot be perceived through the eyes of tourists, the archaeological zone is the dominion of the antiguos, dating back to the decades during which the custodios and their families lived within the archaeological zone. Only about half of Chichen's current custodial staff can count themselves as antiguos, for this elite status is derived from having once lived inside the archaeological zone is not shared by all. From the 1940s until the early 1980s, Chichén's custodios and their families lived within the site center. Through these four decades, the INAH workers created a community among the archaeological ruins. Though not officially a pueblo, or town, Chichén Pueblo functioned as such for its residents. Fifteen houses stood along what was then the main road running through Chichén Itzá, just fifty meters from the Castillo. A school, refreshment and gift stands, and small ticket booth all operated by the families of the INAH custodians complemented the scene that visitors encountered upon their arrival to the world-famous archaeological zone.

Oral history accounts of daily life within Chichén Itzá from the former inhabitants, most of whom now live in Pisté, portray the zone as having been a quiet, family-centered community. The workers' duties were to sell tickets, keep the grounds free of litter and debris, clear the reconstructed monuments of weeds, and maintain the visitor paths that provided access from one part of the zone to another. Nearly all of the families operated side businesses devoted to providing basic tourist services. Other family members—wives, daughters, and young sons—took advantage of the steady flow of foreign and national tourists to supplement the family's income. Buses stopped twice a day at Chichén as they traveled the Mérida-Cancún highway that cuts directly across the zone between the houses and the Castillo. Visitors without the comfort of accommodations at the Mayaland or Hacienda Chichén Itzá hotels adjacent to the zone were happy to take advantage of the beverages and meals sold by the families near the ticket booth. Occasionally, tourists would "tip" workers to see inside their houses. One can only surmise that their motivation was to see and experience, amid all that is ancient, something of the contemporary lives of Maya people.

After tourists were gone for the day, adults played baseball in the wide plaza and in front of the Castillo. Perhaps it is hard to imagine the walls of Chichén's Great Ball Court serving as boundary markers for an informal game of futból for a group of teenagers as occurred throughout the 1950s, '60s, and '70s. During these decades, sons of the first generation of custodians grew up and began to have children of their own, many of whom would continue the family tradition of working for the INAH.

Living in the archaeological zone was not simply a matter of convenience. It was an obligation. Indeed, part of the job of custodios was to simply maintain a living presence at the archaeological zone. As a matter of course over four decades, the everyday activities that accompany life in a small community necessitated different kinds of infrastructure at Chichén. Children went to primary school in the immediate vicinity of the housing area, and some went on to secondary school in nearby Valladolid or Mérida. Families attended mass in the chapel of the Hacienda Chichén Itzá less than a kilometer away. Residents at the hacienda, who were employees of the Barbachano family's two hotels, and those of Chichén Pueblo celebrated the feast day of May 15 to the patron Saint Isidro

Labrador. In their communal solar several families kept domestic animals such as chickens and pigs. All families had dogs, which made everyone feel safer during the dark, unelectrified nights.

The employees' duties then, as now, included selling tickets, keeping the grounds free of litter and debris, clearing the reconstructed monuments of weeds, and maintaining the visitor paths that provided access from one part of the zone to another. Women, the wives and daughters of the custodians, supplemented the family income through selling food and drinks to visitors. Don Pepe, a contemporary antiguo, describes his family's tradition of caring for Chichén:

> My grandfather worked in Chichén Itzá, keeping the structures he had helped reconstruct clean and free from weeds. . . . The next generation of custodians came to love this place, too. Not only did they work there, but they made it their home, just as my grandfather had. My grandfather passed on the concept of the protection of the archaeological zone to my father. And he, too, loved it. Thus they became, along with their other compañeros, the most protective [*celosos, or jealous*] guardians of the site.

In the early 1980s, state development plans for improving tourist services at the zone necessitated the demolition of the custodians' houses. After losing their homes and their intimate presence in Chichén, these INAH workers would devise other ways to keep Chichén "in the family" as a special kind of patrimony. The antiguo workers claim that the knowledge, ability, and sensitivity required to properly care for Chichén Itzá is in their blood. From an outsider's perspective, their commitment to the past and future of Chichén Itzá is admirable, if a bit romantic. Perhaps the site does benefit from such skill and dedication passed along from generation to generation, especially from the perspective of archaeology and cultural resource management. Yet the transformation into a local elite of these Maya workers—self-identified by virtue of their intimate proximity to the economic resources of this cultural heritage site—has occasioned contentious broader community concern for equitable access to the archaeological zone.

The dominant role of the antiguos in the micropolitics of the zone is a source of great consternation for other social actors heavily invested in Chichén, including non-antiguo site workers, archaeologists, and INAH administrative officials. Indeed, through the inheritance of job positions in the zone, the antiguos have, in a sense, kept this World Heritage in their families. But in a slightly more sinister reading of their activities, one archaeologist went so far as to call the antiguo dynasties at Chichén a "mafia."

Instead of claiming inheritance to Chichén based on descent from the ancient Maya, Chichén's antiguos base their patrimonial claims to the archaeological site on what I call "patrifruct" principles. The arguments work in the following manner: Chichén is theirs not by right of cultural affiliation to the ancient Maya but by their twentieth-century presence living and working in the archaeological zone. In today's tourism industrial complex, rapidly becoming transformed by neoliberal agendas, is there a place for alternative kinds of claims to cultural patrimony such as this? The predominant discourse on indigenous claims to cultural and intellectual heritage requires, for the most part, a demonstrable link between ancient civilizations and their contemporary descendants. These cultural affiliations are notoriously complex, caught up in a confusion of identity politics in an unholy alliance with the scientific rigidity of the archaeological record.

But the antiguos—these second- and third-generation federal employees at Chichén Itzá—have formed a very powerful claim to Chichén Itzá that cleverly rearticulates the relationship between ancient material culture and contemporary indigenous people. This rearticulation skips over the fraught debates of identity politics, cutting straight to the heart of the matter. He who has the knowledge to care best for the archaeological zone has the right to benefit economically from this endlessly renewable resource.

The claim on the archaeological site as inheritable family patrimony is maintained through the articulation of two overlapping notions. The first is based on consanguinity and the second on the collective memory and tradition of working in the site. While the first is a patrimonial link by default, the second complements the importance of blood ties to another key body fluid, to put it crudely, the sweat of one's brow. Birth is important, but the labor carried out by one's hands is perhaps equally important in demonstrating one's ties to Chichén. Custodianship of the archaeological zone becomes a usufruct right as it is equated with agricultural cultivation. Working the monuments and the land around them is a kind of traditional outdoor work not unlike clearing weeds from a field, planting a crop, or keeping a watchful eye over one's prize harvest so no man or beast can intrude. Indeed, Chichen's first custodios were local men chosen for their skills as campesinos, and it is only very recently that other skills—such as archaeological knowledge and language competencies—are sought.[8] Over the course of three generations, these two notions—right by birth and right by work—are nearly indistinguishably mapped onto each other in such a way that their correlation is seamless. Though justifiable, a question of fairness arises regarding the patrimonial claims made by Chichén's antiguos to keep exclusive rights to benefit from Chichén Itzá, this site of national and international patrimony.

ABOLISHING THE ANTIGUO MONOPOLY

The first encargados of archaeological zones were elevated custodios placed in charge of the sites. They spoke Maya, were accustomed to life in the campo, and rarely had formal education. These early encargados established a system of worker patronage at the zones. When a position needed to be filled, the encargado would present a name to the INAH central office, usually that of a relative. Due to a patron-client relationship of *confianza*, the inherent confidence and trust in the encargado, the name would be accepted for employment without question. The authority of the encargado ensured the satisfactory performance of the workers on a site-by-site basis. This system worked for more than four decades.

The patronage system of hiring site custodios raises issues of nepotism and the dual-edged "benefit" of strong family networks among INAH custodians. Until very recently, the family networks served to hold the system of custodianship in place of other kinds of local infrastructure. The most obvious infrastructural deficit was in the field of communication: regular communication was very poor between the archaeological zones and the INAH central office in Mérida. Complicating the matter was a lack of intercommunication among the zones themselves. I am referring here to literal modes of communication—roads, radios, and telephones even today do not conveniently or reliably reach some of the sites under regular INAH custodianship. Thus, the autonomy of the encargados was by default and necessity. Staff in the central office in Yucatán's capital city could not micromanage the zones even if they wanted to!

On the other hand, the de facto circumstance of the discretionary power of site encargados has become a source of consternation for officials at the INAH central office in Mérida. If authorities attempted to sanction one custodian for a job-related infraction, such as excessive tardiness, absenteeism, or drinking on the job, often the whole family would take offense and protest the sanctions. Thus the attempt to resolve issues regarding the job performance of one worker can result in the protest of an entire work team of a particular zone. The issue is further exacerbated when family networks extend across multiple zones, even in different areas of the state. For example, the labor history is one of genealogies crossed in complex ways among sites as far-flung as Chichén Itzá, Uxmal, and smaller sites on the Ruta Puuc and even Cobá in the neighboring state of Quintana Roo. Added to this mix are strong union participation among the majority of custodios and the political prominence of certain encargados and workers in their home communities, usually the towns closest to their work.

NEW WORKERS, A DIFFERENT FORM OF CUSTODIANSHIP

Fully one-third of the custodios at Chichén are not antiguos. Only in the past decade has the INAH state office opened local competitions for custodial positions. For the first time, job opportunities opened up for "outsiders" to join the ranks of custodios, most from Pisté and one from outside the state of Yucatán.[9] Though some had worked at the site daily for eight or nine years, they remained *los nuevos*, the new ones. The INAH state office in Mérida, despite pressure from the antiguo-controlled labor union,[10] knew the system would have to change.

In 1994 an open competition for custodio positions was held in Pisté. An examination concerning Mexico's cultural heritage, developed through INAH-labor union negotiations, was presented to all applicants. Of twenty questions, ten were representative of the INAH custodian exam administered throughout Mexico, and ten were put forth by the union. Eighty people presented themselves along with their official documents to compete for six positions. Current university students and those who had already completed a university education were not permitted to enter the competition. Acceptance into the available positions was based on the highest scores. Only those already living close to the archaeological zone were chosen, with the objective of benefiting local communities with these stable and well-paid federal jobs.

The custodial positions stand in great contrast to the current labor economy in Pisté and nearby smaller towns. While many residents are engaged in economic activity closely associated with the ruins, the kinds of work required, number of hours, and days off do not compare with those enjoyed by the custodians. Hundreds of people work within the archaeological zone and along its perimeter as cooks, launderers, gardeners, and the like. Of those informally or self-employed, many make and sell handicrafts (Castañeda 1996; Peraza López and Rejón Patrón 1989; Quintal Avilés 1995).

Almost all of their jobs are for forty-five hours a week rather than thirty-five as is the case for most employees at other zones. The Chichén custodios' work schedule is ten days on followed by four days off. Seven of the ten days on are dedicated to patrolling in uniform around the zone. The remaining three are out-of-uniform, shorter workdays for performing maintenance such as cutting the grass, hacking down overgrown areas, or spraying herbicide on weeds that push between the stones of the restored structures. However, in the time I carried out my research at Chichén, it was rare to find any custodios actually carrying out these activities. Instead, it was from these three days out of every two weeks that vacation and compensation days were taken.

The number of compensation days seemed rather high but was explained to me in the following manner. All federal employees get a certain number of days off, most of which are national holidays. The archaeological zone is open to the public every day of the year, which means that employees have to work on holidays. They are compensated for these days by being allowed to schedule other days off during a regular work period. Patrolling during the hours that the zone is open to the public represents the greatest need in terms of manpower; thus workers are unlikely to get any of the first seven days of each two-week work period as a compensation day.

Traditional work—understood as the labor of a campesino—is being replaced by the increasingly high degree of tourism development at the site and the corresponding high volume of visitors. Another way to describe this transformation would again be through the performance metaphor of onstage labor, involving public presence and constant, direct contact with visitors, replacing the backstage labor more commonly associated with the traditional tasks of the campo.

The period from the mid-1980s to the mid-1990s marked a transformation in labor activities of caring for the patrimony at Chichén Itzá, in both the duties of a custodio and the technologies of the modernization of labor. It appears that the everyday duties of a custodian are quite particular to the extensive development of Chichén Itzá and perhaps increasingly at Uxmal as well. At other zones, where there is little tourism and no state infrastructure or promotion, the work of custodianship remains within the concept of traditional masculine outdoor activity.

The following example defining the duties of custodianship at a less developed site in Yucatán is telling. When one position opened in the archaeological zone of Ek Balam, three men competed for it. Part of the examination was to test the men's skills in *chapeo*, or clearing brush and weeds from paths, monuments, and other areas in the archaeological zone. Each was given an area twenty or so square meters to clear. The

applicant who performed this task the best in addition to achieving a com-
petitive score on the written examination became an INAH employee.

The transformation from the traditional work of the campo to a
new labor regime of custodianship in Chichén Itzá is situated within
modernizing practices of the heritage assemblage. Caring for the monuments at Chichén has been greatly affected by the site's infrastructural development as a tourism destination and by a host of new ideologies of
service-industry labor. Today, new custodios are required to have good
people skills, as their jobs entail face-to-face interaction with national and
international tourists. A customer-oriented politics of politeness is part of
the new professionalization of custodianship. Not simply a matter of atti-
tude on the part of Chichén's workers, the customer-oriented atmosphere
requires new skills.

Though not federally mandated as yet, custodians are encouraged to
develop at least minimum standards of foreign-language proficiency. One
might encounter in the archaeological zone on any given day guards
able to give directions and answer visitors' questions in English, Italian,
or German—in addition to Spanish, of course. Although there is usually
an ambulance on-site staffed with paramedics, custodios know that they
might shoulder the responsibility of first response to any accidents inside
the zone. From these few examples and those that follow, the genealogy
of labor at Chichén Itzá reveals that the archaeological site is no longer
the campo—it is a space of complex, fluid modernity.

THE DAILY GRIND

Forty-five hours a week in an archaeological zone is a long time in a busy
yet seemingly unchanging place. After the first several weeks of my
ethnographic work, I experienced a period of intense boredom during the
daily walk or bike-ride to Chichén from Pisté, knowing that each day
would be remarkably similar to the one before it. I kept hoping, rather
darkly I suppose, that something would *happen* in these long and tedious
weeks, maybe a fall from the Castillo, a lightning strike, or a slip and fall
into the Sacred Cenote. My heat-affected imagination struggled to run
wild. Yet the most exciting event was the summoning of the on-site ambulance to the Observatory late one afternoon. A small child had been
stung by a bee on her foot. Her slight injury was attended to in relatively
short order, followed by a quick cruise around the site in the ambulance
as a reward for her halted tears. How could such a wondrous place be so,
well, boring?

By the time I had been visiting Chichén for several months, I had nearly forgotten this early ennui. Some days found me traversing the zone several times, meeting up with custodios at their assigned locations to chat or conduct taped interviews. Other days I would spend hours in the same spot, usually with a site worker, finding a new work rhythm for myself. This, in retrospect, seems to have derived a good deal from the custodians' own pace and perspective of their work routine. I used this personal experience of Chichén Itzá as my own worksite to think through how it functioned for others performing a different kind of labor.

"Fabulous place" (Castañeda 1996) though it may be, certainly the significance of the zone changes for a person who works there, day after day, year after year. But as in almost any job, INAH workers tactically manipulate their job sites and descriptions to maintain a sense of meaningful activity and pride in their positions. One explanation would go like this: "Certainly many observers see workers, men for the most part, as developing considerable skill in making 'the best of a bad job' in using their human imagination and ingenuity in turning work into more than just a job" (Morgan 1992: 79). While I have to qualify this statement in light of the case at hand—no one considers the work of a custodio to be "a bad job"—I find that this passage raises an issue important to characterizing work at Chichén. What extracurricular activities produced by site workers' "imagination and ingenuity" make the job of custodianship more than "just a job"? Here I will point out three significant activities that help add texture to the everyday life of Chichén Itzá.

The first is social activity, something that is certainly not exclusive to archaeological site workers. INAH workers incorporate social activities into their daily routines, leaving their patrol areas and meeting up with compañeros at another, stopping to talk to others while crossing through the zone to enter a work area, or arranging break-times in pairs or small groups. For example, one group of three to five antiguos—two of whom worked at the Mayaland entrance ticket booth—cooked on site and ate lunch together nearly every day. They prepared meat in an underground pit oven (*piib* in Maya) in the ground behind the ticket booth. Chicken and pork cooked *piib'il* style, in a homemade underground oven, is a popular dish in Yucatecan regional cuisine, in homes as well as in restaurants oriented toward tourists.

In addition to this kind of group activity, custodios socialized with other people engaged with work at the site. Most of these were tour guides from Pisté, Cancún, or elsewhere who made daily trips to Chichén with groups of tourists. This form of socializing led, in one case, to building business relationships between tour guides and one custodian. Inside the zone, the custodio sold sets of photographs of the monuments to the tour guides, who in turn would sell them to tourists. While technically not "legal," INAH officials who were aware of the situation were initially unconcerned. One set of photos, however, turned out to be of an area undergoing excavation that therefore was closed to the public. The archaeologists working on the project were especially upset, as their own research results and photographs had not yet been made public. The worker involved was reprimanded but not formally sanctioned.

Another form of social activity on the job at Chichén takes place through walkie-talkies. Though these are costly and difficult to maintain, many of the guards on duty in the archaeological zone will use radios for communication with each other and the zone's headquarters. In a zone as large as Chichén Itzá, a guard might be as far as several kilometers from a colleague or from headquarters. Apart from the conveyance of critical security-related information, radios also made a handy tool for girl-watching. Radio communication was used to signal to the employee at the next post of the approach of attractive women. The INAH does not supply a radio unit for each worker on duty at a given time; only about half of a shift will have communication units with them. Of the available units, most were donated by the Barbachano family, while a few others were personally owned by custodios.

Radio communication takes place in code, using numbers in place of location names and activity descriptions, much like a police radio system. As much as was revealed to me by the custodios concerning every aspect of daily life at Chichén and the work of the custodios, radio codes were sacred and therefore secret. When they did speak outside of the number code system, the workers often communicated with each other in Maya rather than Spanish. In this way, the Maya language functioned as an everyday code in the presence of tourists.

I include these descriptions to emphasize not the uniqueness of Chichén Itzá but its ordinariness as a workplace. However, in some ways INAH custodianship is not just another job. Indeed, membership in the INAH ranks at Chichén Itzá has its privileges. The degree to which workers are able to spend long hours together under relatively light supervision, the fairly predictable volume and behaviors of the crowds of visitors, and the necessity of close collaboration when confronting serious problems all tend to promote a strong camaraderie among the custodios. But as we will see, this camaraderie is not without its caveats.

PRIVILEGES OF MEMBERSHIP

That which a certain group of the site's guards and caretakers are keeping under their watchful eye, or better stated, their controlling collective thumb, is not simply the monuments per se. Instead of playing their "legitimate" role as federal employees, Chichén's custodios are divided among themselves about the direct control over rights to profit from the World Heritage Site and international tourism destination. These workers are not merely functionaries of the state as their job titles would suggest. They are Maya entrepreneurs who have historically been able to intervene in the national heritage assemblage, making the stuff of the public good that of private enterprise.

The contention for the archaeological zone's resource potential was not an open issue until the state-sponsored major infrastructural development plan of the early 1980s to modernize Chichén threatened to wipe out the kinds of claims and practices the antiguos and their families had been building upon since the late 1930s. This modernization agenda has included the construction of hotel facilities and food, souvenir, and handicraft vending areas, most of which are now located on the perimeter of the area declared as federal property. Thus, Chichén's modernization was not an abstracted process: it was very much accompanied by the increased, felt presence of new regulations and restrictions within the zone's territory. The intensification affected the structure and organization of labor relations at the site as well as the relations between the site and the surrounding residential and business communities.

The antiguo lineages are known today not only within the archaeological zone but in Pisté, where most members reside. Here, the antiguo label is neither neutral nor simply descriptive. Rather, it carries a host of other characteristics that arise from the historical dimensions of the genealogies of the family lines themselves and of the wealth of privileges that membership in an INAH family carries. Due to generations of secure federal employment, INAH workers tend not to be subject to the same precarious economic dependence on the fluctuating tourism economy like many of their neighbors. Numerous paid holidays afford leisure time unthinkable for those who have to sell handicrafts in the streets on a daily basis to make ends meet. Clothing allowances and educational opportunities are also among the job benefits.

Successive years of federal INAH employment have led to capital accumulation, making investment in new local business opportunities possible. Already among the most privileged in their employment, INAH workers

FIGURE 4.4. *A concrete marker (left) denotes Chichén Itzá's UNESCO World Heritage status where the houses of INAH employees stood until the early 1980s. Photograph by author.*

also are entrepreneurs. Since the 1940s, INAH families have used their presence in the archaeological zone to directly provide tourist services, primarily through selling refreshments. The relatively small-scale sale of a cold drink or a plate of food in front of one's home, as was the business practice until the zone's modernization in the early 1980s, raised few eyebrows. Coinciding with the tourism boom in Cancún, the cultural resource presented by Chichén Itzá piqued the interests of officials, particularly at the

state level. The workers' inhabiting of the nation's patrimony—their residence within the ruins—became an image problem. A contemporary
Maya scene of rambunctious children, laundry hanging out to dry, and
roaming dogs and chickens alongside the monuments was incongruent
with the modern representation of tourist destination.

If they could not live in the archaeological zone, raising their families,
planting their crops, and providing services for tourists, the antiguos were
determined to be compensated for the loss of their homes and to find another way to maintain the dominion they had held over Chichén Itzá for
decades. When bulldozers leveled the last of the INAH employees' houses
in the archaeological zone, cash compensation was promised to each head
of household to purchase property and build a new home elsewhere. Left
unresolved was the greater concern for many of the antiguos: their exclusive presence in the zone that had afforded them opportunities to earn
over and above their federal salaries through providing tourist services.
The situation was shortly "rectified" through an under-the-table agreement the custodians made with state officials and federal INAH representatives to establish two refreshment and souvenir vending stands under
the control of the custodians and organized as cooperatives.

Shortly before workers knew that structural and infrastructural
changes would soon instigate their eviction from the zone, the José Erosa
Peniche primary school ceased functioning. A group of then-resident
custodios drummed up a plan for a way to profitably exploit the vacated
structure: they would outfit a small store to serve the other workers, including those employed at the hotels Mayaland and Hacienda Chichén
Itzá, not to mention the ever-growing influx of tourists to the site. Seizing
the opportunity that had presented itself, they pooled enough resources to
begin to outfit and stock the modest space. Just a year later, when they had
barely gotten the shop up and running, the demolition was imminent.
They were "left with nothing," said Don Rosendo, one of the oldest and
most formidable of the antiguos and an original investor in the primary
school bodega. He described the situation, curiously enough, in the third
person:

> The truth is, the families didn't want to leave the site. They were very
> accustomed to living there, and some people had lived there their whole
> lives. It was painful for some, not because they felt like they were *own-
> ers* but because they were accustomed to the ambience of the site: the
> sounds of the night, the sounds characteristic of the archaeological
> zone. So it was difficult for them to leave.

Though Don Rosendo plays up the emotional connection of the resident INAH families, the removal of the employees and their families from the site was reckoned with as if a simple business transaction. The employees' loss should be properly compensated by the state and federal entities involved in the site's redevelopment.

In response to this demand, the state government worked in conjunction with the INAH and the affected workers to come to a settlement agreement. The exact parameters of the agreement and amounts of money it entailed were conveyed to me by those involved and others (friends and neighbors) in wildly varying accounts.[11] According to one informant, custodios were promised three thousand pesos each, which would have been enough to resettle a family in modest quarters in Pisté. Another informant—whose statement was widely backed by many others—claimed that no fixed cash settlement was ever distributed. In lieu of cash compensation, workers were offered a settlement-in-kind in the form of an arranged mortgage on a house in Pisté.

INAH custodios were, to say the least, dissatisfied with the phantom or inconveniently contingent nature of the compensation plan. They set their sights on alternative ways of securing the economic benefits they held when living inside the zone. Along with the mid-1980s construction of Chichén's parador turístico, two palm-roofed vending centers (*palapas*, or thatch huts) were built inside the INAH's jurisdiction of the zone. But who would control these potentially big money-making enterprises? The twelve custodios had invested in the old school building claimed that they were owed compensation, but not a specific amount of money. Instead, they requested and—after much negotiation—received permission through an accord between the INAH, CULTUR, and the Barbachano family to establish a vending cooperative in one of the two palapas inside the zone. It was the mid-1980s, when the tourism influx that centered on Cancún and trickled down to Chichén and Pisté was seemingly limitless and unstoppable.

The vending cooperatives thus established only included among its beneficiaries one group of former site residents. Soon, the others—led by two wives of custodios—mobilized to establish their own cooperative in the second palapa, advantageously located some three kilometers away at the Sacred Cenote. Representing the business interests of their husbands— longtime custodios who had become physically incapacitated through illness—the women had to battle for the palapa, in which a refreshment stand had already been established through the Barbachano family.

The establishment of the two palapas and their associated cooperative members gave rise to an important distinction among custodios that is still very much operative today. Those INAH workers who once lived in the zone and secured an economic interest in the palapas after Chichén's re-development all became antiguos, even though those who established the second palapa were technically newer workers on the site. Thus the "antiguo" label stands as much for economic rights as for longevity in INAH employment.

The "nuevos," on the other hand, never lived in the zone. They came from Pisté, San Francisco (a nearby *rancho*), Santa Elena (the largest town near the site of Uxmal), and Peto. Some had more than ten years on the job at Chichén and resented being called "new." But they preferred this label to *antiguo*. Outside the zone, at home in Pisté, this cohort was particularly sensitive to the town's opinion of INAH custodians. "They group us all together. . . . Most people don't realize that we nuevos don't share in the money made by the antiguos with their palapas inside the zone and their other businesses in Pisté," said José María, a nuevo in his thirties who had been at Chichén for six years. Though his family has a longevity of several generations in Pisté, no one among his relatives had previously worked in the INAH. Tired of waiting tables at the Mayaland Hotel and elsewhere, he relished the opportunity to work inside the zone. And the steady salary along with its other benefits was a safe, secure way to support his family.

José María was particularly vocal in speaking out against the system of economic benefits that antiguos developed. His complaints have an interesting discursive simultaneity—invoking the site as both "cultural patrimony of all" and as a place where the nuevos should have their "fair" chance to earn more than their salaries by working there. While attacking the "injustice" from the standpoint of undermining the practice in terms of its illegitimacy according to policies and regulations concerning patrimonio cultural, he wanted equal opportunity to profit from the site. Why should they earn so much money in "*mi* Chichén"? His possessiveness is more than a pride in the cultural patrimony of the Maya, of Yucatán, or of Mexico. He was from Pisté and worked at Chichén—he was not just one of the passersby who flood the zone on a daily basis. It was his Chichén, and he wanted his financial rewards.

While José María's critique articulates the ambivalence of Chichén Itzá as both everybody's and nobody's, the antiguos assert their own logic for rationalizing and legitimizing the existence of the cooperatives in their present form. They do not appear to seriously consider what they call the "petty complaints" of unfairness by nuevos. However, the custodians involved in the cooperatives do see the state government as presenting a threat to their business inside the archaeological zone. The following

FIGURE 4.5.   *INAH employees' cooperative palapas inside the archaeological zone cater to visitors' refreshment needs. Photograph by author.*

explanation demonstrates one palapa owner's attempt to protect his interests inside the archaeological zone by appealing to the contemporary popularity of the nongovernmental civic association as an institution working for the public good.

> These cooperatives are not cooperatives [in the legal sense]; they are *asociaciones civiles*, they are *comercios* [businesses]. If they [the nuevos] want to join, yes, the door is open, but you have to give your part [an investment in the group enterprise]. When the palapas were formed as asociaciones, they were not formed under the name of one person; rather, they carried the names of all [antiguos] who were present at this historic moment. That is why it is an *asociación civil*.

He continued to rationalize the exclusivity of the enterprise by claiming Chichén as an INAH-family patrimony:

> The cooperatives were formed as entities completely separate from the business of Chichén. They do not receive any of the income of the archaeological zone, and since they are separate, membership is not the right of just any worker. . . . It is a very special, historically justified situation. These people who have no roots in Chichén are not a part of this. It is an exclusive right for the families who once lived in the zone.

This statement requires a bit of unpacking, mostly in the terminological realm. Interestingly enough, he admitted that the palapas are not technically cooperatives, which is correct. But then he proceeded to identify them as asociaciones civiles (A.C.'s). According to a lawyer I consulted, the enterprises inside the archaeological zone are actually *sociedades anónimas* (S.A.'s): for-profit business associations. The rationalization for calling the *cooperativas* by the name asociaciones civiles is highly important in justifying the existence and continued functioning of the refreshment and souvenir stands inside the archaeological zone. The A.C., a nongovernmental organization (NGO), has a coveted nonprofit status and carries the flavor of civic duty, performing disinterested public work, benefiting society, and "doing good" in general. Thus, this labeling recasts what from one perspective looks like a "mafia" organization motivated by personal greed into the light of public good. The term "mafia" likewise carries with it a set of distinguishing characteristics: family-oriented business that is heavily involved in illegal activities. Unlike the hyperstructured organization or bureaucracy, the mafia organization has a personalistic ethos. A mafia might be described as a kinship group with consanguineous, affinal, and fictive kin relations. "In the absence of a legitimate system of effective power, the mafia emerged as a system of parasitic power" (Alba 1985: 36).

In my own research and corroborated to some extent by an INAH official, I found no legal provision for the palapas. The owning organizations do not appear to be cooperatives in a legal sense. Instead, the day-to-day operations and business practices appear to be those of a for-profit corporation. Rationalized as a product of historic patrimony and situated as they are in a site of Maya heritage, the palapas, as one antiguo explained to me, are "cultural foundations." Yet for more than fifteen years the antiguo vending cooperatives continue to operate private, quite profitable business enterprises within the federal borders of the archaeological zone. Though legally suspect, the vending cooperatives are justified by the antiguo families on the basis of patrifruct rights to economically benefit from the archaeological zone. Because their fathers worked the land of Chichén Itzá, they have inherited the right to a presence in that space. They too imagine their duties as a way of working the land of Chichén Itzá, not as the campesinos of earlier generations but as caretakers of the nation's patrimony at an international tourism destination. One third-generation custodio, son of a well-respected encargado, rationalized the establishment of the vending cooperatives: "No one can own cultural patrimony . . . it belongs to everyone. Therefore, we have to claim our part of our heritage that we deserve."

Indeed, the antiguos themselves claim to abide by the principle of cultural patrimony as "commons," but only for its rightful heirs. One young antiguo said,

> For a custodian . . . every day you go to Chichén Itzá, there you spend your time, and on the side you have a little business. For me, this is something that should be respected by history, the people, and the government. After all, how many men have dedicated their lives to the archaeological zones? How many descendants have stayed on to maintain the same site?

Now, why would officials buy this rationale and even allow the establishment of the refreshment stands—especially given that all archaeological zones in Mexico are under a constitutional mandate declaring them under custodianship of the nation? The answer comes in the form of a caveat to the genealogy of antiguos at Chichén Itzá.

Recall the circumstance of landownership: the whole archaeological zone is actually privately held land, having been purchased in bits and pieces between the 1920s and 1950s by a single very wealthy Yucatec family. In this site of cultural patrimony of the Mexican nation, only the monuments are technically under federal control—not the land upon which they sit. Because the refreshment stands do not interfere in the built architectural space of the monuments, they are on the land owned by the descendants of tourist agent and hotelier Fernando Barbachano. The antiguos need only pay steep rental fees to the property owner to continue their own enterprises within the zone. Today the Barbachano family owns and operates multiple hotels, two of which are technically inside the borders of archaeological zones, along with restaurants, bus lines, and guide services. All of this is made possible by a patriarch's keen vision of the future of Maya ruins in the international tourism industry.

Alongside the strong private-sector presence in Chichén Itzá represented by the Barbachano family, the antiguo vending cooperatives do not look quite so exclusive. But that is not the perception by the various "publics" that have vested interests in the archaeological zone. Why, other local residents ask, should only a privileged few benefit so directly from what is, at least rhetorically, patrimony of the whole nation? The question is one not likely to be resolved any time soon, especially as the interests of all of Chichén's stakeholders are increasingly under the threat of formal privatization of national patrimony in Mexico.

Over the past several decades, the antiguos have demonstrated a remarkable flexibility in shaping their patrimonial claims and in their ability

FIGURE 4.6. *Heading off: A custodio walks his bicycle along the path linking the parador turístico entrance to the site center. Photograph by author.*

to maneuver around de facto legalities (perhaps not unlike the "mafia" they have been labeled) regarding who has the right to benefit from cultural heritage resources in Mexico. However we want to call them, these antiguos, these "mafiosos," these Maya, these workers, these indigenous people are just one segment of one local population that finds itself engaged in the everyday negotiation of the global political economy of tourism.

There is something about the splendor, mystery, and magic of Maya ruins that conveniently produces a sense of wonder and obscures the intimate politics of the everyday production and maintenance of an archaeological site. A focus on the genealogy of labor intervenes precisely in this antipolitics of heritage by foregrounding the political economy and the "everyday life" of Chichén Itzá. Historically, Maya workers have produced the site literally through the reconstruction projects of the 1920s through 1940s and continually reproduce the site through maintenance and provision of tourist services. Looking closely at the ambivalent heritage-claiming practices of Chichén's custodios, we can see that it is not always and exclusively the state or even the big-business private sector that sets the terms for the commodification of cultural resources and the interpellation of these properties into the heritage industry.

The workers' assertion of patrifruct rights to Chichén Itzá represents a doubly significant form of privatization. The economic activities of the custodio-run cooperatives within the archaeological zone coincide with any workaday definition of private-sector business activity. At the same time, the antiguo employees are practicing what I would call a "privatization of meaning" at Chichén Itzá. By narrating the past century of the site's history as deeply intertwined with their own family histories, the custodians make the zone theirs, protectively and even "jealously" guarding Chichén Itzá.

CHUNCHUCMIL: AMBIVALENCE IN
A HERITAGE LANDSCAPE

Chapter 5

*Two hundred thousand Maya toil for foreign masters today in the
henequen fields of Yucatán, all memory of their former significance
gone as completely as if it had never been. . . . With such a glorious
past, it would seem as though his future might be made of greater
promise than this. With proper educational facilities, with fair
agricultural opportunities, and intelligent help over the rough
places in the road, he must travel from his own simple past to the
complicated world of today, and there is every reason to expect
that he may again fashion for himself a destiny worthy of his
splendid ancestry.*

SYLVANUS G. MORLEY, *NATIONAL GEOGRAPHIC*, 1925: 86

*Every inheritance is alike beneficial and baneful; even historically
conscious society has had to reassess that balance for itself.*

DAVID LOWENTHAL, *THE PAST IS A FOREIGN COUNTRY*,
1985: xx

One weeknight just after dark, I attended a slide show of archaeological
wonders presented by the INAH-Yucatán's head of security in Kochol. I,
along with thirty or so women and children, watched the scuffed, uneven
wall on the side of the darkened *molino* (corn mill) light up with images of
Chichén Itzá, one after another. The occasion for the slide show was an
invitation extended by archaeologists of the Pakbeh Archaeological Project to the INAH representative in an effort to educate the community
about Maya cultural patrimony. The Pakbeh Project, originally known as
the Chunchucmil Regional Economy Project (CREP), a group of archaeologists mostly from U.S. universities, was in the midst of its fifth season
of excavation at the ruins of Chunchucmil, a few kilometers from where
we were gathered—archaeologists, INAH representative, ethnographer,
and Maya residents—to watch the slides of famous archaeological sites,

Maya glyphs, and artifacts. The slides showed thousands of national and international tourists gathered at Chichén Itzá on March 21, the spring equinox.

Here we were, almost two hundred kilometers from Pisté and Chichén Itzá, in the same state of Yucatán, but in a sense a world away. At the site of Chunchucmil, only recently declared by the INAH an officially delimited archaeological zone, there are no restored monumental structures. There are no emblematic pyramids visitors may climb and snap a triumphant photo such as on the Castillo at Chichén Itzá. In fact, there were very few visitors to the mounds at Chunchucmil at all, including these local community residents, even though most of the land comprising the site center belongs to the community members as an ejido land grant. From my own perspectives on the history of archaeological site development in Yucatán, especially through my research at Chichén Itzá, the words of the INAH representative showing the slides rang true. "Maybe none of you will live to see the *cerros* (mounds) on your ejido look like the Castillo, the Great Ball Court, or the Temple of the Warriors at Chichén Itzá, but maybe your children or their children will." Though attentive and even entertained, were these local residents eager to find "real" cultural heritage right in their midst? Did their hopes for their children and their community's future coincide with the promises of heritage development?

That evening it was difficult for Maya residents of Kochol looking at the evidence of what Morley called "a glorious past" to conceive of a future in ruins. Indeed, how could one imagine that the tree-covered hills in the fields once studded with henequen on the outskirts of town might somehow hide beneath them likenesses of the grand monuments such as those at Chichén Itzá? After all, the few seasons of archaeological work at Chunchucmil could not compare with the decades of excavation and reconstruction efforts in the ruins of Chichén.[1] As it stood, Chunchucmil was a dubious heritage site, not only because it lacked the visual coherence and intelligibility that come with structural restoration but also because for many local Maya residents, the mounds were simply not heritage.

What the Pakbeh archaeologists, the INAH representative, and I shared while we watched the slides that evening in Kochol was a competing and more powerful discourse of ruins-as-heritage. Despite the local perspective positing the ruins as "not heritage," archaeological work at Chunchucmil interpellated these unintelligible mounds into national cultural patrimony. Indeed, the undercurrent framing the slide show event was a set of tourism development plans, already in the initial stage, that would bring the communities around the archaeological site into the business of commodifying this newly deemed cultural heritage. Backed with scientific legitimacy and powerful private interests, Pakbeh archaeologists were poised to bring these communities out of an unsavory past into a future "in ruins."

The ruins of Chunchucmil are part of a historically ambivalent landscape. At Chunchucmil, the mounds were—at least until a few years ago—neither ruins nor cultural patrimony. The inception of an archaeological project in 1993 introduced a new patrimonial discourse in Kochol and neighboring communities, including the town of Chunchucmil on the opposite side of the archaeological zone. This is the discourse of ruins as both Maya and Mexican cultural heritage. The material stuff so clearly identified and promoted by the Mexican state as national patrimony was not a part of the everyday understandings articulated by local residents toward the mounds. In fact, the sixteen square kilometers of the archaeological zone is more significant for locals as federally granted ejido agricultural land. The land was granted to former henequen hacienda debt peons in the 1930s, fathers and grandfathers of current local residents.

As we will see, the heritage assemblage has yet to fully incorporate or territorialize these particular cerros, these hills on the otherwise flat landscape. Yet it would be remiss to conceive of the site as somehow "unterritorialized," as an open field unmarked by memory or history. Indeed, other territories already layer the site and linger among these ruins like thick and compelling counternarratives to monumentalization. Not least of these were the hacienda days, when row upon row of spiny henequen plants covered what is now a monumental zone of national cultural patrimony.

This chapter is about the nonmonumental spaces of heritage in and around the archaeological zone of Chunchucmil. While the land itself is the material embodiment of heritage or patrimony, a wealth of intangible heritage lives in these communities. This intangible heritage is the stuff of neither the state's nationalist vision of Mexican heritage nor archaeology's scientific valorization of the Maya and the ancient past. Not officially identified as such, this heritage lives within and between legal and institutional frameworks, ideological constructs, and disciplinary practice. The nonmonumental heritage of Chunchucmil consists of cultural and familial legacies, inherited beliefs, and transgenerational practices of taming, cultivating, and respecting the land. A troublesome and messy heritage, it is subtle yet enduring for contemporary community residents. Rather than a univocal heritage of ancient Maya culture firmly affixed to the ruins, this nonmonumental heritage is peripatetic. Nomadic as it is, this heritage is not completely rootless.

NORTHWESTERN YUCATÁN IN THE ETHNOGRAPHIC ARCHIVE

Consider this: while Edward Thompson was dredging Chichén's Sacred Cenote for its ancient treasures, wealthy *hacendados*, owners of henequen haciendas, were still delirious with the "green gold" fever of the late nineteenth century. Kochol and Chunchucmil were among the more than four hundred communities in northwestern Yucatán organized under the feudal hacienda system to produce henequen monoculture, beginning in the 1870s and intensifying through the turn of the century. As the CIW began to hire local Maya from Pisté and other communities to work in the excavation and reconstruction projects at Chichén Itzá, land reforms had not yet reached the thousands of Mayas laboring in debt servitude. Not for several years would these hacienda properties be expropriated and the land distributed to its cultivators. Today, while neighboring residents enjoy the flows and weather the ebbs of the tourism economy that encompasses Chichén, former hacienda communities barely subsist in a generally downward-spinning economic spiral due to lack of socioeconomic infrastructure and viable state development projects.

These contrasts are just a few of the reasons Chunchucmil seems a world away from Chichén Itzá. The state of Yucatán has for more than a century been characterized as divided into two regions. Southern and eastern Yucatán, where Pisté and Chichén Itzá are located, are historically known as the milpa region; northwestern Yucatán is still known as the henequen region, though it has been decades since this sisal-hemp plant has been profitably cultivated in the region and nearly a century since henequen production was at its height. The contrasts between the henequen and milpa regions appear most prominently in their agricultural production and in their underlying social organization. During the nineteenth century through the early twentieth century, southern and eastern Yucatán were populated by "free Maya," meaning their free access to land to grow sufficient corn and other subsistence products. In the northern and western areas of the peninsula, most indigenous Maya were forcefully incorporated into life tied to the henequen haciendas as debt peons.

Ethnography of Yucatán has consistently portrayed the regionalism of Yucatán in a manner privileging the milpa region over the henequen region. All four of the communities presented in Redfield's *Folk Culture of Yucatán* (1941), for example, are situated south and east of Mérida. Redfield began his social anthropological study of Maya communities in Yucatán under the auspices of the CIW's archaeological project headquartered at

Chichén Itzá.[2] Redfield's most intensive research was carried out in Chan Kom, a Maya community on the outskirts of Chichén Itzá. In his study *Chan Kom: A Maya Village* (1934) Redfield focuses on the concept of cultural change through the lens of how varying degrees of contact with "civilization" (modernity) differentially affect "folk culture" throughout Yucatán. He presents civilization and modernization through a spatiovisual image of civilization moving across the Yucatán, originating in Mérida in the northeast corner of the peninsula and spreading to the south and west, growing weaker (2). If this region was the seat of Yucatecan culture, where did the haciendas of northwestern Yucatán fit into this schematized image?

Arnold Strickon had the same question in a 1965 article, "Hacienda and Plantation in Yucatán" (36–37), in the journal *America Indígena*:

> It was widely recognized, as soon as *The Folk Culture of Yucatán* appeared, that Redfield had all but ignored the henequen plantations of the northern part of the peninsula. In terms of the economic role of the henequen industry for the whole peninsula, and in terms of the proportion of the Yucatecan population which was directly or indirectly dependent upon it, this zone and these plantations constituted the most important sector of the Yucatecan economy, society, and polity. It is my contention that the henequen estates of Redfield's time were critical to an understanding of Yucatecan culture as Redfield saw it.

It was thought that the slavelike debt-bondage system encompassing hundreds of population centers in northwestern Yucatán had overly influenced or even destroyed the traditional cultural aspects of Maya life. There are few exceptions to the ethnographic bypassing of the henequen region.[3]

Factors distinguishing the milpa and henequen regions are ecological, agricultural, and industrial, all layered onto a distinction of the cultural atmosphere of the regions. Contemporary conditions have exacerbated these contrasts, at least on the level of imagination, as the peninsula has been remapped, so to speak, into new kinds of connections and networks related to the national and international tourism industry upon which the state relied heavily for revenue, jobs, and regional political stability.

I was initially drawn to this other side of Yucatán not through the lure of difference, of "otherness," but for the fact that very little comparative ethnographic work had been done between the south/eastern and north/western regions of the peninsula. While an outsider might be tempted to think that just the other side of the same state would be quite the same, I quickly realized this was not so. Certainly throughout all of Yucatán one definitely finds general and generalizable features of language, dress, lifestyle, and occupation. But what connections link these re-gionalist characterizations and questions of heritage? My own research questions on local and national instantiations of the conception of cultural patrimony led me initially inside the borders of archaeological sites in these two regions of Yucatán. Upon learning something of the "extra-archaeological" territory of Chunchucmil, I found it necessary to step out-side of the discourse on cultural heritage-as-artifact into the more contin-gent realm of heritage-as-practice to look at the ways in which the same geographical space might serve as a locus for different notions of heritage.

Based on oral, official documentary, and other historical sources, I highlight elements in the late nineteenth century through the twentieth century that weave a social historical context of this microregion as back-ground for the current archaeological excavation projects at the site of Chunchucmil. My discussion is divided into three parts, each of which presents a different instantiation of the articulation of patrimony and the production of space within the landscape. In the first part, I explain the rise of the henequen monocrop culture and the reorganization of land, labor, and everyday life for the Mayas of northwestern Yucatán. Here I trace the social history of land patrimony from territorial control of the sover-eign Spanish Crown to the transference to white Yucatecan elites. In this schema, Maya people are disarticulated from territory, thereby losing their patrimony along with their land claims. We will see how the hacienda owners, the hacendados, reorganized the region of northwestern Yucatán through establishment of a new socioeconomic framework for articulating the land and labor of the Maya people.

Next I narrate the conversion of the henequen haciendas into collective ejidos through the agrarian reforms of the 1930s. Similarly to the "prove-nance" of the archaeological zone of Chichén Itzá, I use ejido records and the public property state registry to trace the genealogies of the haciendas and the establishment of the ejidos from the division of their lands. Finally, I discuss recent purchases of former hacienda properties by tourism de-velopers. Just as the archaeological project introduced the discourse of the ruins as cultural patrimony, the "hacienda tourism" development trans-forms the ruined buildings of the henequen plantations into historical cul-tural patrimony, the major selling point for the high-priced luxury hotels for a mostly international niche tourism market. Figuring prominently throughout the discussion are the key terms thus far developed in various ways: patrimony and privatization. And we will find redeployments of these concepts through their local and historical specificity.

HACIENDAS AND HENEQUEN

These days, a tour of the Maya ruins means a visit to our henequen haciendas. (Ermilo Abreu Gómez, *Canek*, cited in Joseph 1982: 228)

Certainly Abreu Gómez was not thinking of the future in hacienda tourism in 1940 when he penned the words above but rather in the ever-present past of the havoc that henequen has wrought on the region's Maya population. For the contemporary Maya in Chunchucmil Pueblo, Kochol, and hundreds of similar communities, the ruins of the hacienda system are indeed more immediate than ancient monuments. In recent years, the Yucatecan landscape has something new to offer more discriminating visitors to the peninsula: the Hacienda Route. Packaged as romantic trips through Yucatán's nineteenth-century splendor made possible by henequen, the route offers a picturesque itinerary through more than one hundred kilometers of the Yucatecan countryside, with lavishly refurbished hotels for overnight stays. Indeed, throughout northwestern Yucatán, the architectural remains of the hacienda system punctuate the perceived monotony of the landscape. Internet advertisements for hacienda tours are sure to highlight these markers of European-influenced civilization, such as this description offered by a tourism Web site, The Net Traveler: "With the passage of the history of Yucatan, the haciendas left deep traces of grandeur that remain perceptible in the deteriorated architecture of their installations."

The hacienda system was the territorializing legacy of the Spanish Conquest of Mexico in the sixteenth century, following upon the mechanisms of the colonial *encomienda* system to control lands and their indigenous inhabitants. Though my concern in this chapter is the territorializing legacy of the hacienda system—especially the post-Independence henequen haciendas in northwestern Yucatán—it is important to understand the influence of colonial land tenure and ownership on their development. The Spanish encomienda system as well the establishment and growth of estancias directly inform the land and labor arrangements upon which the hacienda is predicated. In the early colonial period, lands were distributed to Spanish settlers as rewards under the encomienda system, one of indigenous labor tribute. During the first decades of colonization, lands were territorialized by the Spanish Crown, and their original inhabitants became its subjects. While in the rest of Mexico 55 percent of settlements were held in the encomienda system, in Yucatán the figure reached 90 percent (Strickon 1965: 42). Thus the system had a greater reach—and a

FIGURE 5.1. *Chunchucmil Pueblo's casa principal and its henequen processing buildings, behind the property caretaker, dominate the village landscape. Photograph by author.*

greater longevity, lasting until 1785—than in any other part of Mexico (ibid.). The system was arranged so that the indigenous inhabitants would be obligated to the Spanish Crown for the use of these lands. It is important to note that the encomienda did not imply territorial property ownership: it was only a royal dispensation to collect tribute from the communities under a particular jurisdiction for a set period (Millet Cámara 1984: 19). Yet the effects of the system were to reorganize indigenous work practices and relationships to the land, as Wells (1985: 19), further describes:

> The Maya, who for centuries had lived and worked in communal villages, were now forced to work a prescribed number of days each year for the Spanish encomendero. Significantly, Indians in the Yucatán countryside, although at times badly exploited by the encomienda, were not uprooted from their traditional lifestyle. So long as labor was considered a more valuable resource than land, little pressure was put on the Indian to alter his routine.

The encomienda survived in Yucatán until its abolishment in 1785.

Because the poor soil of the peninsula dramatically affected the productive power of the land for cash export crops, cattle ranches, known as *estancias*, preceded the formation of haciendas. These estancias did not require large populations of laborers, and Mayas were, for the most part, allowed to continue the subsistence cultivation of their staple crop, maize. During the latter half of the eighteenth century in Yucatán, the "classic" haciendas developed. These were combined farming and cattle ranching centers with one unprecedented feature: not only did they offer a secure agro-economic system, but they also began to set in place a social system that would dominate the countryside of Yucatán for almost two centuries (Patch 1976: 32–33).

In the seventeenth century, haciendas were established to give land-owners of Spanish descent their spoils of conquest as well as to give the colonial administrators greater control over territory and population. Unlike the cattle ranches, which required relatively few workers, in the hacienda system, workers and their families lived in the immediate vicinity of the plantation's production center. Thus, during the first half of the nineteenth century, haciendas, as well as some cattle ranches, developed into population centers, often with larger numbers of inhabitants than villages (Bracamonte 1989: 78): "The establishment of each new hacienda was at the same time the birth of a small *aldea de sirvientes*," or village of servants. In Kochol and Chunchucmil, these populations and their descendants tended to remain connected to the agricultural production centers established in this period even after the twentieth century agrarian reform dismantled the hacienda system.

The forced debt peonage of tens of thousands of Maya people came about through a curious confluence of circumstances in the second half of the nineteenth century involving the availability of large land tracts, an already imperiled indigenous population, and the invention of a bale-binding machine. Throughout the nineteenth century, large tracts of land were easily privatized by the white Yucatec elite. They only needed a profitable export crop. Social unrest surrounding the Caste War had displaced and impoverished many Maya communities across the peninsula. Under such conditions, it was easier—and more easily legitimized—to relocate these communities onto haciendas. Meanwhile, hacendados turned to the cultivation of henequen, a fibrous agave plant that grew easily in Yucatán's challenging environment and had a certain demand in the international market as the raw material for industrial-strength rope. Though still in its early stages in the 1870s, a boom in the henequen market was just around the corner. Overseas demand for henequen fiber, especially in the United States, grew exponentially after the invention of the twine binder by Deering in 1879 and McCormick in 1881 (Joseph and

Wells 1996: 99; Topik and Wells 1998: 96). The twine binder is a mechanical attachment to reapers that bound the cut bales of hay. The binder required a tough, organic fiber that would neither decompose nor harm animals feeding on the bales of hay. This confluence of circumstances and events meant unparalleled riches for hacendados and a new level of misery for the Maya of Yucatán.

The care and cultivation of the henequen plant (*Agave fourcroydes*) is both delicate and backbreaking. Even after mechanization techniques for processing henequen fiber were introduced to haciendas, the harvesting of the plant's long, spiny leaves and the maintenance of the plants themselves had to be carefully done by hand. It was not difficult for the hacendados to devise a labor system that would work to their advantage and maintain high levels of profit. The colonial *repartimiento* provided a ready-made model for the exploitation of indigenous labor in Yucatán through debt peonage. Through the repartimientos, indigenous labor became tied to agricultural production on haciendas. The repartimiento system put the indigenous laborer into a never-ending cycle of economic and psychological indebtedness to the hacienda.

Yucatec hacendados relied upon this instrument to ensure a cheap and submissive workforce to develop the henequen economy (Villanueva Mukul 1980: 45). The cultivation, harvest, and processing were difficult and labor-intensive.[4] Labor was forced, docility encouraged, and punishment inevitable.[5] Labor requirements constantly intensified as hacendados planted more and more henequen to increase profits. Mayas who had been milperos, subsistence corn cultivators, were systematically converted into peons by the last decades of the nineteenth century. As they lost free access to land, these debt peons existed in de facto slavery.[6]

The largest of the henequen haciendas reached sizes of two to three thousand hectares, but the typical size was one to two thousand hectares. Not all of this land was used for henequen cultivation, especially as cattle were imported with henequen profits during the boom years. Hacienda populations averaged from 100 to 150 persons, most of whom were Maya resident peons, though some Maya were employed as nonresident day or seasonal workers. There was no such thing as retirement: one would work until his or her death. Children as young as five began work in the henequen. Even with unrestricted access to the labor power of the Maya, the hacendados sought more workers for the ever-increasing yields demanded by the market; at the turn of the twentieth century, they brought indentured laborers from other parts of Mexico, most of them Yaquis from Sonora, as well as from China and Korea.[7]

Henequen labor as controlled and regulated through the hacienda system represented a hybrid form of juridical and disciplinary power, according to Foucault (1977): a transformation occurred in eighteenth-century Europe from sovereign or juridical power that was characterized by brutal, haphazard, and punitive enforcement to disciplinary power—precise, continuous, and routine enforcement in which those subject to authority become self-policing. Foucault carefully distinguishes the projects of docility from slavery. While slavery systems display forms of the juridical exercise of power, as evidenced in the hacienda system, the disciplines "were not based on a relation of appropriation of bodies; indeed the elegance of the discipline lay in the fact that it could dispense with this costly and violent relation by obtaining effects of utility at least as great" (137). The effect of carrying out disciplinary techniques was the production of docile bodies.

While the hacienda system certainly carried holdover characteristics of juridical power, the several techniques of "control of activity" outlined in Foucault's *Discipline and Punish* (1977) fit appropriately. These include the timetable—to establish rhythms, impose particular occupations, and regulate cycles of repetition; correlation of the body and the gesture; and exhaustive use, or non-idleness (149–155). Men I spoke with in Kochol can hardly describe henequen work without making the great sweeping motion used to cut the tough, spiny henequen leaves. People still recall, with the greatest precision of detail, the daily work schedule imposed, as it is explained, not by a person but by a loud bell. The ceaseless ringing of the bell was an attempt to curtail even the tersest of conversation between people in the street or in front of their houses.

It is important to recognize the different forms of power and exercise of authority that enforced the hacienda system in Yucatán and subsequently to attempt to draw connections between these historical formations and the contemporary. Yet, due to the specificity of the rise of the hacienda system in Yucatán, one cannot automatically assume an exact parallel historicity with those states and institutions described by Foucault. The hacienda system is a "ruin" in itself, a relic retaining older forms of sovereign power as a conventional, top-down mechanism of authority based in physical coercion. Yet it is combined with distinctively modern techniques of disciplinary power such as surveillance, the establishment and enforcement of work production quotas, and the debt that distinguished these peons from technical slavery.

This particularly modern form of disciplinary power took aim directly toward the efficient use of labor in agricultural production. The state dictated the laws legalizing the operations of the haciendas. Peons were not allowed to leave the haciendas upon which they worked without certificates establishing that they had completed their work contracts, that they owed nothing to the haciendas, and that they were at liberty to find other work. As can be imagined, this rarely happened. Instead of fulfilling their debts, the amounts consistently grew and grew, compounding as a matter of survival. The debts themselves became a terrible patrimony, an unwanted legacy passed from father to son (Villanueva Mukul 1980: 45).

The hacienda system represents a form of territorializing not only the physical landscape but the bodies of workers and their families. Descendants of those laborers now excavate the same land for its archaeological treasures. The monetary debt visited upon the father and son stands as just one symbol of the heritage of the hacienda. But it is a heritage nonetheless, an element of the nonmonumental heritage that informs the social and physical landscape in and around Chunchucmil. Hacienda heritage is not ancient history in the communities that persist in the former henequen area. Given that there is not, it seems, a stratigraphic method for excavating the hacienda heritage at Chunchucmil, I choose another route.

APPROACHING HERITAGE AT CHUNCHUCMIL

Physical space has no "reality" without the energy that is deployed within it. (Lefebvre 1974/1991: 13)

In front of a small building adjacent to the casa principal of Kochol is a meter-high stone sculpture, now broken at the base and toppled over on its side. Many contemporary residents of Kochol tell of a time when the statue had a "twin," a second stone carving that stood alongside the remaining one. The twin was stolen some years earlier, and no one was sure of its whereabouts. It was thought by most that the statues had a certain potency and that touching the pieces would cause a person to become ill with fever or even to die. This potency was lost when one of the statues became weakened in a flood and toppled over—as demonstrated by the fact that the tellers of these events were actually seated upon it as they recounted its history to me.[8] In one family's backyard in Chunchucmil, where I resided for a time, two ancient stone metates served as animals' watering containers. Columns from ancient temple or residential structures served as stools in front of another contemporary dwelling, my own favorite spot to sit and wait for a truck or collective taxi to come by and go to Maxcanú, the nearest town, about twenty kilometers distant, with regular bus service to the capital city of Mérida.

I first came to Chunchucmil not through my own itinerant travels across Yucatán but through a meeting with Pakbeh Regional Economy Project members at the Fiesta Americana Hotel in Mérida. The project co-director was looking for an ethnographer to join her team to work in the communities surrounding the project's excavation site. The project was specifically looking for an applied anthropologist to facilitate the communication between the U.S. archaeologists and the local Maya residents as both archaeological investigation and site development plans progressed. The Pakbeh Project staff found this necessary for two reasons. The first involved questions of the legal rights as well as the ethics of the archaeologists excavating on the communally held agricultural lands of the site's neighboring communities. In the initial couple of years of mapping, excavating, and clearing the site, some misunderstandings occurred between the archaeologists and community residents. Specifically, the archaeologists' conception of the territory of the state-defined official archaeological zone of Chunchucmil conflicted with another territoriality preceding the archaeological interest in the space. The land, coterminous with the zone, was already divided up into the agricultural lands of five communities according to the ejido distributions of the 1930s. The project therefore was required by these communities to get access permission to work in the various ejidos as well as contract laborers from the communities specific to the area of the zone in which they were working.

The second reason for the project staff's desire to bring in an ethnographer was to facilitate plans for tourism development in and around the site. Ambitious plans were proposed for an artifact museum in the town of Chunchucmil a few kilometers from the archaeological site center and a "living museum" within the archaeological site on Kochol ejido land. The working model for the latter was based on Colonial Williamsburg—in which local community residents would move out of their towns into the archaeological zone to demonstrate daily life practices of the ancient Maya. These as well as other site development ventures required complex, ongoing negotiations between the project and community leaders in order to succeed.[9]

I proceeded in my research at Chunchucmil as a guest researcher instead of a development project facilitator. From this position I was able to enjoy a close affiliation with the archaeologists, sharing their living space and gaining insight into their perspectives on the site and neighboring communities. I modified the model for ethnographic research I had developed for Chichén Itzá to fit the quite different context of Chunchucmil. For me, the most important ground rule for my research was to avoid focusing exclusively on the archaeological project, its members, and relationships between archaeology and the local communities. What I found more compelling is what we could call the "pre-" and/or "extra-archaeological" context surrounding the site and its current development.

In Chichén Itzá I had found that more than one hundred years of archaeological work at the site—which led to its becoming a major international tourism destination—had greatly influenced local conceptions of what Maya heritage is and how the site is inflected with varying understandings of the articulation of the ancient Maya to the contemporary world. In multiple ways, local residents use the site at Chichén to make claims to the cultural patrimony that is simultaneously theirs and that of the Mexican state. Would this phenomenon express itself differently around a site that has only five years of archaeological work?

For ten weeks in the spring and summer of 2001, I carried out ethnographic research in the excavation site of the archaeological zone of Chunchucmil. Most informants I worked with were from the Maya community of Kochol, approximately four kilometers from the site center. Because of my lack of training in archaeology and my hybrid disciplinary status, I spent most of my time in the excavation sites working alongside the laborers from Kochol, carrying out the same (for the most part!) assigned tasks. During these weeks, I lived with project members in the casa principal of the former hacienda of Chunchucmil. After an hour or so of language study each morning, usually in consultation with the archaeologists' cook and maid, I would bike to the excavation sites, often two or three in proximity to each other. I usually timed my arrival with the workers' morning break, at 9 A.M. I typically spent the break-time with the workers chatting, teaching English, and practicing Maya.

When each break was over I went back to work with them, digging, hauling rocks, or looking for ceramic shards and bone and obsidian fragments at the sifting table a few meters from the excavation area. With a tape recorder in a pocket and my notebook in the back of my pants, I used the time I spent working alongside the excavators to hold conversations and interviews. Though my work as an ethnographer was tied in some very obvious ways to the archaeological project, the openness and sensitivity of my informants enabled them to view my heterodox position with a careful discernment of my role vis-à-vis other project members and the directors as well as the discipline of cultural anthropology and its methods and subject matter. To put it simply, they knew that I was not an archaeologist. At the same time, they were quite aware that I too was conducting an investigation in the area, the parameters of which were best mutually understood as concerning "history" and "culture." "History" was taken to primarily refer to the henequen era, and "culture" signified what was locally understood to be traditional Maya beliefs and lifeways.

Something that continually struck me as I worked in the excavation site was how history had revolved around the stretch of land between the pueblos of Chunchucmil and Kochol, encompassing the archaeological zone between the two. The same land upon which they were contracted by the archaeological project to work as seasonal wage laborers was their federally granted ejido land, where they were technically permitted to be carrying out cultivation, mostly of corn. I am more concerned here with the social history of the space of which this land is only one component, that is, the ways in which people have historically interacted with land in accordance the changing political economic and social regimes.

While neither archaeological data nor scientific methods of investigation figure in any way into my own research, the activities of archaeology, particularly as they relate to the local communities, serve as a springboard for much of my ethnography. But unlike other conceptions of "ethnography of archaeology" (see, for example, Edgeworth 2006 and Hodder 1996, 2000), I did not restrict my investigation to the local communities' perceptions of the mounds, archaeology, or a combination of the two. Instead, the archaeological project was only an occasion upon which other local histories were narrated, political ideologies were espoused, and community gossip was aired. That fall, well after the archaeologists had finished their work for 2001, I returned to Chunchucmil for ethnographic fieldwork and then more research in Kochol through the summer of 2002.

Out from under the auspices of the Pakbeh archaeology project, I spent endless hours inside people's homes or yards, sitting in the few small shops that served as community gathering places, or in Kochol's extensive papaya fields. I had long conversations with the three caretakers of the empty, looted shell of the casa principal of the Kochol hacienda. This privately owned house and adjoining property sitting at the very center of Kochol continue to serve as a powerful visual trigger and rich source of individual and community memory. In the functioning days of the hacienda, the main compound consisted of the casa principal, a chapel, the company store, and the engine room that housed the decorticating machine. These buildings were distributed around a large, rectangular courtyard. Workers lived in traditional-style Maya houses, not far from the *casco*, or collection of buildings on the hacienda's main property.

The casa principal of Kochol is not nearly as well preserved as that of neighboring Chunchucmil, possibly because it was used as a storage facility for the Banco Nacional de Crédito Rural (BANRURAL) for many years after its owner defaulted on his mortgage. Whether told on the steps of the casa principal, in the fields, or at the excavation site, few narratives omit a reference to the henequen days. Indeed, Abreu Gómez's words a half-century later still ring true for the people of Kochol and Chunchucmil: the ruins at the center of their lives are not the archaeological monuments but the henequen haciendas.

The Time of Slavery

The people of Kochol and Chunchucmil remember the hacienda days through the stories of their parents and grandparents, and refer to this time as *el tiempo de esclavitud,* the time of slavery. The term refers to henequen boom of the 1850s until the Cárdenas land reforms of the 1930s, when the debt-peonage hacienda system fell and ejido lands were granted. Narrations of life in the hacienda make little reference to the cerros as a distinct part of the landscape. "Not even my dead grandmother knew how this place used to be," commented Rodolfo, an archaeological laborer from Kochol, as I worked alongside him digging a one-meter-square test pit. "The first time I ever came out here was to work for the archaeologists. We in Kochol are *gente humilde* [humble people]. We are *campesinos*, not very well educated and know little about things like what might be inside the cerros."

Eliciting oral histories in Chunchucmil and Kochol proved to be a tricky ethnographic task that depended on the particular turn of phrase when asking questions to older residents of the two former haciendas. There is a very strong sense that what has not been seen with one's own eyes should not be recounted. Therefore, a question posed to an octogenarian regarding life conditions under slavery would be more often than not answered with a flat "That was before I was born." So, upon my post-archaeological-season return, I had to ask questions in the following way: "What did your father or grandfather tell you when you were young about what life was like on the hacienda in the times of slavery?" At first frustrated, I grew to appreciate the eyewitness or firsthand testimonial commitment on the part of the oldest living generation in the two towns.

Throughout what follows, I concentrate on the historical contexts of Chunchucmil and Kochol for the purpose of setting the groundwork to illustrate that heritage, patrimony, and descent are complicated issues in these communities. Here, as earlier for Chichén Itzá, I create spatial genealogies intertwined with oral history to demonstrate how, to paraphrase Redfield (1932), ruins are not heritage. But as we will see, contrary to notions that slavery under the hacienda system stripped indigenous populations of their lifeways and their beliefs—their very identities—there is indeed heritage to be found in these communities. It is just not what or where one might expect.

As we have already seen, the hacienda system began coming into shape at the end of the eighteenth century in Yucatán. Chunchucmil and Kochol have, it may be said, royal lineages. Millet Cámara (1984: 18) speculates that Chunchucmil was founded in the late eighteenth to early nineteenth century as a cattle estancia. Estancias in Yucatán were typically founded upon land obtained through a *merced real*, or royal grant from the Spanish Crown, although some properties were bought by non-Maya elites. It was often the case that settlements of Maya communities holding lands were forced to sell them under the duress of owing large sums of tribute.[10] These transactions were carried out under the authority of the governor. Millet Cámara (1984: 19) points out, "Generally, it was alleged that they were for the payment of tributes, but in the case of Chunchucmil, the transaction in 1783 for the sale of land was carried out by indigenous Maya from Maxcanú, who claimed to need funds for the creation of a granary."

The casa principal at the Hacienda Chunchucmil was founded in 1872 by Rafael Peón Losa, a member of Mérida's *casta divina*, or divine caste, a term first used by Salvador Alvarado, the general who brought the Mexican Revolution to Yucatán and was its governor from 1915 to 1918, to mockingly address the wealthy planter class that dominated social, political, and economic life from their mansions in Mérida and across the Yucatecan countryside through their henequen haciendas. These rich and powerful families controlled large portions of property, interests in transport and storage of henequen, and banks and credit firms, as well as government positions.

The Peón family can be counted among the most powerful families at the height of the henequen era. As opposed to some of the period's powerful nouveaux riches who rose from obscurity to high prosperity as the henequen export market grew, the Peón family was more typical of the Latin American landed elite families, with important ties in Yucatán throughout the eighteenth and nineteenth centuries (Wells 1985: 78). Though their roots in Yucatán did not go back to the original Spanish conquistadors, "the Peóns supported and participated in society's most respected institutions, such as the church and the military, and indeed they can be said to have embodied the aristocratic ideals of patronage and property that had become traditional in colonial times" (ibid.). For more than one hundred years, beginning in the first half of the nineteenth century, the Peón family controlled an economic mini-empire in Yucatán based in large part on henequen production. The Peón family was prepared to take full advantage of the rise in henequen exports as they bought up large tracts of land, mostly cattle ranches, following the Caste War. Through focusing their power regionally, the Peón family was able to control all phases of henequen production in certain geographical areas, including the area around Maxcanú.

Wells (1985: 61) describes the typical impression of hacendados such as Peón Losa:

> Gorged with windfall profits unjustly reaped from the toil of a beaten and dependent labor force, this member of the casta divina built fabulous palaces on Mérida's fashionable Paseo de Montejo. He traveled and educated his children abroad and generally pampered himself. Looking to the far-off capitals of the Western world for inspiration and design, the prosperous henequeneros built ornate palaces with marble pillars, intricately carved facades, and ostentatious stained-glass enclosed porticos.

Local memory in the former hacienda communities of Chunchucmil and Kochol fails to sustain a vivid impression of the hacendados. As much as this is due to the passage of time, it is probably helped along by the fact that the hacienda owners were known for their physical absence from their rural properties. However, the notion of their wealth continues to be articulated, tied as it is to the decaying grandeur manifest in the ruins of the great mansions that still loom large in the center of each town.

In the early stages of my fieldwork in Chunchucmil and Kochol, I simply could not take my eyes or my mind off of each casa principal, as they did not cease to lord over the towns. In Chunchucmil I had, perhaps, a better rationale for my preoccupation: I was living in the house as a guest of the Pakbeh archaeological project. During my time living in Chunchucmil's casa principal, I became familiar with the history of its ownership (as I describe above), thanks mostly to the acute recollections of the property's longtime caretaker. Kochol's casa principal was a different story: completely gutted and crumbling, this house was seemingly uncared-for and its history lost from local memory. Given this, I took on the task of documenting the history of ownership of the house and its associated properties. I had little firm evidence from which to begin.

Hours grew into days sifting through nineteenth-century property records in Mérida, and I eventually came up with a list of names and dates regarding the ownership of the Kochol hacienda and after expropriation in the late 1930s, the remaining pequeña propiedad. Suffice it here to say that the property was founded and maintained through the Lara family line for several generations until the last Lara, Doña Mercedes, transferred the property to her son, Luis O'Horan. He was the owner of record until the foreclosure on the property in the late 1950s. It has since been purchased by a cultural foundation under the auspices of the Banamex corporation, which holds nearly thirty such properties in Yucatán. Though I found information, per se, I had no narrative to tie these names and dates to the experiences of the hacienda's laboring population and even less to provide a context for contemporary perspectives on the hacienda system.

I looked instead to how the hacienda property figures in contemporary everyday life. For today's residents of Kochol, the precise ownership of the property is not something that matters more than the symbolic presence of the casco. It evokes and reminds residents such as Don Nico of the times of his parents and grandparents. Don Nico, seventy-seven years old at the time of my fieldwork, is a lifelong resident of Kochol. His parents were also born in Kochol, but his grandparents came from other pueblos of Yucatán and Campeche in the boom years of the henequen hacienda. The hacienda system, he said, reorganized the people and where they lived. People were thus separated from families and home communities because of economic necessity. His grandparents were *esclavos*, slaves, during the Porfiriato and were forcibly relocated to Kochol from a small fishing settlement on the Gulf of Mexico.

A significant historical event of the early twentieth century for the two former haciendas was the visit of President Porfirio Díaz to the Hacienda Chunchucmil in 1906 for a luncheon as the guest of Rafael Peón Losa. The year 1906 marks the near-conclusion of Díaz's thirty-year dictatorial presidency (1876–1911) of Mexico. Known as the Porfiriato, the era of Díaz's regime is characterized as Mexico's push toward modernization under the banner of "order and progress." In Yucatán the Porfirian years were experienced by the indigenous Maya populations as a time of intensifying oppression through the hacienda system. Nico remembered his father's retelling of that presidential visit. Although he did not stop for as much fanfare in Kochol as in Chunchucmil, the recountings of the day's impressions and circumstances are similar, although Kochol has no plaque to commemorate the president "passing through" Kochol on his way to

Chunchucmil. Don Nico, fully cognizant of the great irony of the situation, described how the hacienda workers lined up in their freshly laundered and ironed white clothes of *manta cruda*, a rough-hewn cotton, and *xanab*, the typical sandals, usually made of henequen and deer hide, to greet Porfirio Díaz. Yet he also said that was not a time of pride but a terrible time of human injustice in which "people were sold like burros or horses."

Brannon and Baklanoff (1987: 3) point out that at the time of Díaz's visit Yucatán was one of the wealthiest states in Mexico. Caste War chronicler Nelson Reed (1964: 232) also writes that "Mérida blossomed. The streets were paved with macadam, had electricity to light them at night, were traversed by horse-drawn streetcars and numbered in the scientific way, all this in advance of Mexico City." This image stands in stark contrast to life on the haciendas. Life was extremely difficult in the years the hacienda operated. The hacendado was like a slaveholder or a feudal lord. Rather than using any form of money, hacendados relied on tokens or scrip. Many of the larger haciendas minted their own "coins," which held value only within that hacienda. The coins, which have since become collectors' items, are printed with such phrases as *Un mecate chapeo*, signifying the labor of clearing twenty square meters. In this manner, labor was directly converted into a kind of credit that could be used at the hacienda's store.

Further exploiting the laborers, writes Villanueva Mukul (1980: 46), "All of the peons were obligated to carry out certain free labor known as faginas in addition to their normal work from sunrise to sunset." *Fagina* labors consisted of all of the work necessary to keep the hacienda running and in good repair besides the normal henequen cultivation and processing. Faginas thus included road clearing and repair, grounds maintenance, construction, and building repair. In Kochol, there were two faginas each day. Every morning a bell rang at 3 A.M. to signal the day's first fagina. At 8 A.M., the bell would sound again, signaling the beginning of the paid workday. Upon the workers' return home at 3 P.M., the ubiquitous bell ringing would begin again.[11] The second fagina of the day was due to begin by late afternoon, and would last until 8 P.M.

By nightfall, married couples would return to their own houses, and young unmarried men retired to the bachelors' quarters. There was none of the evening socializing that characterizes life in present-day towns throughout Yucatán. People, especially women and children, simply did not spend any time on the streets. Workers' lives were strictly controlled, and they had no free time during at least six days a week. Sunday was the only day off, which rather than implicating leisure, more often than not entailed a full day's work in one's milpa or solar. It was also a day of heavy drinking of aguardiente sold directly from the hacienda store. According to some, drinking was a problem on the haciendas, and the provision of alcoholic beverages through the *tienda de raya* (company store) was yet another mechanism through which the hacendado manipulated and controlled the lives of the *acasillados*, the hacienda's resident laborers.

Formal education was technically available, but neither encouraged by hacendados nor sought by hacienda workers. It was not unusual for children and women to help in the henequen fields in order to meet the high production quotas imposed on each worker by the overseer. Because of the stresses and rigor of everyday life, it was often the case that a family on the hacienda was without a male head of household. This obviously made more precarious the financial situation of the family, and the burden usually fell on the shoulders of the oldest sons. "I went to school for one year," a Kochol town elder explained. "And I even liked it. But how could I continue when there were so many mouths to feed?" Today, most men of Kochol's oldest generation have rudimentary Spanish language and reading skills, and most older women speak no Spanish and do not know how to read.

Control of workers' bodies through labor extended to their personal and social lives. Nearly every older resident I interviewed told me a similar story about the hacienda marriage practices. The hacienda patrón himself or the plantation overseer kept a large book, the *nohoch cuenta*, with data on the entire population of the hacienda. It was he who decided when and to whom a young person would be married. After arranging the union, a short ceremony would take place, and immediately following this, the bridegroom was sent off to a distant area, perhaps even another property owned by the hacendado. The absence of the young man following the wedding permitted the patrón access to the young, presumably virgin bride. It would be impossible to say how many children born to Maya women were fathered by hacendados.

It is well known that a group of *chinos* lived in Chunchucmil in the early part of the twentieth century. The immigrant laborers were most likely Koreans, not Chinese, who had come to Yucatán as indentured laborers beginning in the late nineteenth century, as henequen boomed. "Oh yes," recalled Doña Candelaria, a resident of Chunchucmil then more than ninety years old, "the chinos didn't live near us, but over toward the *planteles* [henequen plots]." She pointed out the door of her grandson's shop toward an area behind the casco of the hacienda, but it was difficult to judge exactly where she is gesturing as her eyes were covered with a thick, milky film of cataracts. School had just gotten out for the day, and my interview with Doña Candelaria was competing with a couple of ten-year-olds trying to outscore each other on a twenty-year-old video game that was so loud as to almost drown out my shouted questions and the elderly woman's thin-voiced replies. "I didn't know them myself, but my father did. He worked with them cutting *pencas* [henequen leaves]."

Her hands sat quietly in her lap, folded around a newspaper. Her grandson saw me glance toward the paper and came out from behind the counter to join us. "You know, she reads the newspaper every day," he said. I complimented her, and told her that my grandmother was ninety and also read the paper every day. Nobody said anything for a minute or so. Then Candelaria spoke up, her mind lit by a spark of memory: "The chinos didn't eat the same food as us. They didn't eat tortillas! To this day I don't know how they survived without eating tortillas."

Land Reform: A New Production of Space

As I have emphasized, heritage is a social relationship. The meanings and historical contingencies of heritage, so conceived, never fail to exceed heritage as it is defined by and confined to material cultural objects. The social relationships of heritage manifest across the twentieth century at Chunchucmil are directly tied to the relationships between local Maya, wealthy landowners, and the paternalistic state. Further, we are concerned with the relationships between each of these social actors and the land—who owns it, how it is distributed, its productive capabilities, the volume and kind of labor required to work it, and its resource potential beyond agriculture.

Next we will look at the effects of land reform in the first decades of the twentieth century. Just as with Chichén Itzá, I turn to the most compelling documentary evidence demonstrating the genealogy of heritage and the historical politics of patrimony in these former hacienda communities: materials that predate the recent archaeological heritage site of Chunchucmil. Land records, in the form of hacienda property titles and ejido land-grant distribution documents, help to piece together the story of the present-day archaeological site of Chunchucmil as a battleground for many decades. These documents, along with contemporary ethnographic description and oral histories, help to recreate the spatial political economy, or, in Lefebvre's terms, the production of space. Before the land expropriations beginning in the 1920s, Chunchucmil's ruins were not heritage per se. But the land itself was an inheritance due the former peons of the henequen haciendas by the patrimonial Mexican state. We will see how the privately held hacienda properties were transformed into collective agricultural landholdings. This process institutionalized what one current Kochol farmer called *patrimonio ejidal,* or ejido heritage.

Though the process of expropriating lands from the great haciendas began more than a decade earlier, it was not until the mid-1930s that the thirty thousand adult male peons living with their families on henequen haciendas in Yucatán were touched by the slow bureaucracy of land reform (Fallow 2001: 11). The presidency of Lázaro Cárdenas (1934–1940) is locally remembered and revered as marking an epochal shift from the time of slavery to that of liberty. Under Cárdenas a new political economy based on state-subsidized peasant labor was initiated, as we have already seen in previous chapters, through massive ejido land distributions. What I am most interested in is how the socioeconomic transformation brought about by the liberal reforms instituted by Cárdenas articulate with changing conceptions of not only what constitutes patrimony, but how this patrimony can be possessed.

The establishment of the ejido system, materially hinged to the expropriations of the privately held hacienda properties, reterritorialized the Yucatecan landscape. This reterritorialization was effected through redrawing boundary lines on the earth as well as restructuring the relationships residents held with the land and their social communities. Not only did slaves became farmers, but different plots of earth were reworked under changing labor conditions.

The expropriations in northwestern Yucatán took place much later than in the southern and eastern parts of the state, the milpa region, and most initial land parcels were granted to the former hacienda workers in 1937. However, this was not the case for non-hacienda settlements of the henequen area. In other words, the Maya communities not tied to haciendas received ejido grants nearly a decade before communities such as Chunchucmil and Kochol. The establishment of these two ejidos began with land grants received by non-hacienda polities.

In March 1925, the large landholdings of Chunchucmil *hacendado* Rafael Peón Losa began to be expropriated. The initial expropriation was for the creation of an ejido for the nearby *ranchería* of Coahuila.[12] According to the hacienda expropriation laws, a community could apply for ejido status and receive an amount of land dependent on a ratio between the number of adult men in the community population, and the quality of surrounding lands. Lands for the initial ejido establishments were either hacienda properties or from *territorios nacionales,* federal lands. The rule of the seven-kilometer radius went into effect with each ejido application, meaning that any hacienda with territorial extensions within seven kilometers of the requesting community would most likely be affected. Peón Losa protested bitterly, arguing against the expropriation to Coahuila on the grounds that this community had falsified information on their grant application (CAM-RAN Exp. 177).[13]

There are no documents in the agrarian archives demonstrating support in his favor, nor do we know if his letter was taken at all into consideration by agrarian officials. Just two months later, Coahuila received 1,368 hectares of the Chunchucmil hacienda property.[14] By 1935 the community had grown and was seeking to enlarge its ejido landholding through an *ampliación*, or land extension. On September 5, 1935 (CAM-RAN Exp. 348), a notice was published once again in the *Diario Oficial* to the property owners within a seven-kilometer radius of Coahuila. This time the ejidatarios were requesting an extension of their original land grant, citing poor soil conditions, much of which had to lay fallow for ten to twelve years. Not only was the soil worn out, they argued, but the territory itself was of insufficient area to meet their agricultural needs. "We have found ourselves without enough land to carry out our cultivation," declared the ejidatarios, "and for us this constitutes a tragedy" (ibid). Once again, property owners protested the call for further land expropriation.

It was not until the spring of 1939 that the ejido of Chunchucmil was founded, not in its own *dotación* (original grant) of ejido lands but rather through an ampliación (extension) of the ejido of nearby Coahuila, a settlement with the political title of ranchería, not hacienda. Although I cannot say with absolute certainty who were the residents of Coahuila, it is more than likely that they were part-time hacienda and cattle ranch workers. They were definitely not *peones acasillados* like the resident laborers at Chunchucmil. Instead, they lived in a "free village," or in this case, ranchería, and traveled daily to work in henequen cultivation.

In the original dotación granted to Coahuila in 1925—8,480 hectares, of which 480 were designated for henequen cultivation—the 97 peons and workers of the Hacienda Chunchucmil were counted into the 119 *capacitados*, men over age sixteen who were able to work (CAM-RAN Exp. 177). Once again in the ampliación, the 97 peons and workers of the Chunchucmil hacienda formed part of the now 142 capacitados counted in the official agrarian census. They solicited the recognition of a new *centro de población agrícola*, or agricultural population center (ibid.). While Chunchucmil was battling Coahuila to establish its own ejido, Kochol was embroiled in similar circumstances with the larger town of Halacho.[15]

As we saw, in the expropriation of the Hacienda Chichén Itzá, the ruins figured importantly in the final outcome of which particular pieces of land stayed attached to the pequeña propiedad that the hacienda owners were legally permitted to retain as their holdings. However, in all of the archival documents I reviewed relating to the ejidos of Coahuila and Halacho and the subsequent extensions established at Chunchucmil and Kochol, nowhere are "ruins" mentioned, even in the topographers' indications of the "quality" of the land.

In some cases, the descendants of the original hacendados held the titles to the pequeñas propiedades that remained after the expropriations of the first half of the twentieth century. In other cases, the properties passed through a series of hands, becoming decreasingly valuable in succession. In almost all cases, the casas principales were vacant and in ruins, apparently abandoned with the sense of their contemporary worthlessness. As indicated above, the last locally known owner of the casco of Kochol was Luis O'Horan, but he has since passed away as well. Don Luis was locally infamous for liking drinking and cockfighting, among other activities. He was unsuccessful at sustaining the hacienda, and under the strain of debts, he sold off everything from the casa principal. The casco was left to his daughters, who "abandoned" it. Now, according to many, there is no owner, and the casco belongs to the community. Or at least it should.

The ruins of the hacienda system are everybody's and nobody's. I belabor the history of property and land tenure in Chunchucmil and Kochol for a specific reason. This is to lay out the historical conditions that deeply inform the ways in which current residents of these two former haciendas will come to make their own claims to the heritage of Chunchucmil.

Contemporary Perspectives

Yucatán's henequen industry is a classic example of how paternalistic government intervention in an economic activity can retard rather than advance development. (Brannon and Baklanoff 1987: 185)

In Don Nico's account, the dismantling of the hacienda system was foretold to local people by a seer in nearby Halacho. The seer said that in addition to the ejido grants, soon would come a paved roadway. This was to be followed by the previously unknown circumstances of having to purchase drinking water and the introduction of electricity. One of Kochol's oldest residents, Don Maximiliano, like many octogenarians in Kochol had lost most of his eyesight to cataracts. During a long afternoon we spent together talking about the tiempo de esclavitud, I was struck by the lack of bitterness in his memory. He fondly recalled the adventures of his youth and his narrative stressed the importance of his connection with the outdoors and agricultural work. As we were finishing up, he leaned across his hammock to pat the head of his youngest grandchild, eighteen-month-old José. "I was about this size the first time my father took me to the monte, and that's where I have worked my whole life."

Don Ernesto, another octogenarian ejidatario, still bicycles, albeit slowly, to his milpa in what the archaeologists call the site center of the Chunchucmil archaeological zone, about four kilometers from Kochol's town center. Ernesto, like other Maya milperos, used a pointed wooden stick between four and five feet long, a *xul*, to make small holes of about three inches deep in the rocky ground. Farmers in Kochol and Chunchucmil still, for the most part, use this traditional method for planting corn, without fertilizers or pesticides, considered too expensive for the relatively small subsistence crops.

PROCAMPO, the Programa de Apoyos Directos al Campo, introduced direct cash subsidies to farmers in 1993. PROCAMPO aid is available to milpa farmers in Kochol and Chunchucmil, though the actual monetary amounts are low, only eight hundred pesos (about eighty U.S. dollars) per year per hectare. As the soil has worn thin over the years, even traditional milperos are becoming increasingly dependent on fertilizers to produce a subsistence-level yield. "I can hardly do this anymore," Ernesto told me as we walked over the mounds, planting. "The henequen took all my strength."

Residents of Kochol and Chunchucmil worked in henequen cultivation for several decades following the abolishment of the hacienda and the establishment of the ejido. Henequen cultivation was the principal occupation for Mayas in northwestern Yucatán until 1970. Immediately following the establishment of the ejido system, the Yucatán state government took over the role of the hacienda patrón. In other words, the state maintained the monocrop cultivation of henequen, which had become an unprofitable and therefore heavily subsidized industry. Both prices and demand markedly declined after World War II, and to make matters worse for the henequen industry, synthetic fibers developed in the 1970s presented stiff competition in the marketplace. By this time, Yucatán had clearly lost its early-twentieth-century status as one of the wealthiest states in Mexico, having become instead one of the poorest: it became "rich in population growth and poor in capital and technical resources" (Brannon and Baklanoff 1987: 3). As part of economic modernization programs on state and federal levels, subsidized henequen production ceased entirely in the 1990s, and around the archaeological zone of Chunchucmil, cultivation stopped. Viewed in retrospect, it is clear that henequen production in Yucatán followed a path of neoliberalization, marked most notably by the parcelization of collective ejido lands and the withdrawal of the state over the past two to three decades.

Since the passage of the reforms to Article 27 of the Mexican Constitution in 1992, the national protectionist stance toward the ejido has loosened considerably. Ejidatarios, the beneficiaries of land reform, only received rights to use the land in legal theory and could not alienate it as if it were private property: if an ejidatario could no longer farm his or her land and had no successors in the family able to do so, the plot should revert to the community for redistribution to some other potential beneficiary. In practice, however, land titles have been bought and sold in ejidos, and the land might be rented to capitalist entrepreneurs from outside the agrarian community for long periods. But these were informal and illegal practices until December 1991, when the neoliberal administration of President Carlos Salinas de Gortari amended constitutional Article 27 in ways that would in practice make legal sales of ejido land possible for the first time and allow ejidatorios to use their land as collateral for loans. The land re-reform has been characterized widely as privatization of the ejido.

Carrying out the Article 27 reforms required the establishment of a new bureaucratic arm, the Procuraduría Agraria, or Office of the Agrarian Attorney General. The Procuraduría Agraria is the federal institution in charge of the defense of ejido members' rights and enforcement of agrarian law. It provides legal support to ejidos in their dealings with third parties. This agency serves as the watchdog of ejido-related institutions and must investigate and denounce cases of land concentration, administrative faults, and noncompliance on the part of civil servants or the agrarian justice system. PROCEDE, Programa de Certificación de Derechos Ejidales y Titulación de Solares Urbanos (Program for the Certification of Ejido Land Rights and the Titling of Urban House Plots), which operates through the Procuraduría Agraria, is the land rights certification program designed to pave the way for privatization. Begun in 1993, this voluntary land certification and titling program has had limited success nationwide.[16] After certification, each ejidatario would hold an individual certificate to a specific plot of land. However, the sale or transfer of this plot to someone outside of the ejido would have to be approved by a majority vote in the assembly of ejido landholders. Now, through PROCEDE, a community can obtain certificates as titles to particular parcels of land. With a supporting vote of the ejido, these pieces of land may be sold outside of the ejido.

After the final liquidation of state-subsidized henequen production and the establishment of PROCEDE, through which land titling would take place, the avenue for ejido privatization was cleared. But the road was not a smooth one for all. To date, Kochol has gone through PROCEDE's certification process, and ejidatarios do now hold certificates to specific parcels of land. The Chunchucmil ejido, on the other hard, has not passed through the process, nor has the municipal seat of Maxcanú. These eji-datarios do not hold certificates to their land. This is due to a decades-old dispute between Chunchucmil and neighboring communities, especially Coahuila. In the past few years, both critics and supporters of the 1992 "reform of agrarian reform" have realized the problems with Mexico's land-titling program. Mexico's experience echoes across Latin America. "There is a widespread belief that land privatization (i.e., the granting of individual property titles) and abolishing of old restrictions are important instruments for producing a more efficient—and more equitable—distribution of the land, and creating a basis of sustainable land use" (Zoomers 2000: 59).

Yet modernization and democratization have hardly been the results of most privatization featuring land-titling programs. Instead, a variety of problems plague the registry and titling programs. In the case of Mexico's PROCEDE, four years into the program only slightly more than 40 percent of Yucatán's ejidos had completed the certification process (Baños Ramírez 1998: 30). The reasons for lack of conformity with the titling program are multiple. For some ejido communities, the actual extent of ejido land and boundary lines continue to be in dispute with neighboring ejidos, in some cases, such as Chunchucmil, since their establishment. Land certification and titling has only proved to exacerbate these local disputes and promote deadlock in terms of continuing with the PRO-CEDE program. For other communities, land registration and titling is a complicated formality that some see as not really worth the effort. If an ejido has enough land for those who wish to farm and no intervening factors to inflate property values (such as archaeological vestiges, beachfront property, or historic built heritage), goes the argument, why bother getting a piece of paper that says what is already agreed upon in practice?[17]

Given this situation, do former hacienda communities like Chun-chucmil Pueblo and Kochol stand to lose their land—their heritage?

What is more, does the presence of prehispanic ruins covering a large part of these communities' ejidos factor in the post-1992 land re-reform process? If local residents, especially the ejidatarios and their families, claim this land as their cultural patrimony, any change in usufruct or ownership status would implicitly change the ways that this heritage might be claimed and ultimately what this heritage means. I will later address this problem framed as a clash between patrimonio cultural on the one hand and patrimonio ejidal on the other. I will identify, in other words, the tensions that arise as the local discourse on heritage shifts from the posting of (ejido) land as heritage to monuments as heritage. The 1992 land re-reform plays only a partial role in exacerbating this tension. An equally if not more important part is played by two distinct yet collusive groups of social actors: archaeologists and tourism developers. We will see how these two parties join forces in their territorialization of Chunchucmil and its environs. But first I want to focus on how the private sector has territorialized the heritage landscape of northwestern Yucatán through purchasing former hacienda properties (those that remained intact following expropriation by the state) and creating a tourism route of luxury hotels replete with all of the nineteenth-century charm of the henequen hacienda boom.

LUXURY HACIENDA HOTELS: REPRIVATIZATION, REPATRONAGE

If one were inclined to survey the contemporary communities of Kochol and Chunchucmil in search of built cultural heritage, one's attention undoubtedly would train on the imposing houses, machinery halls, and outbuildings erected more than one hundred years ago to serve as the center of hacienda life. For most former henequen hacienda communities, these collections of buildings known as cascos sit in near-ruins at the center of town. Certainly this is the case with Kochol. Though in Chunchucmil the casa principal or *casa grande* (big house) is still habitable thanks to dedicated caretaking and some restoration work. Just as the archaeological mounds have not yet been completely brought under the umbrella of heritage, neither have these historic buildings been the concern of large-scale, state-sponsored preservation or restoration efforts. Instead, as we will see, one particular initiative from the private sector has sought to purchase cascos across the state of Yucatán into neighboring Campeche with the goal of creating luxury "hacienda hotels." A reprivatization of the former hacienda properties has occurred in Chunchucmil and Kochol. Just as ejido privatization is at its core a question of patrimony, so too is this privatization of the symbolic centers of the henequen haciendas deeply intertwined with heritage.

Early one morning I found Don Gregorio on the property of Chunchucmil's casa principal clearing an overgrown corral with a *coah*, a scythe-like tool. Clearing the property of its head-high tangled brush is a twice-yearly job for the caretaker. Gregorio, in his mid-seventies, had been caring for the house for almost thirty years. In contrast to the Kochol property's three (much younger!) custodians, Gregorio worked alone. The work was overseen by Alejandro Patrón, part owner and manager of both hacienda properties. The work of clearing brush is physically brutal, and Gregorio worked alone all morning while awaiting the three Kochol workers who were supposedly on their way to Chunchucmil to help. Because of the intense heat, Gregorio worked outdoors from seven o'clock in the morning until eleven. The ground was wet from the previous day's rain, and the mosquitoes moved about in swarms. The smell of the freshly cut weeds mixed with that of animal dung, the former not quite balancing out the latter.

We sat on the remnants of a low wall that at one time separated two corrals. "There was a time when these corrals were full, full of cattle," Gregorio told me. He took a long drink of water from an ancient two-liter Coca-Cola bottle he carried with him to work on a henequen fiber rope he knotted around his waist, as do most local men when working outdoors. "And the trees!" he gestured to the area above the high wall that separates the garden from the corrals. Avocado, sweet orange, sour orange, lime, and mango flourished under the hand of a local gardener in the boom days of the henequeneros. One avocado tree still stands, but this year it did not bear fruit. The garden was neatly kept but did not give any sense of lushness or abundance. Not a single mango achieved maturity during the previous archaeological season, when much to the chagrin of some of the houses' residents, young boys grabbed and ate even the greenest of the fruits.

During my fall 2001 stay in Chunchucmil, I saw Don Gregorio first thing most mornings. He was never surprised to see me, and it became a habit that he passed to me the heavy set of keys to the casa principal, held together by a Houston Astros keychain. "You need to use the bathroom?" he asked. Long over the embarrassment at what under other circumstances are rather private affairs, I nodded and took the keys, my fingers automatically sorting through them to find the small key for the padlock on the tall, heavy double doors of the bathroom. The facilities at the casa principal are among the only indoor plumbing in Chunchucmil and therefore highly prized by myself. Whenever I returned the keys each morning, Gregorio took the role as both secretary and mentor for my day's research. "Did you make it over to the comisario's house last night?" "Did you find Doña Magdalena in her daughter's home as I told you she would be?" I developed a sense of who was at home in the morning, who spent these few cooler hours of the day in their milpa, which families had most of their members gone during the weekdays working in Mérida, and what few people remained through the week to make their living locally, operating one of the several small shops or working in other agricultural ventures such as raising papaya. Sometimes, discouraged, I had to answer "no" to Gregorio's inquiries into the progress of my research, though much of what he asked he already knew the answer to—I stuck out like a sore thumb in this small, quiet town, and it was not difficult to track my movements.

It was already eight-thirty in the morning and hot. He asked what I had planned for the day, contributed his advice, and wished me a good day. He thought I had strange work, though he was neither suspicious nor close-minded. Through this daily exchange, Gregorio introduced me to social networks in Chunchucmil. The "map" of Chunchucmil that he unfolded for me was of one of various communities within the pueblo. The primary network is one centered on the Pentecostal church and its members (*hermanos*) and their relations. Gregorio's *templo* was one of two evangelical Protestant churches in Chunchucmil, which also has a Catholic church congregation.[18] Gregorio's participation in the religious life of the Pentecostal templo informed his own telling of his life history. Before he converted to Pentecostalism, Gregorio drank. Afterward he completely abstained from alcohol and avoided companions who were drinkers.

He is the father of twelve by two wives, as he remarried after the death of his first wife. His youngest son was at the time a slight, precocious boy of nine years—Gregorio Jr., or "Gordo" as he was known around town. Gordo taught me how to ride a horse and use a slingshot, achievements locally appropriate to a boy of his age, though they presented a startling challenge to this adult woman. Returning the curiosity, Gordo often accompanied me to interviews I conducted with his neighbors. Though I am sure this is no comment on the high drama of the routines of ethnographic fieldwork, he usually fell asleep before fifteen minutes had passed.

Another morning, I met up with Gregorio as usual, only that day he was not hacking down weeds but opening up the various outbuildings on the hacienda property to check for roof leaks and rain damage. It was almost the dry season, but afternoons still brought torrential rainstorms. The century-old structures were for the most part still standing but approaching the danger of collapse. I helped Gregorio sweep puddles of water out the doors of the former plantation store. We observed the roof beams. One principal beam was supported by a tree branch wedged between floor and ceiling, and chunks of plaster had fallen and smashed on the floor around it. Though the structural damage would condemn the building in the United States, Gregorio considered it a "good building," only a shame that the owners were not quicker about restoring the property. Satisfied that the interior would dry, we left the doors unlocked and open, moving to the next job: "Let's go see Don Alé's house." I laughed out loud at the irony of Gregorio's innocuous statement. The house, built in the traditional oval Maya style, was modest, to say the least. Here we found more puddles and a definite rotting stink. "Don Alé" is Alejandro Patrón Laviada, brother to Yucatán's governor, Patricio Patrón, and an enormously wealthy businessman in his own right. The image of Patrón residing in a ramshackle traditional oval Maya house with thatched roof on the dusty streets of Chunchucmil Pueblo could not be more preposterous.

Immediately behind the gutted and seemingly haunted building that housed the *desfibradora* machinery was another house in Gregorio's care. Also built in the typical oval Maya style but with a modern door and windows, it had a recent thatched *palapa* addition to the back and large, clean solar equipped with running water. This house along with the other buildings forming the casco of Chunchucmil is—as in the case of Kochol—owned by a cultural foundation backed by Banamex. Rather than calling it "Don Ale's house," Gregorio referred to this one as the house of the co-director of the archaeological project. "Why is it his house? Did he ever stay here?" I asked. Gregorio answered no but thought it would be a good idea for the director of the archaeological project to live in this house after he retired from his academic job in the United States.

"Where else can you see something like this?" Don Gregorio paused to look back at the expansive grass quadrangle framed by the casa principal, machinery building, and storage buildings. I thought the question was rhetorical and let a moment pass while he basked in his pride. But then I realized he was looking at me, expectantly. "Well, I think that in the United States we would call this a quadrangle," I said, awkwardly translating the term as *cuadrángulo*, a nonexistent word in Spanish. He nodded. "There is something like this, for example, at my university in Texas," I added. "But it's not as pretty as this, is it," he did not so much ask as state.

I looked across the grass field, closely shorn by random grazing animals, to my right at the stark presence of the machinery building, gutted now for years, its façade littered with graffiti. To my left, at the slumping bodega, a series of single-story connected buildings alternately having served as the hacienda foreman's home, the plantation store, and a cantina. And finally directly in front of me was the large house, a heavy, columned structure, said to have been grandiose in its time, the nicest in the countryside, still standing while most of its contemporaries have decayed. I knew that this question was indeed rhetorical, for I did not know how to answer anyway.

The current ownership status of the historic hacienda properties across Yucatán signals a new wave of cultural heritage privatization. For the past several years, representatives using the front of a nonprofit cultural foundation have been buying up former hacienda properties around northwestern Yucatán. Along the Maxanú-Chunchucmil corridor, in a stretch of about twenty-five kilometers, one will pass five former haciendas. One casco, that of Santo Domingo, is owned by the community. Restored with state and municipal funds, the casa principal in Santo Domingo is attractive, painted with the traditional colors of red and white, and serves as a center for community activities and events. Three of the five cascos—Santa Rosa, Kochol, and Chunchucmil—are owned by the nonprofit Fomento Cultural Banamex, A.C. To date only Santa Rosa is fully restored and operating as a luxury hacienda hotel administered by the Grupo Plan enterprise of Roberto Hernández, former owner of Banamex. Many residents of Kochol and Chunchucmil claim not to know precisely who the casco owners are, arguing that they are indeed the well-deserved property of the community. Santa Rosa, a few kilometers from Kochol and Chunchucmil, is quite different. Originally the property of the hacendado brothers García Fajardo, Hacienda Hotel Santa Rosa is a nineteenth-century hacienda that was restored, remodeled, and updated into a beautiful and comfortable replica with such conveniences as a gourmet kitchen and swimming pools that would be expected by visitors paying top dollar for lodging.[19]

An undated article in *Gatopardo*, an online magazine, refers to what I call here the "repatronage" of northwestern Yucatán in the following manner:

> In the early 1990s a group of adventurous hoteliers began to buy some of the abandoned hacienda buildings in order to construct very exclusive hotels outside of the conventional tourism routes. At first, the idea seemed a little absurd, but there was something deeply romantic to it and as the years have passed, it has had excellent results.

In the state of Yucatán alone, banking magnate Roberto Hernández has used the nonprofit cultural foundation arm of the Banamex corporation to purchase around twenty-five former haciendas, several of which are already converted into luxury hotels, while many more are slated for upcoming development projects.[20] One particularly well-known property is the Hacienda Temozón, where then-president Bill Clinton stayed on a trip to Yucatán in 1998.

As economically depressed as any rural former hacienda community in northwestern Yucatán, Santa Rosa had high hopes for any development project that could pull the small community of several hundred inhabitants out of its decades-long economic slump, which intensified after the henequen liquidation of the 1990s. When the foundation purchased the property and began the major renovation project in the 1990s, residents clung to the promises of revitalization that would come with the opening of the Hotel Hacienda Santa Rosa. After several years in operation, the reality of the relationship between the hotel and the community has set in. Promises of local jobs for many community residents forced to travel to the capital city for work were fulfilled only for a small number. The eleven-room hotel could not possibly sustain employment of more than a dozen or so workers, the majority of whom occupied low-paying, unskilled positions.

Knowing the outcome of the hacienda renovation at Santa Rosa, do the residents of Kochol and Chunchucmil hope for or await similar development? The answer is different for each town. Chunchucmil, the former hacienda with a reported population of 900 to 1,000 inhabitants is, on the whole, slightly more enthusiastic than Kochol, whose residents seem to have low expectations for hotel renovation and tourism development. These differences in outlook stem from a variety of reasons. In the first place, the casa principal at Chunchucmil that would serve as the core of a hotel facility is in much better shape than Kochol's casa principal. One would surmise that it is simply easier to imagine a luxury hotel in Chunchucmil because it presently stands as habitable. In fact, the house has been occupied for at least six months each of the past several years by members of the Pakbeh archaeological team. Also for this reason, perhaps, residents of Chunchucmil are more accustomed to having foreign visitors residing within the former hacienda for temporary, though extended, periods.

Another reason that support would be higher in Chunchucmil than in Kochol is that property owners of the structures of the compound have made better efforts to communicate with the residents of Chunchucmil than with those of Kochol. Property owners have also made deals with

Chunchucmil political leaders to negotiate, for example, where Catholic residents would attend mass when the chapel is renovated and closed to access and where people can play soccer on an alternative field. In summer of 2002, residents of Chunchucmil began to see certain realities of the refurbishing project taking place as one of the casco's main buildings, which had served as the overseer's residence, a cantina, and then a storeroom underwent reconstruction.[21] The archaeological project is creating the development package with support from banking mogul Hernández and his associate Patrón Laviada, brother of the governor of Yucatán.

The purchase of the hacienda properties in Chunchucmil and Kochol by the Banamex foundation calls into question the usufruct rights that residents of both former haciendas have enjoyed without issue for years. In Chunchucmil and Kochol, the extensive grassy courtyards (kept trim by grazing goats, horses, and sheep) around which the structures are situated are sports fields. Regular soccer games are played in this area, and a government-sponsored recreation development program in the 1980s installed basketball courts in these areas as well. The courtyard in Kochol also serves as the location for the annual community fiesta. Each May, a bullring is constructed in front of Kochol's casa principal, complete with a two-tiered pole and palm leaf spectator area.

In both former haciendas, the cascos thus serve as community centers, though this should be carefully qualified. Children of both communities feel free to climb the steps and sit on the porches of the main house in each town as well as, in the better-tended Chunchucmil property, eat the mango and *guaya* fruit from its trees. In Chunchucmil a couple with whom I stayed for a time was married in the late 1980s in the hacienda's chapel and had the wedding party on the house's long, shady porch. Not to be dismissed in terms of another social function, the old machinery building in Chunchucmil is a favorite hangout for men drinking together, especially in the evenings.

In both towns, community residents show a noticeable lack of specific information regarding the property ownership of the hacienda cascos. In terms of legal property rights, the cascos do not belong to the communities. In Kochol few residents know exactly who owns the properties, and many assume, by nature of the way in which the space is used, that they indeed belong to the community. Several prominent ejidatarios that I spoke with in the course of my research blame a former town official for losing the casco to Banamex during his administration. They argue that he sold the "communal" property to Banamex for his own personal profit.

Current and former town officials who were involved in some of the legal maneuvering by the Banamex foundation in the purchase of the casco point out the property lines and argue that the community has not fully lost its control of this land. The ejido of Kochol retains part of the casco property, nearly half of the courtyard, situated between the Maxcanú-Chunchucmil road and the casa principal.

As a guest researcher with the Pakbeh archaeological project in the spring and summer of 2001, I too lived in the casa principal of Chunchucmil. The house was run-down but picturesque and surprisingly cool even in the nearly unbearable heat of late afternoon. The old, leaking roof had been sealed the year before with a smooth cement cap, yet anyone who attempted to sleep without a mosquito net risked a face full of falling plaster in the middle of the night. The house's double bathroom with modern plumbing was one of the biggest bonuses of the living arrangements. Improvements to the house were made at the expense of the property owner, Banamex.

Members of the archaeological project on many occasions expressed certain anxieties toward living in the casa principal of a former henequen hacienda. Some felt quite keenly the undeniable geography of power that the house, as a potent symbol of the hacienda system, represented. An interesting slippage of terms complicates this anxiety: most project members during the time of my stay referred to the house in everyday speech not as "house" in either English or Spanish (*casa*) but as "the hacienda." At the same time, older Maya residents continued to use the term *hacienda* to refer to their town, whether Kochol or Chunchucmil. Rather than finding an intentional agreement between the two uses of this term, I find the opposite—a quite unintentional equation of a variety of elements in play on the part of archaeologists and of local residents. This ensemble of elements orchestrated around the term "hacienda" include: older residents' continued use of the term, which carried the weight of the political categorization of the settlement in their parents' times and possibly in their own youth; a metonymic inversion or reversal of the term for a socioeconomic system—the hacienda system—for its material embodiment through the physical structures that are, in effect, the topoi of local memory of the hacienda system; and a colonialist (in the general sense) notion of living "on the hacienda" associated with privileges of race and wealth.

Earlier I pointed out that as I began to work with local residents in the excavation work at Chunchucmil, I was struck by a profound irony embedded in the local landscape. I am not speaking here of the valuable artifacts that lay below the surface of the community ejidos. I am referring instead to how the changing significance of "heritage" has transformed residents from debt peons to landholders and now into wage laborers engaged by archaeological practice. My main purpose here is to point out that the ruins of Chunchucmil were made into heritage only of late, and a strong notion of heritage already prevailed within the landscape. Thus, I have illustrated how changing relationships among people, land, and institutions of power may be understood as different kinds of patrimonial regimes. Through oral, written, and official documentary historical sources, I have attempted to create, as I did in the case of Chichén Itzá, genealogies of space to illustrate the complex historical embeddedness of three essential elements: henequen, haciendas, and hotels. Each of these territories has occasioned a new production of space in the social and economic landscape. Each demonstrates a specific kind of ownership and principle of usufruct, and, concomitantly, a different representation and practice of heritage. As I have demonstrated here, hacienda heritage anchors the roots of patrimonio ejidal: which has become an ambivalent heritage following land re-reform that opened ejidos to privatization and archaeology, examined next in greater detail.

As much as the hacienda system has shaped contemporary everyday life in these communities, residents of Kochol and Chunchucmil are ambivalent toward the heritage in their midst. The legacy of the hacienda is both a terrible and a proud inheritance for the Maya residents of former hacienda communities. While the system was terribly oppressive, the hacienda experience is not exclusively remembered in a negative vein. Instead, those I interviewed about the tiempo de esclavitud, the time of slavery at Chunchucmil and Kochol, speak proudly of two aspects of that time that I will mention here: first, that they were able to successfully survive the harsh conditions of life and second, that they were good workers—that they were able to turn the harsh and stubborn land into abundant yields of henequen, green gold. The power of finding pride in the deplorable conditions of debt peonage was made clear to me through the words of one of my informants. An octogenarian who as a young boy was taught by his father how to cut and stack henequen leaves in the fields, which are becoming an archaeological zone, put it like this: "*como dice la biblia* [as the Bible says], the meek will inherit the earth." Indeed, the descendants of the hacienda slaves did inherit the earth comprising Chunchucmil. And this patrimony is certainly hard-won.

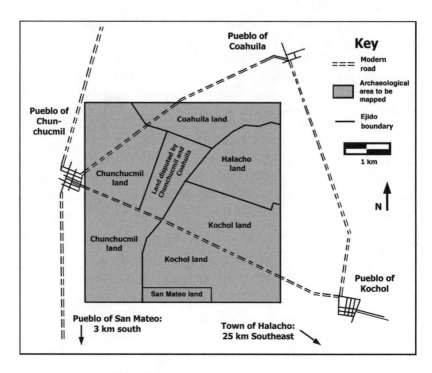

Key

=== Modern road

▨ Archaeological area to be mapped

— Ejido boundary

◼◻ 1 km

N ↑

Pueblo of Coahuila

Pueblo of Chun-chucmil

Coahuila land

Land disputed by Chunchucmil and Coahuila

Halacho land

Chunchucmil land

Kochol land

Chunchucmil land

Kochol land

San Mateo land

Pueblo of San Mateo: 3 km south ↓

Town of Halacho: 25 km Southeast ↘

Pueblo of Kochol

MAP 6.1.   *Map of Chunchucmil archaeological site center and ejido boundaries. Map © 2004 by Scott Hutson.*

*One could perhaps say that certain ideological conflicts animating
present-day polemics oppose the pious descendants of time
and the determined inhabitants of space.*

FOUCAULT, "OF OTHER SPACES," 1967/1986: 22

The archaeological zone of Chunchucmil in northwestern Yucatán is situated in a landscape replete with ruins. From the roadway between the
Maya communities of Kochol and Chunchucmil, even the casual observer
may note up to a dozen mounds, some eighteen to twenty meters high. In
the dry season, the mounds are more noticeable as crumbling yet imposing structures of cut stone. This is in part what attracted archaeologists to
the area in 1993 to begin surveying and mapping the sixteen-square-
kilometer site just inland from the Gulf of Mexico. Through examination
of settlement, subsistence, and household patterns, archaeologists of the
Pakbeh Project, a group representing various U.S. universities, believe
Chunchucmil to be a "demographically enormous site and one of only
two known specialized trading centers dating to the Classic Period in the
Maya lowlands" (Dahlin et al. 2000: 1). The project is funded by the U.S.
National Science Foundation, National Geographic Society, and other
sources to carry out survey, mapping, excavation, and other investigations
at the Chunchucmil archaeological site. Surveying and mapping by archaeologists had been going on for several years, and excavations began
in the summer of 1998. Though mapped and defined in accordance with
the theories and methods of archaeology, the production of a univocal,
universal, or ideologically dominant interpretation of the site has yet to
emerge. The territorializing machinations of heritage have yet to fully incorporate Chunchucmil: not only is the site undeveloped in terms of archaeological heritage tourism, it also lacks a coherent logic of vision that
allows a landscape to be properly ancient. In other words, local residents
do not yet know how they are supposed to "see" how these tree-covered

hills that dot community agricultural lands are—or may become—Maya or Mexican cultural heritage.

Here we will examine how the onset of archaeological investigation—particularly excavation work—at Chunchucmil has newly inflected the local landscape with monumental ambivalence. Not only is there a deep ambivalence toward the promises of archaeological tourism development, but there exists an even more profound ambivalence as to whether the mounds are indeed monuments. For the generations of local people, the mounds that only relatively recently caught archaeologists' eyes were neither new nor discovered. For many (especially older) residents of the surrounding communities, the mounds are part of the natural landscape, having been the shape of the land since their grandfathers' times. Thus, a mound, impressive to the casual outsider's eye as mysteriously and unidentifiably "ancient," is for a local person a natural feature of the terrain. Residents of Kochol and Chunchucmil tend not to think of the mounds as archaeological features. Instead, they are fully integrated within the agricultural landscape. This land is their ejido, a communal land-grant designated to the people who had been debt peons to the wealthy and powerful henequen planters. From the local perspective, the mounds are, echoing Redfield's (1932) words, "not a heritage." But the land is.

In the days of the henequen haciendas, a father's patrimony to his son was a terrible legacy—his lifelong accumulated debt to the hacienda's tienda de raya. But now, decades later, patrimony is valuable, productive, and protected. For residents of Chunchucmil and Kochol, their patrimony is their land. Although the term *patrimonio ejidal* is not in general circulation among these landholders, the concept it describes is a common-sense understanding of the role and value of the lands granted to these communities through the ejido system. The concept of patrimonio ejidal exists even among the younger generations, although many who have little or no agricultural experience have left the towns to seek employment in a clothing factory in nearby Maxcanú and in Mérida. I will demonstrate how the concept of patrimonio ejidal already codes and territorializes the space of the archaeological zone. How does archaeology, with its reliance on the concept and material markers of cultural patrimony, contend with its patrimonial competitor—patrimonio ejidal?

Property titles and ejido distribution records from the 1920s and 1930s reveal the complex histories of land allocations and tenure among Maya communities in and around the Chunchucmil archaeological zone, several of which have ejido or federal land-grant holdings overlapping the zone's boundaries. Land—how much is held, for how long, under what legal frameworks, and perhaps most important of all, by whom—is the primary signifier in the organization of everyday life in these communities. In the past few decades, the land's signifying power surpassed an exclusive association with henequen and the socioeconomic system of the hacienda that had supported its cultivation. Local communities, on five- to seven-year cycles, have attempted to stick with agriculture. Through thick and thin, these communities, particularly Kochol, have tried various crops and cultivation methods to regenerate their local economies. Habanero chile, grapefruit, and most recently, papaya along with the ubiquitous corn milpa are not only crops but signs of economic life and diversification in these communities, which some might see as struggling or merely surviving in the shadows of the decaying structures of the former haciendas.

Many current residents of Kochol and Chunchucmil, including the farmers who regularly trek the communities' ejido lands, claim to have no knowledge of the mounds only three to four kilometers from each town center. Some even say that their participation as hired laborers in the excavation project has been their only interaction with this particular landscape. But others have stories about the mounds. I first met Don Emiliano as we worked side by side digging, sifting dirt, and hauling rocks as part of the 2001 field season of the Pakbeh Project. Emiliano, a laborer on the project, Kochol town elder, and former *comisario ejidal* (ejido commissioner, the most important elected ejido authority, overseeing everything involving the ejidos and the ejidatarios) and I, cultural anthropologist and ethnographer, found many reasons to take breaks from the hot sun and heavy work of excavation to share conversations about ourselves, where we came from, and, most of all, about the mounds that covered nearly the entire expanse of Kochol's ejido land. Don Emiliano's grandfather was a henequen cutter in the time of slavery who worked for Rafael Peón Losa, patrón of the hacienda. At the time, stories were circulating around the hacienda speculating on what might be inside the *muul'ob*, or mounds that cover the peninsula's rocky karst topography. One day, the henequen workers, despite their better judgment, went to work digging down into the top of the largest mound on the orders of the patrón. They worked all day dismantling the twenty-meter-high structure. The work was quite difficult, involving moving hundreds of large stones. By six o'clock that evening, the end of the workday, the men had not nearly completed the job of the mound's "excavation." The foreman of the job suspended work for the day, and the workers returned to the hacienda. The next morning, when they all returned to the site to finish the excavation, the mound was completely reconstructed back to its original state without a trace of the dismantling carried out the previous day.

This story has several variations, one of which does not involve the direct orders of the hacienda patrón. In this version, a man and his son go out into the monte one day and come upon a large mound. Overcome by curiosity, the older man begins digging into the top of it, persuading his son to join him in the difficult work. Exhausted after a few hours of work, they settle down for a meal and a rest. With their backs to the mound, they sit on some rocks and eat their *pozole*. When they turn back around toward the mound, it has changed back to the state in which they found it, showing no trace of its dismantling. This is an ambivalent image of the mound: both constructed and deconstructed. In this story, what is taken down by one hand is reconstructed by another.

The image serves as an allegorical comment on the impossibility of the work of cleanly dismantling—or deterritorializing—the assemblage of the archaeological zone. It is an image of the impossibility of the existence or persistence of, in the words of Deleuze and Guattari (1987), a "fully coded signifying regime" that defines the archaeological landscape. The existence and persistence of multiple meanings and multiple (de)territorializing practices demonstrate that significance cannot be contained by a geographic notion of space and that history and memory play an important role in the way the space is practiced today. Through an analysis of the territorializing practices of modern archaeological science, heritage institutions, and private enterprises, I ethnographically examine how various groups of people including foreign archaeologists, nonprofit cultural foundations, and the residents of the Maya community of Kochol practice and imagine the transnational space of the archaeological zone of Chunchucmil.

(DE)TERRITORIALIZATIONS OF THE LANDSCAPE

The physical space of the archaeological zone of Chunchucmil is a network of coexisting territories—site of "ancient Maya civilization,"[1] henequen hacienda, ejido, and archaeological zone—each implicated in the others and each with its own history, practices, and embedded ideology. Together these territories form Chunchucmil's social landscape. While a landscape may be thought of as the features of a terrain bestowed by nature, recent appropriations of the term by cultural geographers and archaeologists demonstrate the recognition that "landscapes are created

FIGURE 6.1. *An ejidatario from Kochol plants corn in the traditional style atop an archaeological mound within view of an excavation site. Photograph by author.*

by people—through their experience and engagement with the world around them" (Bender 1993: 1).

The concept of landscape is particularly useful for understanding that ruins are not isolated from the space of social relations. In other words, landscape (as an analytical concept) moves beyond treating ruins as autonomous "things in space" to a consideration of their existence in a contingent, relational field. This approach distinguishes itself by acknowledging that ruins are indeed embedded within wider contexts, whether historical, economic, environmental, scientific, or even aesthetic. Further, the landscape approach also pays significant heed to the role of human populations—ancient and/or contemporary—as their activities shape these contexts.

Landscape archaeology has begun to reveal the ideologies embedded in space and place, as well as the contestations of these ideologies.[2] Bender and Winer (2001: 3) distinguish, for example, the elitist way of seeing landscape that emerges alongside the development of mercantile capital in western Europe because this point of view "ignores the labor that has gone into landscape and obscures the relationships between landscapes." Instead, a broadened definition of landscape utilizes landscape "to understand the way in which people—all people—understand and engage with the material world around them" (ibid.). The concept of landscape adds nuance to the concept of ownership. "To possess or to own a landscape means to identify it systematically; it entails its intellectual creation and implies responsibility for maintaining it. . . . If landscape refers to an ideological framework, it cannot be 'owned' in a typical material property sense" (Ayres and Mauricio 1999: 299). The authors go on to suggest that landscapes, as cultural heritage resources, are a kind of intellectual property, a confounding idea for typical Western notions of property ownership based in materiality.

While I find landscape archaeology sympathetic to the kind of spatial analysis of archaeological zones I am developing here, I see some of its limitations. In the case of Chunchucmil, where "heritage" does not necessarily signal either archaeology or the built environment, the significant reliance on material culture as a grounding point of reference in landscape studies preempts, I believe, a full account of the (non-archaeological) production of space. Not all the territories of an archaeological site are tied to the presence of ruins. In the pages that follow, I will discuss in detail the shifting significance of both "archaeology" and "ruins" as the (geographical) site has only recently become a target—or perhaps, a pawn—of monumental heritage discourse.

I relate how the concept of patrimonio ejidal has come into conflict with both state policy and a local archaeological excavation project. Finally I pull these ideas together through a curious event held at Chunchucmil in the summer of 2002. We will see how and why archaeologists appeal to the heritage of Maya cultural "tradition" as recorded within the ethnographic record as they sponsor a public ceremony to "cleanse" Chunchucmil and ask the spirit guardians of the monte to ensure the safe and satisfactory progress of their excavation work.

THE MULTIPLE TERRITORIES OF CHUNCHUCMIL

First I unpack the landscape at Chunchucmil by examining three territorializing practices that I witnessed during the course of my fieldwork in and around the site and the neighboring residential communities. In the first instance, "zoning" is a spatial practice that emanates from and thus reflects the statist logic of defining and containing heritage properties of and for the nation. The second territorializing practice is seemingly unrelated to archaeological heritage, as I identify agricultural practice as representing a tactical resistance to the statist strategy. In this example, we see how farmers test the new limits imposed upon the landscape through the delimitation of Chunchucmil as a federal archaeological zone. In terms of a third territorializing practice, I focus on archaeological labor—a key site of monumental ambivalence.

Zoning as Territorializing Practice

Although ruins are a part of the natural and cultural landscape of Yucatán, particular legal regulations define and demarcate what areas are technically archaeological zones, legally protected and administered by the state, via the INAH. Although according to the Mexican Constitution, all archaeological vestiges are the property of the nation, not all are defined and administered equally. The delimitation of archaeological zones is the responsibility of the Subdirección de Registro Público de Monumentos y Zonas Arqueológicas (SRPMZA) within the INAH.

As proper "archaeological evidence" (Sánchez Caero 1995: 187) takes the form of artifacts or monumental architecture, delimitation becomes the primary means of safeguarding heritage under the law. Until the 1980s, delimited areas were based on "monumentality," meaning that in a delimitation process, site centers—determined through research as being ceremonial, religious, or civic centers—formed the core of an archaeological zone. In the 1980s the practice changed to create more expansive and inclusive archaeological features of an area within a zone's official boundaries. Zones were created to include, along with monuments, ancient living and cultivations areas, adding to the monumental architectural vision a human and ecological dimension (ibid.: 193).

Delimitation of an archaeological zone is an intermediate stage in the declaration of an official archaeological zone. Delimitation works hand in hand with a process of cataloguing or inventorying the archaeological monuments and materials. Little more than 1 percent of archaeological zones in Mexico are delimited, and eighteen have been protected through presidential decree. In a delimited and declared archaeological zone, a variety of regulations come into effect regarding land use, sale, and expropriation. A site delimitation establishes two categories of area internal to the zone. In the center, or Zone A, land use is restricted to archaeological investigation, maintenance, and services basic to the good functioning of the zone. In Zone B, the surrounding area, partial restrictions regarding land use apply (ibid.: 195). But are they always put into effect? And what about questions of compensation if the zone is coterminous with ejido land? The process of delimitation and declaration is just one aspect of what I call "zoning." In the following accounts from the archaeological site of Chunchucmil, I will explore how this "zoning" includes not only the spatio-juridical practices of the INAH, but concomitant local, national, and international processes in the cultural, social, and economic realms of everyday life of a zone and the different sets of actors involved in practicing this space.

The Pakbeh Project has been employing Maya laborers from Kochol in the work of land clearing, test pitting, excavation, and masonry for architectural consolidation. Foreign projects are allowed in Mexico only through explicit permissions and guidelines set by the INAH. Though the existence of the ruins at Chunchucmil has been officially recognized for decades, no sustained investigation had taken place in the site before the Pakbeh Project.

In 2001 the site of Chunchucmil was granted by INAH the official status of zona arqueológica. Still the site has no guards or night watchmen, its boundaries are not marked, and ejidatarios from Kochol regularly use the land to make milpa and other crops. This "zoning" is a territorializing practice par excellence: it codes both the landscape and the relationships people have with that landscape. The spatio-juridical process of establishing a *zona* determines what can and cannot happen in the space as well as what may or may not happen. It sets forth rules as to how close to the mounds farmers may plant and prohibiting their accustomed slash-and-burn agriculture to clear the land and enrich the poor, thin soil of the region.

But zoning is not a primal territorializing practice on an otherwise smooth space or empty, unmarked landscape (Deleuze and Guattari

1987: 474–500). Historically, the area has been demarcated, bounded, and parceled. Upon the foundations of an ancient Maya commercial center, the land has been continuously over several centuries cleared and planted, built and leveled, to make way for a variety of human activities. Now that the land is finally in the hands of the Kochol ejidatarios, many see it as a target for yet another territorialization, this time in its most physical and visual sense. Perhaps meant to be a statement of fact, though perceived by residents as a threat, archaeologists have repeatedly made reference to the INAH's legal right to enclose the site with a fence or wall.

The possibility of this radical territorialization dramatically alters the status of this community-owned ejido land: "Soon I myself won't be allowed on my own land without paying an admission fee!" said an angered and worried ejidatario from Kochol, echoing the sentiments of his colleagues. "The INAH will have to come here and present a plan to all of the ejidatarios." Said another:

> Look, this isn't Chiapas, and here in Yucatán we are *tranquilo* [peaceful], but if this happens, we'll have something to say about it. . . . If we are respected, we will be respectful. If the archaeologists want to come and work here, *adelante* [go ahead]. But they are going to have to answer to the people. *Nosotros campesinos tenemos derecho, tenemos terreno. Somos ricos por el terreno.* [We campesinos have rights, we have land. We are rich for the land we have.]

Planting as Territorializing Practice

Throughout the first three years of excavation work with laborers from Kochol, talk about the project and its members, the finds at the sites (though these have, to date, been undramatic to the untrained eye), and the excavation work itself have definitely been food for thought and are growing into terms for debate. In one local political contest, two factions within the same political party were divided along lines delineated by, among other issues, positions favoring or opposing the archaeology project. The ejidatarios and other residents of Kochol are hearing more and more about plans being implemented by the archaeologists and their hired development consultants to open the area to tourism development, but this is not a tangible reality for many community residents who are uncertain and even unwilling to give up the ejido land—much of which lies within the new boundaries of the archaeological zone—that they have only held for two or three generations.

In late June 2001, three ejidatarios began clearing three mecates (sixty square meters total) of land to plant a new papaya field in the space deemed the site center by the archaeological project, just meters from an excavation site. Papaya growing is an agricultural industry started in Kochol in 1998 as yet another stab at reinvigorating the local and regional economies of former henequen haciendas in northern Yucatán. Beginning in the 1980s, various government-sponsored agricultural programs were introduced. For example, a women's cooperative began to grow habanero peppers, but the intricacies of growing the delicate product made its cultivation unpopular and expensive. Economic crisis reached a high point in Kochol in the late 1990s as an unprecedented number of men and women left the pueblo to seek employment in Mérida. In came the papaya program, and something clicked with the people of Kochol. In the past few years, almost 80 percent of the families have become involved with papaya cultivation.

Twenty-four-year-old Efraín is part of what one may slightly romantically call Kochol's "Lost Generation," those who spent their teen and young adult years away from the day-to-day activity of the pueblo, working and living in Mérida, about an hour and a half away by bus. But his is a lost generation that has, in a very literal sense, come home again. "When I was very young," Efrain explained to me as we toured his two mecates of papaya, "I would go out with my father to the henequen fields. I did that for about five years. Then I went to work en el otro lado [the other side, referring to Mérida]."[3] He continued, "Now with the papaya, I can stay here in my pueblo."

Pueblo life is eminently preferable for most residents of Kochol over city life in Mérida, and the sentiment is reiterated in many parts of the peninsula. "In Mérida, if I need a tomato, I have to go buy a tomato. If I need a lime, I have to go to a supermarket and pay for it," said town elder and former comisario ejidal Don Emiliano. "In Kochol, I can get all of these things from my own *solar*." He and his two grown sons worked several rotations on the archaeological project in an arrangement between the directors of the archaeological project and the secretary to the comisario ejidal.[4] Under this arrangement, men of Kochol who had completed their community service, or fagina, were eligible to work for two weeks with the archaeologists, earning by local standards a decent wage.

Because of the self-selected labor pool, any given two-week rotation of workers brought important Kochol community leaders to the excavation sites (former comisarios, the Pentecostal church pastor, and of course, the secretary of the local ejido government, who assumed the position of foreman of the workers). The younger workers might have spent their teens and twenties away from the pueblo six days a week in school or working in a nearby clothing factory or as masons in Mérida, and the excavation work brought them out to ejido lands that they had not set foot on in several years. For the older generations,[5] the three-kilometer bike trip from Kochol proper to the archaeological site center provided an opportunity for other outdoor activities: some came to the sites with machetes strapped around their waists to cut wood before returning to the pueblo, others would trek to nearby cenotes or natural wells to bottle the water they insisted was *agua purificada*, purified water.

Through the time I spent working alongside the people of Kochol, I came to realize that clearing land, digging, and hauling rocks, which make up the primary activities of archaeological labor, have a perfect symmetry with the agricultural work that is the primary occupation for many *kocholeños*. For members of all generations, the 6 A.M. to 1 P.M. excavation workday was just one of many scheduled work activities. Many went back to town just for a bite to eat with their families and a quick rest before continuing the workday harvesting or maintaining their papaya fields—often well into the evening when large trucks picked up the fruit for transport out of state—or, depending on the month, burning or planting their milpas.[6]

Does this discourse of the land with all its meanings and potentials collide with the configuration or emplacement of "the land" in other territories such as that of the archaeological zone? It certainly does, as demonstrated by the following example involving the ongoing dispute among residents of Kochol, archaeological project members, and the INAH regarding the name of the archaeological site. The beginnings of excavation at Chunchucmil in 1998 initiated the ascription of new regimes of value and ownership in Kochol's ejido land. Just as a milpa yields corn and papaya fields produce a cash crop, the archaeological landscape yields a material bounty: pieces of ceramic, slivers of obsidian, and the occasional pottery vessel.

Though there was little to impress the layperson, the excavation did yield some artifactual treasures from the earth within the Kochol ejido. "What happens to the artifacts taken out?" the hired laborers from Kochol were quick to ask. The current practice of the project is to keep all findings at project headquarters in the casa principal of the Chunchucmil hacienda. Large or important pieces are periodically transported to storage at the INAH regional anthropology museum, the Palacio Cantón, in Mérida. The sentiment that "What is taken out of the ejido land is ours" caused such controversy in the 2000 season that project directors, in an attempt to neutralize the arguments, changed the name of the project to the Pakbeh Project, thereby removing the name "Chunchucmil" from the labels on shard bags. The problem is greater than this simple label change can solve. As far as the INAH is concerned, the site is officially designated Chunchucmil. Compounding the problem is the historical relationship between the pueblos of Chunchucmil and Kochol.

Ejido land surrounds the pueblo of Kochol, and most of the more than three hundred ejidatarios agree that the amount of land itself is sufficient to meet demand for growing papaya. Some future-looking papaya growers paint the picture a little differently, pointing out that a papaya crop only lasts for a year and a half before the soil has to be left fallow for at least a year. With much of the ejido land parcels immediately surrounding the pueblo filled with papaya, this means growers soon face the problem of sufficient land to plant the next crop. In coming seasons, they will move away from the lands immediately surrounding the pueblo to ejido lands two and three kilometers from town, into the area that the INAH has now officially designated as an archaeological zone.

One morning in early July I pulled my bike up alongside Don Oligario's on the main road that connects the five pueblos between Maxcanú and Chunchucmil, and we pedaled out to his new papaya field in the site center, hailing his various buddies, one of whom, Don Abelino, was planting corn in the traditional Maya style just at the roadside on the slopes of a ten-meter-high mound. Don Oligario is what you might call an agricultural guru of Kochol. Locally respected for his knowledge and success in planting and raising various crops, most recently papaya, Don Oligario had accumulated enough capital to purchase and install a gas-powered water pump to irrigate fields where there is no available electricity.

Having come to understand the deeply personal and political significances of the self-sufficiency and economic security that come with the ability to use the resources they have at hand, I still wondered about the real motivations of planting the papaya alongside the excavations. I broached the question awkwardly, "So you're running out of land closer to the pueblo and you all really need to use this land out here?" "Yes, that's right." He smiled. "This is virgin soil, very fertile." "You know," he continued, "the archaeologists were out here yesterday questioning me. I thought you might be one of them. They were bothered, but then I told him we wouldn't go anywhere near the mounds." He smiled again, nervous because I might be one of them? Or knowing, because we both knew this was exactly the right thing to say. We stood together in the hot morning sun

FIGURE 6.2. *Project workers gather on the steps of Chunchucmil's casa principal at the end of a workday. Photograph by author.*

and watched his compañeros walk through the cleared area with their herbicide backpacks and spray guns.[7]

Archaeological Labor

Another form of territorialization that began to take effect on the Kochol ejido within the archaeological zone of Chunchucmil is based in labor. Scientific investigation of the site introduced a new wage-labor economy to the Kochol ejidatarios as they began to be hired by the project to work as day laborers in the site excavation. Just as we saw in the series of twentieth-century transformations of labor at Chichén Itzá, the development of the Chunchucmil site involves historical transformations as well, but in a different socioeconomic framework. The sons and grandsons of the debt peons who worked in slavelike conditions for the owners of the henequen haciendas were now laboring on the very same parcels of land where henequen had been cultivated. Archaeological labor, for these men who are living in a space still layered with the memory of slavery to the patrones of the henequen hacienda, is another kind of working of the land. And, more importantly, it is working *their* land, granted through the ejido reforms of the 1930s: it is simultaneously a natural and cultural patrimony writ local over and above the national.

As an integral part of my ethnographic research at Chunchucmil, I spent time working alongside laborers from Kochol in excavation work. My ethnographic practice within the archaeological site involved what Ian Hodder calls "interpretation at the trowel's edge" (2003: 58). But instead of producing interpretations within the parameters of scientific knowledge of the ancient past, I sought to use the work of excavation to reveal contemporary understandings of the social, cultural, and economic landscape. In analysis of the production of space and exercise of territory at Chunchucmil, labor figures as a site of intensification in the transformation initiated by archaeological development.

From the perspective of Kochol's farmers with landholdings in the archaeological zone, excavation labor should follow the same usufruct principles as agricultural land use and tenure. In other words, the rules of the ejido system were transposed onto archaeology's use of the land. Of primary importance to those who held ejido land within the archaeological zone was the maintenance of their usufruct rights no matter what territorializing practices sought to reorganize land use, value, or productive capacity.

At the outset of excavation work at Chunchucmil, archaeologists were not fully aware of the particularities of the ejido holdings in the archaeological site in terms of property and propriety. During an initial season of excavation, project archaeologists used the crews from Chunchucmil Pueblo that had already been assembled to work on various preliminary aspects of the work at the site, namely brush clearing and guiding archaeologists through the monte. When an elderly Kochol farmer went to his ejido land to weed his milpa, he came across a group from Chunchucmil working to clear the land. Though the events only occurred a few years ago, the rest of the story is now legend in Kochol, told each time with higher drama. The stooped, elderly campesino "flew" back to town to inform his compañeros of the "invasion" that was occurring right under their noses. The church bells were frantically sounded; bells that had once been rung to summon exhausted hacienda peons to yet another day of backbreaking work in the henequen fields were now used to assemble the town's ejidatarios for an emergency meeting.

It was an obvious issue of territoriality. According to the ejidatarios, residents of Chunchucmil Pueblo should not be working on Kochol's land—no matter that they were working in the territory of archaeology rather than agriculture. Though archaeological excavation implies a different and seemingly noncompetitive economy of value, Kochol's ejido holders saw people outside of their own ejido community benefiting from the product of Kochol's land. The possibility of invasive or extractive activities taking place in the Kochol ejido drew alarm, then protest from community residents. The problem was addressed and logistically resolved through an agreement between Pakbeh and the Kochol ejidatarios: all archaeological labor performed on Kochol's ejido would be done by Kochol's ejidatarios. Their usufruct rights would be compensated with a wage.

The story of Don Francisco and what he stumbled upon one spring day in the Kochol ejido is most likely to be related in a context of continuing tensions between residents of Kochol and the archaeological project at moments when other disputes arise, minor or more significant, whether the archaeologists are themselves aware of a problem or not. The archaeological project was about to enter the last month of the field season of 2001. Tensions were running a little higher than usual as the director, assistant directors, and other staff members were feeling the crunch of completing their season's work on schedule. The impending end of a six-month field season added the additional financial and logistical pressure of consolidating all excavated architectural features in order to comply with an INAH mandate.[8]

As opposed to the unskilled labor provided by Kochol's ejidatarios, consolidation (according to the archaeologists) required the services of professional masons experienced in archaeological work. Pakbeh archaeologists thus hired a small crew of masons from Maxcanú whose backgrounds included extensive consolidation experience at the newly developed site of Oxkintok. One day I was accompanying five masons from Maxcanú who were working with the assistance of two Kochol residents in consolidating a small structure at one of Chunchucmil's excavated areas. The Kochol men working that day had spent much time throughout

FIGURE 6.3. *A mason mortars stones in the consolidation of an excavated structure.* *Photograph by author.*

the season with the project and appeared to be somewhat put out at the circumstances that have made them *chelanes*, or apprentice helpers in the masonry work at hand. In theory, these helpers would learn the work one season in preparation of leading a Kochol-based crew of masons in the next season. One assistant director became frustrated at these chelanes, complaining that Kochol has sent two old men—one in his early forties, the other a bit past fifty—rather than young people who are more suitable for apprenticeship to archaeological masonry. They spent the entire workday in the wearisome and mind-numbing task of moving rocks, with very little interaction with the Maxcanú masons. It was only into the next weeks of work that a thaw occurred between the Kochol and Maxcanú workers, and they began to join in with some of the trivial banter that helps the workday pass more pleasantly.

Presently in the site of Chunchucmil, there are no entirely reconstructed buildings; only portions of walls, exposed floors, and some stairways are visible. It is difficult for a nonspecialist to surmise what the exposed areas represent. The masons from Maxcanú/Oxkintok distinguish between regular masonry work, known as *obras*, and that associated with archaeological consolidation. This distinction thus implies a specialized knowledge of archaeological structure consolidation, but more importantly illustrates the masons' degree of experience. I was surprised when much of the work went unsupervised and alarmed when direction was asked of me. The masons took it in stride, coordinating tasks among themselves, using experienced eyes to reset stones, reforming collapsed and crumbled walls of ancient structures.

I would have thought the process of consolidation, a task of reconstruction, to be more "scientific" or exact. But when a stone did not seem to fit with the string plumb line tied to two sticks, another was found to take its place. If the facing side stuck out too far, the back was chiseled away. If a top stone sat higher than its neighbors, the bottom was hacked off to lower it. After a row of stones was set in place, another line was made above it, and so on, to form the lower section of a wall about a meter high. The stones were then numbered with a thin white paint, and the wall was dismantled and the stones set in their numbered rows on the ground nearby, away from the structure. The rows were then realigned, more adjustments were made, and they were mortared in place. While the mortar was still moist, it was painted with an earth and water mixture, the proper terra cotta color produced through trial and error.

Painting the mortar around the set stones was the only task in which I was permitted to participate. The head of the group was about fifteen meters away setting up stones at a nearby structure but managed to watch my simple work like a hawk. I did not think it was something that could actually be messed up. But in no time he was kneeling next to me demonstrating a better technique. I quickly caught on, and in subsequent days I was clearly expected to do the painting. The days passed quickly, and soon we were finishing the second week of consolidation. It was one o'clock in the afternoon, very close to quitting time, and the heat of the July day was fully upon us. The head mason used a mallet to knock the final stone of a row into its proper place. The stone refused, and the same mallet helped a chisel shave off a few critical millimeters. The mason stood back to gain better perspective, and something still did not look quite right. He announced to us, smiling, *Suficiente para la patria*, good enough for the nation.

This partial reconstruction of the ruins, as a task of both skilled and unskilled laborers, takes place more or less outside of the "pedagogic regime" of archaeology in which archaeologists explain ruins to the locals as edifices built by their ancestors. The workers had no idea what they were reconstructing. There is no image of a whole structure to which the reconstruction aspires. (There were rumors of a drawing, a plan, but I never saw it. It was later reported to have been lost on the first day of work.) Yet this did not seem to matter, as the more crucial point was to assemble the parts as integral unto themselves, one row, leading to one wall, and so on. Returning to the site several months after the end of the 2001 field season, at the soggy finale of Yucatán's rainy season, I could barely make out the structure I painted at the Mooch Group. I compared the structure overgrown with vegetation to the perfectly cleared, newly restored monuments at Chichén Viejo, which I had visited through the courtesy of site managers just a week earlier. Does the development of the ejido land into an "attractive" archaeological zone, appropriate for tourism, create a "non-work" place (Lefebvre 1974/1991: 24) out of the labor of Kochol's ejidatarios? Will Chunchucmil become a place in which leisure replaces labor in the production of space? Do the landholders of Kochol stand to be rendered invisible in their own land like the INAH workers displaced from Chichén Itzá as obstacles to modernization?

PATRIMONIO EJIDAL, THE STATE, AND ARCHAEOLOGY

"You know what," a state INAH official once commented to me, "sometimes archaeologists get too involved with the local communities. They make complications where they shouldn't." A definite complication arose at the outset of the 2002 field season when project directors met with Kochol ejido leaders. By this time, anxieties had bubbled to the surface that previously only lingered beneath it. The official position of the community regarding the archaeological excavations in their ejidos reached a more public consensus: the workers would go on strike to stop the archaeological project. The labor embargo could be broken, however, if one simple demand was met. The ejidatarios wanted an official document stating the plans and intentions of the archaeologists for the course of their work at Chunchucmil.

The INAH was called into the meeting as archaeologists wished to demonstrate that they were by no means the ultimate authority. Showing that their own hands were tied in the face of the INAH, archaeologists stepped outside, in this instance, leaving the visiting INAH representative to bear the brunt of the frustrations expressed by the Kochol ejidatarios. One archaeologist said as the meeting opened, "For once we are just here to *listen*." Thus, in this instance, the members of the archaeology project were the silent interlocutors of the early spring 2002 meeting. The previous dialogues, discussions, and presentations over the course of several field seasons created a palpable tension that night on the Kochol basketball court, raised in flashpoints of anger expressed by the Kochol residents.

The meeting came at a critical time for the archaeologists, as they had just been denied their 2002 season excavation permit, the official reason being the failure to satisfactorily complete the *informe*, or report, for the 2001 season. Rumors suggested that the problem lay deeper, in the project's proposals of local museum development and various encounters some of the Pakbeh archaeologists had previously with the institution. INAH director Luis Millet stated to me, "An archaeological permit is just what it says: it grants permission for researchers to carry out academic, scientific investigations."

The *asamblea* is the usual format for discussion of issues pertinent to the residents of Kochol. Even though there had been periodic public meetings, a problem of "correct" information dissemination seemed to continue. The ejidatarios' fear going into the meeting was that their ejido would be *embargado*, or confiscated from their hands. They worried that the land would become inaccessible to the very people to whom it supposedly pertained.

Two days before the scheduled meeting, two female members of the archaeological project met with a group of women health promoters to speak about the archaeological project and the benefits that supporting the project and its development plans would bring to the community. This self-selected group of almost thirty local women saw themselves as progressive and community-oriented. One told me just minutes before the women's meeting that those in town who did not support the archaeology project were "ignorant." Other residents of Kochol saw these *promotoras* as the disciples of the local physician, a young woman from central Mexico who was serving her required public-service duty staffing the Kochol clinic, an underfunded facility that served as the main health facility for several communities. She had spent her entire term in Kochol haranguing the people about public health issues. The biggest issue was the abundance of pigs then wandering the streets. When I asked Don Tomás, the *comisario municipal* (town mayor), if he thought it was true that unpenned pigs presented a community health threat, he replied, "Yes. This is what the doctor tells us. If the pigs are loose in the street, they eat whatever they come across. If the pigs eat garbage, then we are eating garbage when we eat the pig." Indeed, a Kochol without pigs now looks like a different, sanitized Kochol.

Disappearing along with the pigs was a substantial amount of litter. Fresh paint adorned the basketball court in the center of town. Did this facelift stand for a new Kochol? A more docile Kochol? Was a path being paved for the town's heritage-based modernization and development projects? The INAH representative sent from state headquarters to speak to community residents at the public meeting arranged by the Pakbeh archaeologists had no forewarning of the complex web he had entered. A lawyer by training, the high-level bureaucrat with considerable experience in negotiating INAH-community relations focused on demystifying the INAH. He detailed the agency's mission, functions, and duties in a down-to-earth manner using little jargon and clear examples. He emphasized the shortfall of resources the INAH was experiencing, exacerbated by the incredible number of archaeological ruins in Yucatán. The 106 municipalities in Yucatán and more than two thousand archaeological sites, he explained, could mean up to twenty sites in each municipality. He stressed that Kochol's situation was not unusual—most archaeological sites coincide with ejido land. For most ejido communities, this does not represent a conflict.

The representative, aware that archaeologists or others might have promoted anti-INAH sentiment in the town, played down the power of INAH, explaining that it is an institution, an office building. In the Mexican context, calling something an institution almost erases its power and capacity for actually affecting anything. The Kochol ejidatarios have completed the PROCEDE process and hold the certificates for their land. Knowing that it puts the land at greater risk, they expressed fears that the INAH would force them to sell the ejido lands within the archaeological zone. In response, the representative made clear that INAH is neither interested in buying nor able to buy lands. The INAH does not *own* archaeological properties, he emphasized, and most are either ejido lands or *propiedades particulares*, private properties.

He responded to ejidatarios' concerns regarding the name of the site. To those who wanted the site to carry the name "Kochol," he countered that Chichén Itzá is not called Pisté, Uxmal is not called Santa Elena,

Oxkintok is not called Maxcanú, and so forth. While he made a valid point, what the representative missed in this example is that the site name *coincides* with that of a contemporary town. The problem arose not strictly because of this coincidence, but because—due to the history of hacienda expropriations—the archaeological site is not spatially coterminous with the entity whose name it shares. The archaeological site "Chunchucmil" shares the territory of five ejidos: Coahuila, Halacho, Chunchucmil, Kochol, and San Mateo.

Because of the overlap in questions of territory, jurisdiction, and land-holding and ownership, there are often points of connection between questions of ejidos and archaeological properties. While practice and circumstance draw them together, juridical frameworks separate them. "Questions about your ejido should be directed to the Procuraduría [Agraria]," the representative advised. "The INAH is not an ejido authority. If the questions regarding the continuation of the archaeological project are based in concerns about the status of the ejido, then the Procuraduría should be consulted. The INAH is not a land authority."

Yet in its ability and indeed its constitutional mandate to territorialize archaeological zones, the INAH does appear in practice to lord authority over the land. Local ejidatarios keenly perceived this. The following excerpt is from a heated exchange at the meeting between the INAH representative (IR) in Kochol and town ejidatarios (KE). This excerpt of dialogue clearly demonstrates the local sensitivity toward INAH's territorializing threat. Kochol's comisario municipal (KC), who initially remained in the background, intervened to break the tension between the INAH representative and an outspoken ejidatario. Archaeological project members were present at the evening meeting in Kochol's basketball court but were purposely not taking a central role in the proceedings. One archaeologist (A) intervened toward the end:

KE: But when the permissions aren't granted, even under the law they can't enter the land to work.

IR: Yes, that's right. This is what the law says.

KE: I wanted to make that clear. Did you come here to help your compañeros [referring to the Pakbeh archaeologists] or to benefit the community?

IR: This is what I am trying to explain.

KE: Already you've been talking for half an hour.

IR: Which compañeros? Do you think that I know them [the archaeologists]?

KE: Didn't you just say you work for the INAH?

IR: Do you think I know all of you?

KE: Exactly. You don't know us.

IR: I didn't come here to support anyone's side. I came to explain what the INAH is.

KE: The people are conscious of what is going on. The more you talk, and talk, and talk, *aquí no puedes lograr nada* [you won't get away with anything here]. . . . You came here to get permission from us for your compañeros to work in our ejido.

KC: While we are interested in the general explanation you were giving, the comisario ejidal was trying to tell you that there are some problems in the mounds where the archaeologists are working. The short of it is, the people have not reached an agreement about their work. We would like for them to present their work plan to us. The archaeologists want to do their project, but the people of Kochol don't want it.

KE: [*addressing archaeologist*] In this area, they are planning on planting coconut trees, and then they will close it off.

A: I never said that!

KE: And then no ejidatario will be allowed to enter his own property.

Several weeks after this confrontational public meeting in Kochol, the ejidatarios asked project directors to draft and sign a statement to be authorized and held by Kochol officials stating that the project had no intentions of confiscating the community's ejido lands. INAH officials were also asked to co-sign the declaration, but the agency representative refused: "If we start making contracts like this with every ejido that has archaeological remains, it would become very complicated for us, both practically and legally." Even without the INAH's signature, the document was drafted and signed by project officials. Around the same time, permissions were finally granted to the project by the Consejo de Arqueología in Mexico City. The Pakbeh Project was back on track, and the 2002 field season continued.

"Our problem is the rumors that have spread around Kochol," an archaeologist said later. "They are worried that the INAH is going to come in and close off their land." Other project members have echoed this sentiment and said that it is not the intention of the archaeological project to restrict access or activity on the ejido land within the boundaries of the official zone. Contextualizing the powerlessness of the project relative to the INAH, project members have frequently and publicly held up the government agency as a threat to the community. Residents of Kochol and Chunchucmil previously had little if any contact with the INAH but greater familiarity with governmental agencies such as the Instituto Nacional Indigenista (INI), an agency lacking an important presence in these communities. The primary orientation of local residents toward institutions of archaeological investigation is solely the Chunchucmil Regional Economy Project. This is not surprising, given INAH's serious shortage of resources and personnel that leads to an inability to maintain any sort of a presence at most archaeological sites in the state.

The project was still required, of course, to obtain permissions for excavation and other investigation practices. A problem arose early in the 2002 field season regarding these excavation permits. The application hit a snag in the INAH's national Consejo de Arqueología regarding a passage in the project report about its involvement in community development programs. The project was in the initial planning stages for the creation of two museums: a living museum to be situated within the archaeological site and an artifact museum slated to be housed within Chunchucmil Pueblo. An interview I conducted in March 2002 with the director of the INAH Centro Regional Yucatán in Mérida, also a member of the Consejo de Arqueología on a national level, left me with little doubt as to the INAH's official position on community archaeology:

> Archaeological projects have one function. For foreign archaeologists, their job is to investigate academic archaeological issues. Now with the issue of development projects—they would have to have other kinds of orientations and authorizations. An archaeological project is authorized as a project with an academic character.[9]

For the director, there is no gray or fuzzy space between academic and community-oriented development endeavors. That the archaeologists at Chunchucmil were being penalized for a suspected boundary-crossing I cannot know for sure. I can say, however, that this issue, invoked as it was by the INAH's regional director, was yet another layer to the turf war playing out at Chunchucmil among local landholders, archaeologists, and government officials.

While the conflict in Kochol is plainly about clarifying the territorial rights of the INAH and the community ejido holders, it is equally mired in questions of the responsibilities of archaeological practice to local communities. As this case demonstrates, these two issues can easily become entangled with one another. Clearly, the archaeologists of the Pakbeh project had some sort of commitment to opening lines of communication and even collaboration between themselves and the residents of Kochol and Chunchucmil Pueblo. Their efforts to include local communities as interlocutors in their work, I believe, goes beyond the call of strictly academic archaeology. For many anthropologists, especially coming from the U.S. context, this kind of undertaking can only be admired.

Yet it clearly did not translate well across the border. And what seemed to archaeologists an ethical imperative looked to INAH officials like troublemaking. Compounding this difference in interpretation of academic boundaries was the way archaeologists presented themselves to local communities. In the course of the many formal and informal meetings between archaeologists and various officials, elders, and ordinary residents of both communities, (perhaps inadvertently) the archaeologists acted as an autonomous group. In other words, as they discussed the site and proposed development plans such as the creation of a community museum, they appeared to many local residents to be independent of the INAH; this would especially be the case for those local residents who were not even aware of the existence of the INAH. When the situation heated up, however, one could argue that archaeologists attempted to hide behind the INAH: the archaeologists argued they did not have the power to territorialize the site—they could not make its borders, put up fences, or charge admission prices.

By now we know that the physical delimitation of boundaries is not the only way in which a territory is marked. What the archaeologists—and the INAH, for that matter—failed to recognize was the shift in the local discourse on heritage that the excavation project boldly announced. As we have seen, the archaeological site had already been repeatedly territorialized: by the hacienda system, the ejido system, and now, the machinations of heritage. In sum, the events I relate above point to one of the central ideas of this study: the making of archaeological heritage is a spatial practice that produces, reproduces, and intervenes in a field of social relations. Perhaps greater attention to the historical contingencies of these social relations—and how they indicated alternative concepts of heritage—could have avoided some of the tensions and "trespassing" of archaeology and the state in the space of Chunchucmil.

CEREMONIAL INSCRIPTIONS

Before the time of the fathers of men now living, there are only myths, the stories, moral or merely fantastic, of the acts and happenings of supernatural races, unconnected with the Maya of today. "A long time ago, in the time of my grandfather, there lived in these parts a race of little people," a typical story begins. The "time of my grandfather" is a time of magical and mysterious events. (Redfield and Villa Rojas 1934/1990: 12)

In May 2002 Pakbeh archaeologists initiated plans to hold a ceremony in the archaeological site center, part of which overlaps the territory of the Kochol ejido. The intention of this ceremony to heal community relations was, at least to me and several of my informants, thinly disguised. There is an established tradition of conducting ceremonies such as these in the history of Maya archaeology, at least in Yucatán. The ceremonies performed at archaeological sites belong to a general class of cleansing ceremonies, the *hetz luum*. These ceremonies also are performed to seek permission for working upon specific areas of land, especially if this work is to be invasive, whether into the soil or the mounds. Why would such ceremonies be held, and what ends do they serve? More importantly, for whom are they performed? Archaeologists? The present-day Maya? Or the supernatural inhabitants of the landscape?

The type of ceremony to be performed at the archaeological site is known as a *loh*. The purpose a loh is "the propitiation and exorcism of evil spirits" (Redfield and Villa Rojas 1934/1990: 175; confirmed in an interview with Don Nico). Loh ceremonies are simultaneously preventive measures and problem-solving strategies. This means that while they are designed to propitiate spirits or other beings that inhabit a cave, a milpa, a house plot, a cenote, or other landscape feature, the ceremonies I learned about throughout the course of my ethnographic research were necessitated by some sort of problem or disturbance—an abnormality—that has already occurred.

The basic activities of a loh ceremony consist in the *h'meen*, a Maya ritual specialist, reciting prayers in Maya and making various food and drink offerings. Loh ceremonies have an important practical dimension, and are accepted and encouraged by a variety of agents: local Maya, Yucatec (white) businessmen, and archaeologists. Ceremonies can be private or very public affairs. Often, a h'meen or *yerbatero* will engage in ceremonial activities to cure an individual of illness brought on by exposure to *malos vientos*, or bad winds. This would take place in a person's own household. Redfield and Villa Rojas (1934: 175) note that "the loh ceremony is apt to be not a private or familial matter, but a communal act, comparable in significance and in seriousness to the *cha-chaac* [rain ceremony]." Loh ceremonies at archaeological sites are typically public affairs with the weight of financial sponsorship carried by the archaeologists.

The Pakbeh archaeologists' idea for conducting a ceremony on the Kochol ejido in the Chunchucmil archaeological site grew out of the project's general orientation toward connecting with local communities in the practice of archaeology. The plans were ambitious and well-orchestrated: proper kinds and amounts of food had to be sought and purchased, plenty of cooking help had to be secured, and transportation would have to be arranged for participants from surrounding communities not within comfortable walking distance. And perhaps most importantly, a ritual specialist had to be found to conduct the ceremony. Successfully covering all of these bases—through a rather heroic amount of work, I might add—there was one that the Pakbeh project members did not premeditate: that many local Maya would perceive the ceremony as not being for them—as part of their traditional practices per se—but as a "show" of Maya Culture.

Comparative study between Pisté/Chichén and Kochol/Chunchucmil offered me insight into a very interesting, and somewhat counterlogical insight. I make the following suggestion hypothetically: in a place with more archaeological development, residents become more comfortable with the markers of "Maya Culture," as they carry a certain currency when oriented to outsiders; in a place with no "outside" audience such as that provided through tourism, residents have less of a connection to those same "telltale" signs of Maya Culture. The illogic of this has to do with the now-commonplace insight provided by social scientists, among others, regarding tradition versus modernity. In this we might look to Robert Redfield as an example, especially with his paradigmatic folk-urban continuum. With higher degrees of development, more contact with the outside world, higher education levels, more comfortable economic situations, and so forth, people should be farther away from so-called folk beliefs. It follows that with a greater degree of isolation, less technology, less contact with the outside, lower degrees of education, and the like, folk beliefs would be stronger and more persistent.

One good example concerns *aluxes*. In the course of talking with relatives of the early Maya laborers who worked with the archaeologists at Chichén I stumbled on a phenomenon remarkably similar to what Redfield describes in his 1932 piece "Maya Archaeology as the Mayas See It." Redfield claims that the archaeology of Yucatán has given rise to a particular set of beliefs among the Maya of the 1930s, particularly in their stories of the aluxes:

> The alux, a people quite distinct, are living today. They are a mysterious and mischievous people whom it is always best to avoid and often wise to propitiate. . . . The alux may easily do one harm, and they never

do one good. Most of the older men have seen these little people, and are familiar with their appearance. They are about a foot high, and look like very small children, except that they are the color of clay and wear beards and crowns. They are hollow inside, so that rain enters them at the top and runs out at the toes. (304–305)

Many stories of aluxes circulate presently in Pisté. What Redfield claimed in 1932 remains, for the most part, true: "The alux are a favorite subject for storytelling; men tell of their uncanny adventures with them meeting them in the bush, or observing the results of their pranks in their homes" (305). I know now where they dwell: mostly in caves or near cenotes. And it seems as though one may keep them away by smoking a cigarette, a warning that humans are approaching.

Redfield, it seems, did not know what to make of the stories of the aluxes, especially as these narratives, as told by the Maya people, were well interwoven with references such as Noah's Ark and the Tower of Babel. He comes to the conclusion that unless the "real" Maya elements of these tales were learned from the archaeologists, they "represent a battered remnant of native tradition" and goes as far to say, "there is no reason why some of these beliefs may not have resulted from entirely new interpretation placed upon archaeological artifacts since the Conquest" (306).

In Chunchucmil Pueblo and Kochol, I had trouble eliciting alux stories. The initial stages of my research in these towns chronologically followed my fieldwork in Pisté, where these accounts were repeatedly, even incessantly volunteered. In Chunchucmil, where I conducted interviews before Kochol, the mere word *alux* was enough to bring a conversation to an uncomfortable impasse.[10] Where there was not an impasse, there were some hesitant offerings, always couched in the grammar of "I have heard other people talk about the aluxes, but I never saw one myself." No one, it seems, had ever personally seen one, yet everyone had an uncle, cousin, or neighbor who might have encountered an alux walking down the road at dusk, in their solar at night, in the monte gathering firewood, or even going to school. But then the dialogue often opened up a bit, after I demonstrated my own avid curiosity. "Well, I haven't seen one, but one day I was walking to my milpa and I heard the sound of rocks being thrown." Or another common account places the protagonist in the evening in a hammock and hearing a sound in the kitchen, of a wooden spoon stirring inside of a cup, such as the noise produced in making a chocolate drink.

What I found in Chunchucmil and Kochol initially surprised me but on second thought made sense. It should not be surprising that residents of the more rural areas are less likely to discuss issues such as belief in the presence of aluxes. This is for at least two reasons. First, there is a degree of guardedness that the residents of Kochol and Chunchucmil practice when speaking of such things, especially to an outsider, in this case an American anthropologist who locally has the status of a schoolteacher. This guardedness may be related to a *vergüenza*, or embarrassment, at the stuff of folklore—what would an educated person from the United States think about aluxes? A second reason is based in the absence of a discourse of promoting Maya Culture in this region of Yucatán. This absence may be attributed to the hacienda history and form of social control it presented to several generations of Mayas in this region; the dearth of appropriate or culturally sensitive social programs; and the communities' geographical locations off the tourism circuits. Simply put, the residents of Kochol and Chunchucmil, on the whole, do not recognize Maya Culture as a marketable patrimony.

Ya pasó la época de los aluxes, the time of the aluxes has passed, said seventy-eight-year-old Don Alberto of Kochol. "They still exist, but they don't have the same power they did when I was a boy," he continued. We were sitting inside his daughter Doña Victoria's small store in one of the old hacienda buildings along the main street of town, passing the worst hours of a particularly hot May afternoon. What was the time of the aluxes like? How was it different from now? I asked him. This was before electricity, he explained. The streets were illuminated with *faroles de papel*, paper lamps with candles rather than electric streetlights. The low light they cast upon the street created a shadowy atmosphere advantageous to wandering *brujos*, or witches. The brujos could move easily on the low-lit streets amid uncorraled animals including pigs and cattle. The designation of a historical period in which aluxes were more abundant is articulated, thus, to degrees of village size, population, and density. Spatial differentiations marking the boundaries between residential areas, milpas, and monte are markers of different realms of alux activity.

Aluxes like to be near humans, as it is from humans that they receive offerings such as food, alcohol, or cigarettes—all of which they like and with which they might be propitiated. Yet, in the bush, a human being has the responsibility of warning any aluxes that might be nearby and unaware that human beings are near. Warning signals the human might give include walking noisily or smoking a cigarette—two decidedly human practices. Also, the presence of certain kinds of technology, such as electricity, affect the auspiciousness of an environment for aluxes.

The issue of auspiciousness was replayed in the weeks preceding the ceremony in the Chunchucmil archaeological site. Many residents of

Kochol were troubled for at least two reasons. The first was regarding the issue of contemporary religious belief and practice. For the many local Protestants, the ceremony was something in which their religious doctrine dissuaded participation. The second was a practical issue for farmers who take seriously the power of the supernatural. If the land was disturbed by the ceremony and the aluxes and other supernatural personages were called forth and propitiated, this would begin a burdensome cycle for farmers of constantly making more offerings to work in their own ejido plots.

Don Marcelo, a h'meen I interviewed and observed, is a Catholic. He felt that his work served a concrete purpose in harmony with Maya beliefs about the spirit world, although he knew not everyone appreciated what he did: *Los que son muy pegados a la lectura de la biblia rechaza el trabajo de los h'meenes, pero la mayoría de la gente tiene creencia* (Those who stick very closely to biblical teachings reject the work of the h'meen, but the majority of the people are believers). Even today, with the popularity of various Protestant groups, Catholicism serves as a "baseline" religious tradition. In Pisté, Kochol, and Chunchucmil, Protestant groups, particularly the Presbyterian Church, have an enormously popular following. But there is always a sense that those who are members of the Presbyterian, Pentecostal, or Assembly of God *templos* are "converts," although in some cases these groups have a thirty-year or longer local presence. According to one elderly resident of Kochol, "We are all born Catholics," though some might choose to join a templo. In Kochol, there are five templos and a Catholic church. All are thriving, yet Protestant templos are more popular for several reasons. Among these are the churches' discouragement of drinking, the ritual informality of their services, their lay leadership, and the presence of activities nearly every night of the week. Perhaps the most appealing aspect of the templo services is the combination of prayer with live music. While a rural templo might not have its own musical group, traveling groups regularly visit areas like Kochol and Chunchucmil for special occasions and retreats.

Spiritual life is alive and well in Kochol, though the seeker of authentic Maya cultural tradition would be disappointed to see it under the banner of Christianity. The strong religious convictions of many of Kochol's residents, whether Catholic or Protestant, produced a decided discomfort with the proposal of a Maya ceremony at the ruins. During a casual conversation between me and three ejidatarios from Kochol on the front step of the tienda near the center of town, Don Chumín, a prominent town elder, pointedly raised the subject of Pakbeh's proposed ceremony. "On the eighteenth of this month there will be a ceremony in the cerros,"

FIGURE 6.4.   *Stirring the pot: Attendees of the Pakbeh-sponsored cleansing ritual in the Chunchucmil archaeological zone prepare the ceremonial food. Photograph by author.*

he offered solemnly, to be hosted by *los que trabajan allá* (literally "those who work there," a typical way of referring to the archaeologists). "[They] want to see a ceremony, so they are going to have it in our ejido." It was all arranged, although the details unfolded little by little—a yerbatero was coming from the nearby municipality of Halacho to perform an as yet unidentified sort of ceremony.

"We are definitely not going," said another group of three ejidatarios as we sat on the steps of Kochol's dilapidated casa principal. This group, easily a generation younger than Nico, Chumín, and Sixto, were highly critical of the "big show" the archaeologists were planning, entrance to which would require a ticket. The final date of the ceremony ended up as June 15, a month after the originally scheduled date. The problem had been with finding an appropriate yerbatero, though there were many to choose from in the immediate area.

The day of the ceremony, I arrived by nine o'clock in the morning. Preparations had been going on for days, most intensely since the evening before. Most of the preparation involved the large amount of food for the ritual and then to distribute among those present. It was a long, particularly hot day marked by intermittent downpours that did little to provide relief from the scorching sun. A dozen or so people were at work, most of them involved in cooking ceremonial foods in huge pots over open fires. As the hours went by, archaeologists made several trips with their field vehicles to the town centers of Kochol, Chunchucmil, Coahuila, and San Rafael to offer rides for residents who wanted to participate in the ceremony. As it turned out, tickets were not being used. In all, no more than approximately seventy-five people attended the ceremony held in the Kochol ejido at the base of a large mound. Those who did come left ambivalent. At the end of the day, none of the local residents who were not directly affiliated with the yerbatero, only a few kocholeños among them, knew what the ceremony was about or why it was performed.

MONUMENTAL AMBIVALENCE IN THE FORMER HACIENDAS

Many residents of Kochol and Chunchucmil were left somewhat uncomfortable with the archaeologists' ceremony, embarrassed at how much money was spent, and even angry at the unfair distribution of the ceremonial food at its conclusion. The example of the loh ceremony at Chunchucmil demonstrates how the archaeological zone is a social space of multiple inflections, the meanings of which exceed the significations of both the "the land" and "the ruins" as well as the practices of agricultural work or archaeology. "Land" is not a *tabula rasa*; it is a space produced and neutralized as a "natural" ground for social relations. The land itself has a spatial genealogy, a history and coexistence of different inscriptions, codes, and territories. This is what makes it particularly meaningful as patrimony or inheritance.

On the one hand, "monumental ambivalence" refers to an enormous or overwhelming ambivalence on the part of the residents of the archaeological zone's neighboring communities toward what they could theoretically claim as their cultural heritage. On the other hand, the phrase "monumental ambivalence" could refer, in a deeper and more complex sense, to their undecidedness, indecisiveness, or uneasiness about the mounds as monuments. In the first instance, the efficacy of a claim that the ruins are the cultural heritage of the local communities would remain to be seen. I am inclined to think that it is a moot point. If anyone attempts to express the idea, indeed the belief, that the mounds were built by another race of people not related to the present-day communities, he or she runs the risk of being judged by archaeologists, site visitors, or officials as mistaken, uneducated, maybe stupid, and certainly not savvy in the heritage discourse that circulates on regional, national, and international levels among academics, heritage professionals, and bureaucrats. The second possibility, that monumental ambivalence is the lack of conviction that the mounds are monuments, is an effect of living in a landscape of multiple territories. Certainly, the mounds existed as physical entities in the Chunchucmil landscape long before archaeology arrived on the scene. Yet as we have seen here, the monumental meanings of the mounds at Chunchucmil as insisted upon by archaeology and the state are secondary, if that, to those monumental meanings evoked by more than a century of changing social, political, cultural, and economic relationships in the space.

Regardless of the commonsense saliency of the local understanding of Chunchucmil's mounds as natural features of the landscape, archaeological development at the site has conditioned the possibility for a new codifying regime to emerge. In this new territory of heritage, ejido holders become wage laborers, local political alliances are shaped by pro- and anti-archaeology factions, and contemporary Maya people are interpellated into a relationship of continuity with ancient Maya civilization.

As archaeological development continues at the site of Chunchucmil, the Maya residents of its surrounding communities increasingly face the question of what is their heritage and how they will negotiate the new semiotics of the landscape. What promises does archaeology make? In terms of patrimony, does cultural heritage enjoy a privileged position over inherited ejido land? Does national patrimony efface local patrimony, the public good over the rights of particular citizens?

Archaeological development at Chunchucmil in the past few years has raised issues both for archaeologists and for local residents around this idea of the land and its meanings, not unlike the cases of hundreds or perhaps thousands of sites around the world. After all, living does not stop at a heritage site's borders. Nor does it begin there.

In closing, I return to the INAH-sponsored slide show in Kochol with the following anecdote. At the slide show's conclusion, a thirteen-year-old girl and lifelong resident of Kochol, pulled me to a quiet corner and asked, "Is it really true that thousands of people come from all over the world to walk around those ruins?" She was fascinated by the images of throngs of people we had just seen touring Chichén Itzá. Though practically living amid ancient vestiges, she did not think of herself as a person who had ever visited Maya ruins. She keenly perceived, however, the differences in register carried by the term "ruins," knowing that crowds of visitors in the unrestored mounds of Kochol would indeed be a sight to see.

DOCILE DESCENDANTS
AND ILLEGITIMATE HEIRS:
THE AMBIVALENCE OF INHERITANCE

*The world is ambivalent, though its colonizers and rulers do not
like it to be such and by hook or by crook try to pass it off for one
that is not. . . . Ambivalence is not to be bewailed. It is to be celebrated. Ambivalence is the limit to the power of the powerful.*

BAUMAN 1991: 179

*Maya Indian farmer Diego Uc returned from his field one day in
December 2000 to find Mexican federal police waiting at his one-
room adobe house in the Yucatán tropics. With barely a word, they
put him in a van and drove him three hours to federal prison in
the state capital of Campeche. "'You have business in Campeche,'
they told me, and they took me to jail," Uc, 58, said recently at his
home. He stayed in prison for nine months, his health failing and
his family living on handouts from relatives. Uc's crime: moving
plain, melon-sized stones on land he owned since 1982. Authorities said the stones formed part of a protected archaeological site,
which Uc damaged. . . . The case pits two sets of national authorities against each other: those who protect archaeological sites left by
Mexico's ancient people and those who promote the rights and culture of living Indians descended from those civilizations. Uc's
stones may well have been put there by his ancestors.*

ORLANDI 2002: I

Who are the proper heirs to Maya cultural patrimony? Through the course
of this study I have suggested several possibilities. Under the notion "that
which is everybody's is nobody's," all and none of us inherit Maya, Mexican, and World Heritage. As tourists, scholars, or any other workaday citizens, perhaps we are content to let this ambivalence go unexamined. But
what about those people who live within the landscape of ruins in Yucatán?
What about those who must negotiate this curious and perplexing am-

bivalence of the ownership of cultural patrimony in order to go about their everyday business? Maya communities such as those in and around Chunchucmil and Chichén Itzá have indeed engaged this task of negotiating monumental ambivalence for decades.

Heritage is a set of values, meanings, and practices differently constituted at local, regional, national, and international levels by social actors and institutions. Distinct regional, local, and even site-specific understandings of Maya cultural heritage exist in tandem and tension with both the Mexican nationalist discourse on cultural heritage and UNESCO's criteria of universal cultural value. For local Maya communities, heritage is part of an everyday experience and common-sense knowledge. The archaeological ruins, especially for those employed in their preservation, form just part of the social, political, cultural, and economic landscape. For regional and national institutions charged with preserving and promoting culture, heritage is composed of material spaces of intervention, such as archaeological ruins, used to produce symbolic meanings that forge identity, belonging, and community at regional and national levels. For international agencies, heritage is a set of policies and practices that create and regulate humanly built cultural spaces.

As we have seen, the precise configuration and expression of the patrimony of an archaeological site differ according to a wide spectrum of factors. At Chichén Itzá, an internationally famous site that has undergone archaeological and touristic development since the early twentieth century, federally employed site guards and caretakers understand the site as an inheritable family patrimony. The care and protection of Chichén, they claim, is "in our blood." At Chunchucmil, local residents—some who are excavation laborers—also articulate a strong connection to the newly declared archaeological zone. However, for these agriculturalists, patrimony is found in the land, not the ruins. The land coterminous with the archaeological heritage site is their patrimonio ejidal, the ejido land-grant heritage they have held since the federal government distributed land to indigenous people in the 1930s.

As they navigate the produced spaces of heritage in Yucatán, Maya people are alternatively positioned—by archaeology, the state, the private sector, and on occasion themselves—as both docile descendants and illegitimate heirs to cultural patrimony. As docile descendants, Maya communities in and around archaeological sites must affirm that they are, to paraphrase Sylvanus G. Morley, remnants of an ancient, glorious civilization. In this construct, modern Maya are the passive accoutrements of a heritage assemblage that seeks to territorialize contemporary landscapes as ancient or "out of time," if you will. They must agree that ruins are monuments and that these monuments are a univocal signifier of their heritage. What is more, they must be willing to share this heritage with the nation and even the world. When the univocality of monumental heritage is challenged— whether explicitly or implicitly, as both case studies demonstrate—the same populations become illegitimate heirs of a national patrimony that was never really available to them by law or by practice.

Diego Uc's case, detailed in the passage above, is just one illustration of the very real consequences of this ambivalence. Diego Uc's alleged crime reminds us of the changing conception of Maya people and their relationship to the material vestiges of ancient Maya culture, those for whom, as Redfield supposed, the ruins are not a heritage. At least, theirs is not a heritage that can be used at the discretion of its heirs. Some may find Uc to be a docile descendant—a legitimate inheritor of Maya cultural patrimony. To argue that Uc's removal of stones is not a serious offense against the state, one would have to argue that the stones were just stones—that they were not a heritage. Though a legitimate landowner, he is an illegitimate heir to the cultural patrimony on his property. He is misusing cultural heritage, privately exploiting that which belongs to the nation. Yet as we saw throughout our case studies, private interests have consistently been allowed—and even encouraged—to territorialize and exploit heritage resources. This contradiction stems from a monumental ambivalence of who counts as "everybody" and as "nobody."

How different is Uc's crime from the activities of the INAH custodios at Chichén Itzá who use a different sort of descent-based patrimonial claim to assert their right to economically benefit from the sale of refreshments and souvenirs inside the federal territory of the archaeological zone? Does Uc's crime stem from his perhaps innocent inconformity to the legal-territorial regime that insists that these stones and landscapes in general be protected and not utilized? Is Uc so different from the ejidatarios of Kochol who wish to reclaim their own ejido land in the center of the Chunchucmil archaeological zone through planting corn or papaya or in the excavation embargo they attempted to effect? Did Uc even recognize these "plain stones" as national monumental heritage? I ask myself, would I?

Maya people who live in and around ruins in Yucatán, like Diego Uc, the custodians at Chichén Itzá, and the farmers at Chunchucmil, are docile descendants and illegitimate heirs. Historically, residents of Chunchucmil and Kochol have been thrust into the role of docile descendants, as for generations they were slavelike laborers in the hacienda system. These local residents' unquestioning acceptance of the archaeological interpretations of the Chunchucmil site and willing participation in tourism development plans would further solidify the construct of Yucatec Maya as docile descendants.

Moving back to the case of Chichén Itzá, the custodios of the archaeological zone, too, are in a sense docile descendants. Their attention to caring for and protecting the zone across several generations demonstrates their accord with the state's discourse on monumental heritage. This position, however, is manipulated by Chichén's workers when they employ it as a justifying rationale for establishing the refreshment cooperatives. As the antiguo custodios claim the archaeological site as a resource for themselves, they utilize the monumental ambivalence of the site as "everybody's and nobody's."

Yet all of these social actors are illegitimate heirs as well. Kochol's ejidatarios have, in a sense, illegitimately inherited the newly established archaeological zone. Legally the land remains theirs, per Article 27 of the Mexican Constitution. But as the mounds become monuments, access to their ejido land becomes tantamount to trespass.

We may draw a parallel conclusion from Chichén Itzá. Indeed, the historical contingencies of usufruct rights and living presence inside the zone pave the way for the entrepreneurial practices of the INAH custodios, over and against legal mandate. For the thousands of other Maya residents around Chichén Itzá, certainly the INAH custodios are flagrantly illegitimate heirs. How does this select group have the right to inherit the nation's patrimony? But for many, this logic needs only the slightest of twists to justify their own interests and practices: they are saying, in effect, "The site is patrimony of all of the nation/world/humanity, and I am Mexican/global citizen/human being."

The heritage assemblage, prone as it is toward creating and sustaining ambivalence, generates the construction of both docile descendants and illegitimate heirs. This assemblage is composed of national law and policy, institutional practices, sui generis international heritage regimes, global economies, and multiple publics. I have argued that the ambivalence of heritage revealed itself at a particular historical moment in Mexico, following the introduction of the 1999 "Privatization Proposal" to open resources of cultural patrimony to private concession. While I have stressed that the proposal, to date, has not passed into constitutional amendment, it provides an occasion and a strong motivation to critically analyze the ongoing relationships between private-sector interests and heritage sites in Yucatán—a main task of this study. As I demonstrated, the emergence of privatization at the intersection of Mexican nationalism and local site development presents both a threat and new possibilities for Maya claims to cultural heritage.

I have stressed the need to stretch our understanding of heritage beyond material culture into the realm of practice. I have thus posed archaeological zones as territorial assemblages: geographical places accompanied by a historically specific production of space. I have examined the practices through which these zones are constituted, managed, used, and represented. Given that these processes are intimately connected to an analytical perspective on the spatiality of these zones, I have used a mapping methodology most amenable to drawing out, connecting, and understanding their complexities. But the maps created are not simple reproductions of the statist cartography of national heritage.

To better grasp a politics of heritage beyond concerns for site management and tourism, it is necessary to map heritage to the overlapping territories of multiple discursive regimes: legal, economic, spatial, and so on. Indeed the social scientific study of the local-level instantiations of the intensification and ever-widening reach of neoliberalism lags behind the rapidly transforming cultural and economic landscape. As more nations transfer their patrimonial resources to the private sector, the ambivalence of "that which is everyone's is no one's" deepens.

Against the notion that private-sector intervention in the nation's patrimonial commons is a new threat signaled by the recent intensification of neoliberal economic and social programs in Mexico and across the globe, however, I argue that a host of informal or partial privatizations have consistently accompanied the state's assertions of territorial control over cultural patrimony. While these interventions are not privatization in the strict sense, they do represent extralegal practices common to the everyday functioning of archaeological heritage sites. I demonstrate that multinational big business is not the only privatizing spectre haunting the future of ruins. Indeed, local indigenous communities, through various entrepreneurial and land-protectionist activities, are vital players in the continuous privatization of heritage resources.

"When we contemplate ruins," writes Christopher Woodward (2001: 2), "we contemplate our own future." Archaeologists, cultural resource managers, museum curators, and others would certainly agree that contemporary preoccupations with the past most certainly indicate concerns about the present and anxieties toward the future. It would not be surprising, then, that other social actors whose lives are intertwined with the heritage assemblage—the images, ideas, ethics, laws, and material manifestations of cultural patrimony—orient their past vis-à-vis their hopes and dreams for the future. Perhaps Chichén Itzá's past is Chunchucmil's future, a future, that is, "in ruins."

NOTES

1. Article 73 reads in full: *Para establecer, organizar y sostener en toda la República escuelas rurales elementales, superiores, secundarias y profesionales, de investigación científica, de bellas artes y de enseñanza técnica; escuelas prácticas de agricultura y de minería, de artes y oficios, museos, bibliotecas, observatorios y demás institutos concernientes a la cultura general de los habitantes de la Nación y legislar en todo lo que se refiere a dichas instituciones, para legislar sobre monumentos arqueológicos, artísticos e históricos, cuya conservación sea de interés social; así como para dictar las leyes encaminadas a distribuir convenientemente entre la Federación, los Estados y los Municipios el ejercicio de la función educativa y las aportaciones económicas correspondientes a este servicio público, buscando unificar y coordinar la educación en toda la República* (as amended on December 21, 1965, and published in the *Diario Oficial*, January 13, 1966). The 1999 Fernández Garza initiative proposed the reform in the juridical and institutional organization of the protection of Mexico's cultural patrimony as stated in two pieces of legislation: the 1972 *Ley Federal sobre Monumentos y Zonas Arqueológicos, Artísticos e Históricos* and the 1985 *Ley Orgánica*.

2. The country's financial problems heightened in the 1970s, leading to the peso crisis of 1982 that resulted from Mexico's default on loans from foreign commercial banks. The International Monetary Fund (IMF) and the World Bank, in their "rescues" of debtor countries including Mexico, imposed structural adjustment plans featuring wage freezes, decreases in public expenditures, and support for exports. This is the root of Mexico's embrace of neoliberal ideology, marked by the decision to move from a fixed exchange rate to a free market rate. The 1990 Washington Consensus laid out the neoliberal path for Latin American economies in crisis (including Argentina, Venezuela, and Brazil along with Mexico). According to this plan, economic stabilization followed by structural adjustment policies would remove constraints on markets and promote privatization. Fiscal discipline, tax reform, and the strengthening of property rights for foreign investors were all promoted as modernizing measures to open up the economies of Latin American as well as post-socialist Eastern European transition economies to the global market and its forces (Babb 2001: 10; Baer and Love 2000: 4).

3. Beaucage (1998) argues that *Salinismo* marked the continuation of a long history of liberalization in Mexico dating back to Lázaro Cárdenas, often thought of

as the president most antithetical to Salinas. After all, Cárdenas was a nationalizer, while Salinas is remembered for the multibillion-dollar privatization programs installed under his administration.

4. The name Chunchucmil refers to both an archaeological site and a residential community. When necessary for clarity, I sometimes refer specifically to Chunchucmil Pueblo, the community, as distinct from the archaeological site.

5. According to Deleuze and Guattari (1987), an assemblage is a group of "things" or parts of "things" that are forged into a common context. The dynamic combination and interaction of the assembled elements produce a range of "effects," whether productive, consumptive, or aesthetic. Though it is neither tightly organized nor coherent (in fact, it more resembles a jumble), an assemblage has a certain set of features or notable characteristics. The components or elements of an assemblage are heterogeneous terms, forming liaisons and alliances among them.

6. This preoccupation is perhaps most evident in the relatively new concept of landscape. Barbara Bender (1998: 5) notes, "Landscape—people's engagement with the material world—not only works between fields of knowledge, but also incorporates everyday life and contemporary politics, and highlights institutional constraints."

7. These include Aplin 2002; Cleere 1984, 1989; McManamon and Hatton 2000. For a brief overview of CRM issues in Mexico see Robles García and Corbett 2001.

8. See, for example, Hooper-Greenhill 2000; Kaplan 1996; Kirshenblatt-Gimblett 1998; MacDonald and Fyfe 1996; Stone and Molyneaux 1994; Stone and Planel 1999.

9. These studies are generally concerned with the effects of tourism on culture, identity, and politics of a specific community or region. See, for example, Abram et al. 1997; Boissevain et al. 1996; Moscardo 1996; Nuryanti 1996; Prentice 1994; Selwyn 1996; Teo and Yeoh 1997. Specific to Mexico or the Maya see Brown 1999; Clancy 1999; Juárez 2002; Van den Berghe 1995.

10. Bartu (2000), Hodder (1998), and Shankland (1996) discuss Çatalhöyük; Bender (1998) and Chippendale (1983) discuss Stonehenge.

11. The heritage-as-artifact approach is not solely confined to considerations of tangible heritage by archaeologists or other specialists of material culture. Indeed, the approach could be applied to analyses of intangible heritage as well.

12. Castañeda (1996) ethnographically and discursively analyzes the archaeological zone of Chichén Itzá as a "Museum of Maya Culture," a monument to archaeological science and the state. Though it is not within the scope of this study, his line of inquiry suggests further investigation regarding the living Maya communities that are in many ways connected to Chichén.

13. There is no singular definition of "practice" to which I am referring in the "heritage-as-practice" approach. Rather, I draw upon a variety of sources and inspirations, from Bourdieu in his *Outline of a Theory of Practice* (1990) to de Certeau in *The Practice of Everyday Life* (1984).

14. I also conducted research in Chunchucmil Pueblo and Kochol during the archaeology off-season. During this time, I resided with a local family. Following this, I made regular day trips to both towns while formally residing in Mérida and Pisté.

15. The following characterization is typical: "The Maya communities outside the henequen zone are, generally, more traditional and more strongly conserve the language and personality of the culture. In fact, of the 44 municipalities considered 'indigenous municipalities,' more than 30 percent of the total population are Maya speakers" (CONAPO 1993).

CHAPTER TWO

1. Bauman (1991: 2) suggests that classification and categorization are characteristic of modernity's drive to exterminate ambivalence: "The ideal that the naming/classifying function strives to achieve is a sort of commodious filing cabinet that contains all the files that contain all the items that the world contains— but confines each file and each item within a separate place of its own." The filing cabinet image of the neat and orderly ideal of modernity stands in contrast to the jumble of artifacts in a cabinet of curiosities. See Bennett 1995; Hooper-Greenhill 1992; Pearce 1994.

2. The prominent place of space in contemporary social theory is addressed by many and the transformation noted most famously by Foucault (1980: 70): "Did it start with Bergson or before? Space was treated as the dead, the fixed, the undialectical, the immobile. Time, on the contrary, was richness, fecundity, life, dialectic."

3. In Chapters Five and Six we will see an interesting example of mounds at the Chunchucmil archaeological zone that many locals perceive as natural topographical features.

4. Harvey (1989: 218) expands this, using Bourdieu's concept of habitus to explain the dialectical relations within the three dimensions of space outlined by Lefebvre.

5. "Heritage assemblage" is not to be mistaken with "heritage industry," which is concerned with deployment of the past and its accoutrements as the ideological response to a crisis in culture induced by capitalist modernization and globalization and which has the characteristic of reinterpreting the past as a glorification of the eighteenth-century ideals of free-market capitalism (Corner and Harvey 1991: 14; Hewison 1987).

6. Of course I am referring to the tangible and intangible heritage that was not deliberately destroyed or that for other reasons did not survive the Conquest.

7. *Terrenos baldíos* are lands presumed to be uncultivated and otherwise unused. As we will see, the presumption of fallow land, first by colonial authorities and later by the Mexican state, was a convenient way to territorialize and privatize the rural landscape out of indigenous hands.

8. This marks a change from Spanish colonial law, under which rights to property had emanated not from natural right but from the Crown. This derived from a papal bull dated May 4, 1593, by Pope Alexander VI that granted the American possessions.

9. The implications of this legislation were perhaps more significant for petroleum and minerals than for archaeological materials.

10. In 1902 Porfirio Díaz initiated a new organization and classification of federal cultural properties (*bienes inmuebles*) that covered archaeological ruins and historic monuments. This law replaced the Juárez law, dividing federal cultural properties into two classes: properties of public domain and properties of the federal government. Public domain property, which included archaeological and historic structures, was nonmortgageable and nontransferable, and it could not be used for the exclusive benefit of private persons.

11. It was not until after the Mexican Revolution that the vast landholdings of Mexico's white elite were appropriated by the state and distributed to the largely landless majority indigenous population. Before the 1992 reform of the land law, ejido land was not constituted as an individual property right but as a usufruct right. Under this system, it was illegal to rent or sell the individual land parcels. No private investor was allowed to own or co-own an agricultural enterprise with ejido members. The proposed change of the agrarian law in 1992 consisted of the abolition of such restrictions over rents and sales of ejidos, bringing the land back into the market as a commodity. For full discussions of the ejido system in Mexico and its transformations from liberalism through neoliberalism see, for instance, Baños Ramírez (1989, 1998), Collier (1994), Cornelius and Mhyre (1998), Randall (1996), and Snyder and Torres (1998).

12. See, for example, Anderson 1983, Atkinson et al. 1996, Gathercole and Lowenthal 1990, Hobsbawm and Ranger 1983, Kohl and Fawcett 1995, Oyuela-Caycedo 1994, and Silberman 1989.

13. In 1825 the first Mexican National Museum was established, followed in 1835 by the creation of the National Academy of History.

14. Gamio was a student at Columbia University of Franz Boas, with whose help he founded the *Escuela Internacional de Arqueología y Etnografía Americana*. This institution was the first in Mexico to offer new scientific archaeological field methods, including stratigraphy (Schávelzon 1990: 76).

15. A 1986 revision acknowledges "protected fossil vestiges or remains of living creatures which lived within the national territory in the past, and whose study, conservation, restoration, recovery or use follows a paleontologic interest" (*Diario Oficial*, January 13, 1986). This decree covers an omission from the 1972 law, which did not mention such finds, and includes the definition of new fields of archaeological research.

16. Mexican delegates have participated in key international meetings such as the United Nations' 1963 Conference on International Travel and Tourism, in Rome; the 1967 Meeting on the Use and Preservation of Monuments and Places

of Artistic and Historic Interest, in Quito; and the 1969 International Forum on the Conservation, Preservation, and Valorization of Monuments and Sites in the Foundations of Cultural Tourism Development, in Oxford, England.

17. This circumstance raises the following question/speculation for further research: Does Mexico participate so actively on the international level in order to more carefully patrol the boundaries of its national cultural heritage?

18. The authors liken the reproduction of generative models following arborescent "tree" logic to the tracing. "The rhizome is altogether different, a map and not a tracing. The orchid does not reproduce the tracing of the wasp; it forms a map with the wasp, in a rhizome. What distinguishes the map from the tracing is that it is entirely oriented toward an experimentation in contact with the real" (Deleuze and Guattari 1987: 12).

PART II

1. The naming of "the New Seven Wonders of the World" is a project of a Zurich-based nongovernmental organization (NGO), the New 7 Wonders Foundation, or N7W, "created in 2001 by N7W founder and Swiss adventurer, Bernard Weber, with a mission to protect Man's heritage around the Globe" (http://cms.n7w.com/index.php?id=2). The foundation is sponsoring an Internet voting competition to select the seven sites of greatest monumental importance across the globe. Voting is expected to be finalized in 2006 and "will culminate with a live, worldwide, telecast on 1st of January 2007 to announce the New 7 Wonders of the World."

CHAPTER THREE

1. For a thorough history of the Caste War see Reed (1964) and Rugeley (1996).

2. Years later, on October 31, 1911, Thompson's Massachusetts hometown newspaper, the *Worcester Daily Telegraph*, reported the story: "Mr. Stephen Salisbury, president of the American Antiquarian Society, to appoint Edward H. Thompson, a former student at the Worcester Polytechnic Institute, United States consul to Yucatan, Mex. Mr. Salisbury was ably and successfully seconded in this effect by Senator George F. Hoar." The official status of Thompson's presence in Yucatán is reiterated in this 1911 article in response to the looting charges brought against him by the Mexican government that same year. Willard (1926: v) clarifies that the appointment was indeed made by the U.S. president, "having been urged by the American Antiquarian Society and the Peabody Museum of Harvard University, both of which were anxious to have a trained investigator on the peninsula."

3. One of the better-known results of Thompson's work at Labná is a mold of the famous Portal (arch) exhibited at the 1893 World's Fair in Chicago. At the request of F. W. Putnam of the Peabody Museum and head of the anthropology

and ethnology exhibits at the fair, Thompson made molds not only of Labná's arch but of architectural features found on the ruins of Uxmal as well. "Ten thousand square feet of moulds were taken by the expedition under his charge, during four-teen months of hard labor and serious risk of life in the dense malarial jungles of Yucatan. . . . Everyone who visited the Exposition will recall the weird effect pro-duced on the imagination by these old monuments of an unknown past" (*Official Report of the Massachusetts Board of Managers, World's Fair* cited in Thompson 1932/1965: 148–149). Thompson is careful to note that the casting project en-joyed the support of Mexican President Porfirio Díaz, who had demonstrated a reluctance to export actual artifacts to the United States, as made clear by the Chacmool case (141).

4. The survey was published in 1898 as *Ruins of Xichmook, Yucatan*, Field Columbian Museum Anthropological Series 2, no. 3.

5. Robert Redfield and Alfonso Villa Rojas (1934: 4, 23) reported decades later that the area around Chichén constituted the "frontier" between pacified and rebel territory.

6. I thank Thomas G. Knowles, curator of manuscripts at the American An-tiquarian Society, for this reference.

7. I again thank Thomas Knowles for providing me with this letter from the society's archives.

8. According to archaeologist William Folan (1970), Thompson made a last attempt in 1910–1911. Following this, it was not until 1960–1961 that another major exploration effort was carried out, this one by Folan under the sponsorship of the National Geographic Society. This project was authorized by the INAH. Another project was initiated in 1967–1968 under the supervision of INAH ar-chaeologist Roman Piña Chan.

9. The author of this article in *La Prensa* of May 27, 1921, most likely the very same Teobert Maler of the newspaper campaign against Thompson a decade be-fore, cites an article that appeared in *La Revista de Mérida* dated July 16, 1910: "With great puzzlement has been received a news item related to Mr. Thompson having asked for a twenty-year concession . . . for the installation of a hotel or boardinghouse and a cantina, in the famous ruins of Chichén, as well as a rail line from Dzitas to the hotel." For centuries, the author argues, residents of Pisté have used the lands at Chichén for making their milpas without incident.

10. During Díaz's same trip to Yucatán he visited the Hacienda Chunchucmil.

11. Not incidentally, Harvard's Peabody Museum of Archaeology and Eth-nology, then under the direction of Alfred M. Tozzer, and the Field Museum in Chicago were named in the Mexican federal suit against Thompson. It was sus-pected that artifacts worth up to $500,000 were in the possession of these museum collections.

12. These include Ticimul, Xkatun, San Rigoberto/Xkalacoop, San Felipe, and the larger town of Pisté.

13. The original text reads: *La dotación de ejido se trata de afectar terrenos pertenecientes a la finca Chichén Itzá y anexas de la propiedad de mi mandante Edward*

H. Thompson, en una extensión de 1,521 hectareas, 48 areas. Como esa dotación es del todo ilegal me apresumo a impugnarla por medio de este memorial ante esa Comisión Local Agraria, a fin de que resuelva que la misma afectación no es procedente.

14. The original text reads: *pero propiamente la hacienda tiene mucha mayor superficie pues su propietario el estadounidense Edward H. Thompson fue adquieriendo tierras, ya sea comprándolas a precios irrisorias o denunciándolas como baldías, tierras que fueron anexado a la hacienda principal, pero sin hacer manifestaciones al Catastro y Registro Público de la Propiedad.*

15. Soon after Barbachano Peón began acquiring land at Chichén Itzá, he also began to purchase large tracts from the Hacienda Uxmal.

16. Título Segundo, Capítulo VIII, Sección 2, Redistribución de Propiedad Agraria, Artículos 115–126, of the 1942 Código Agrario as cited in CAM-RAN Exp. 719.

17. The 1917 Constitution had previously set out the following provisions: 150 hectares for land dedicated to growing cotton or anything else with irrigation and 300 hectares for land dedicated to cultivation of bananas, sugar cane, coffee, henequen, olives, vanilla, cacao, or fruit trees. For raising cattle, rather than specifying a fixed amount of land the clause allows no more property than necessary to maintain a maximum of 500 head of cattle.

18. Folio 69, Libro 1, Tomo 12B indicates that he bought 148 hectares for 1,500 pesos.

19. Subsequently this land was divided by Barbachano Peón into five pieces. Between 1957 and 1970, the parcels were sold to the following parties: Alfonso Cisneros Canto, Fernando Barbachano Gomez Rul, Carmen Barbachano Gomez Rul, Rosario Aguilar, and María del Carmen Gomez Rul de Barbachano.

20. The Mexican SEP, by way of the Subdirección de Población Colonial, working alongside the CIW through the 1930s and 1940s shared the CIW's mission—to reconstruct the buildings into ruins that were comprehensible to the public without altering the original constructions (Peraza López and Rejón Patrón 1989: 16).

21. The delimitation has been reassessed periodically in each subsequent decade, save, I believe, the 1960s. In 1977 and 1978, at the request of the Dirección General of the INAH, a territorial delimitation was carried out in the archaeological zone of Chichén Itzá under the supervision of archaeologist Peter Schmidt of the Centro Regional Yucatán, who remains the archaeological director of the site. In 1984 a northern amplification was made in preparation for elevating the status of the zone to protection by presidential decree, which was formalized in 1985.

22. Locals pay about fifteen pesos in cab fare for this trip, while tourists might pay up to sixty pesos for the same trip.

CHAPTER FOUR

1. In Spanish, *antiguo* may be translated as old, archaic, ancient, or antique, depending on the context. For instance, a *mueble antiguo* is not an ancient piece of

furniture but an antique. The Spanish term most likely to be used to describe an old or elderly person is not *antiguo* but *anciano*. In my fieldwork experience in Yucatán, the term *antiguos* was used to refer to people in only two contexts. The first was a work context in which well-established people with seniority in a workplace were called *antiguos*. In the second context, antiguos were the Ancient Maya. In the case of the custodios, the term *antiguo* is a unique evocation of both of these meanings.

2. The sons of Isauro, grandsons of Juan, live in Pisté and work in the archaeological zone. Four are state-credentialed tour guides at Chichén Itzá, and each is fluent in at least four languages.

3. *Licenciado* is an important title in Mexico and denotes that a person is a university graduate. The encargado at Chichén Itzá was usually referred to as *el licenciado* formally and in personal conversations between the custodians and me simply by his first name.

4. One custodian suggested that if found, the dog should be secured with a chain that it could not bite its way through, and the encargado jokingly suggested using the heavy chain that had been recently taken down from the Castillo.

5. Photography is generally permitted in most areas of the zone. There are, however, a few exceptions. Photography is explicitly prohibited inside the "tunnel" entrance of the Castillo. Film is regularly confiscated from visitors who take photos from or of illegally entered areas. Film is also confiscated from photographers who appear to be "too professional," i.e., using large or fancy equipment, most of which is not permitted entrance without previous authorizations and fees paid. There have been many incidents at Chichén involving the photography of bikini-clad, topless, or even nude women in front of the monuments. This film is confiscated as well under the assumption that the images will be reproduced for commercial distribution, an activity expressly prohibited by the INAH.

6. The artisan invasions at Chichén Itzá are the subject of much anthropological consideration. Castañeda (1996), Himpele and Castañeda (1997), and Peraza López and Rejón Patrón (1989) discuss this in detail. The third source, an anthropological study commissioned by the INAH, looks at the socioeconomic roots of the invasion as a problem to be corrected for the protection of the zone. The other sources take a much more nuanced approach, specifically looking at the (ongoing) issue from the point of view of the artisans and vendors.

7. Himpele and Castañeda's 1997 documentary film *Incidents of Travel in Chichén Itzá* presents a fascinating portrayal of the event in 1995 and again two years later. At center stage in this film are New Age spiritualists who find an important connection between Maya pyramids and their own beliefs.

8. Many of the current custodians have never been campesinos. Among the thirty-six we can find former bus drivers, pharmacy managers, restaurant cooks and waiters, and agronomists who studied agriculture in the classroom, which some say is not akin to learning as a *milpero* (corn farmer).

9. One custodian from Veracruz constituted a special case, as an archaeologist in this position only for the time being.

10. Antiguo groups, though smaller in number, work at other archaeological sites in Yucatán, most notably in the Puuc-area sites such as Uxmal.

11. I found it impossible to get either written documentation or official accounts of this matter from state or INAH authorities.

CHAPTER FIVE

1. It should be said that greater monumental reconstruction would be simply a matter of time: the reconstruction of monumental architecture was not within the purview of the investigation undertaken by the Pakbeh Project.

2. Redfield had already undertaken the first study of a "peasant" community in Tepoztlán in central Mexico. *Tepoztlán: A Mexican Village*, published in 1930, was based on several months of research carried out in 1928. The Tepoztlán study arguably influenced Redfield's developing conception of the influences of modernity, represented by urban centers, on traditional or folk society. Redfield suggested that the "disorganization and perhaps the reorganization" of culture in Tepoztlán under "the slowly growing influence of the city" exemplified a general process by which "primitive man becomes civilized man, the rustic becomes the urbanite" (13–14). In 1930 he moved the focus of his research to Yucatán, where the CIW approved his plan for a study of four locations: Chan Kom, a peasant village; Tusik, a tribal village; Dzitas, a town; and Mérida, a city. Each represented a location on a continuum of intensification of the influences of modernization.

3. Perhaps the best presentation of a well-researched "straight" ethnography of a henequen hacienda community is Kirk's 1975 dissertation, "San Antonio: From Henequen Hacienda to Plantation Ejido." The historiography, however, outweighs the ethnography; Brannon and Joseph (1991), Joseph (1982), Joseph and Wells (1996), and Wells (1985, 1998) have produced the most solid research articulating the politics of Yucatán to Mexico and even the United States through the henequen industry in Yucatán. Several important studies on the political economy of henequen in Yucatán include Brannon and Baklanoff 1987 and Sabido Méndez 1995. Bracamonte (1989) offers a historical study of the period that predates the henequen boom, thus demonstrating the institutionalization of the hacienda system in the early period that set up the conditions for the emergence of the large and highly profitable henequen haciendas. Villanueva Mukul (1984) follows this period, covering the henequen industry during the Porfiriato. Studies of the relationship between identity and henequen work (Varguez Pasos 1999) complement contemporary examinations of the twentieth-century decline and liquidation of henequen in Yucatán (Baños Ramírez 1989, 1996, 1998).

4. Henequen production has three phases. The first is agricultural—growing the henequen plant for its leaves, or *hojas*. The second phase, which moves the process into the industrial stage of production, entails processing the hojas in a machine known as the *desfibradora*, designed to separate the fibers from the leaves. The next phase, also industrial, is turning the fiber into various products.

5. The 1868 Ley de Sirvientes del Campo authorized landowners and administrators to discipline offenses of peons with corporal punishment. See Gabbert 2000 for the relationship of this law to ideas on racial categories and discrimination.

6. Joseph (1982: 29, 79) points out the irony that at a time when slaveholding was being abolished or was irreversibly declining elsewhere in the Americas, it was reaching a new point of intensification in Yucatán, creating a "de facto slave society." This is evident in maize production statistics as Yucatec subsistence farmers' crops declined: maize production dropped from 15,000 hectares in 1845 to 4,500 in 1907 (73).

7. The American John Kenneth Turner twice traveled to Mexico, in 1908 and 1909, disguised as a wealthy investor to see for himself the social conditions created during the Porfiriato. Pretending to be interested in making investments in the henequen haciendas, he was escorted to a hacienda he called San Antonio Yaxche in the northwest of Yucatán. Turner's (1910) work was received as overtly polemical, but others have since found it to be an interesting historical document. He gives the following statistics from the first decade of the twentieth century: "The slaves are 8,000 Yaqui Indians imported from Sonora, 3,000 Chinese (Koreans), and between 100,000 and 125,000 native Mayas, who formerly owned the land that the henequen kings now own" (15).

8. Archaeologists working in the area suspect the bas relief to have come from a concentration of ruins near the contemporary community of Paraiso, several kilometers away, a site that demonstrates similar archaeological findings.

9. See Ardren 2002 for an account of the history of community relations from the perspective of archaeologists working at Chunchucmil.

10. San Bernardo del Buen Retiro in Maxcanú as well as Kopomá are examples.

11. Turner (1910: 27) reported similar circumstances at a henequen hacienda he visited in 1908: "The slaves rise from their beds when the big bell in the patio rings at 3:45 o'clock in the morning, and their work begins as soon thereafter as they can get to it. Their work in the fields ends when it is too dark to see, and about the yards it sometimes extends until long into the night."

12. A *ranchería* in this period was defined as "a collection of milpas and houses under the authority of and dependent upon a parent-community" (Redfield 1950: 2–3). Though not a self-governing community, the ranchería was a population center most typically composed of farmers who maintained subsistence corn plots, many of whom also worked on nearby haciendas as seasonal or day laborers.

13. In a letter to the local agrarian commission dated May 4, 1925, Peón Losa argued that the census data upon which the Coahuila *dotación* was based were falsified. Specifically, he charged, twenty-one of those capacitados claiming legal age—in this case twenty-one men claiming to be eighteen or nineteen years old— were actually minors. Further, Peón Losa claimed that one man counted as a capacitado did not exist at all. To support his protest to the April 18, 1925, census,

Peón Losa challenged that these men could not prove their legal ages. It is particularly interesting that Peón Losa would raise the matter of proof of age. For hacienda workers and peons, vital statistics on birth, death, marriage, and all other dates and personal data were recorded in a large record book held by the hacendado. This management of vital statistics can be seen as an important form of power manifested by the hacendado over the hacienda populations that operated in a disciplinary mode. The Coahuila claimants were "free" campesinos, not hacienda peons, and therefore had no such "official" records of their vital statistics, other than possibly in church records.

14. By May 15, 1925, the Hacienda Chunchucmil, in addition to the 1,368 hectares expropriated to Coahuila, had lost 4,822 hectares to Halacho (CAM-RAN Exp. 177).

15. In the early 1920s Halacho was an established pueblo of considerable size in comparison to Coahuila. Its application for an original ejido grant claimed 3,286 residents, with 809 heads of household. On October 25, 1922, Halacho received 19,416 hectares of land expropriated from seven haciendas.

16. In Yucatán, various sources estimate that 85 percent of ejidos have undergone the PROCEDE program, which is somewhat higher than the national average. However, this has not translated into obvious benefits for the ejidatarios who now hold titles to their land parcels. "With very few exceptions, the ejidos of Yucatan . . . are in crisis—undercapitalized, fragmented, and almost entirely dependent on government support" (Baños Ramírez 1998: 31).

17. Just as the 1999 cultural patrimony privatization proposal carried an ambiguous concept of privatization, so did the land privatization that came with the 1992 agrarian reforms. The idea that this law privatized the ejidos has to be highly qualified. If an ejido community passes through the PROCEDE process and individual members receive certificates and wish to sell, there is yet another set of procedures that must be completed. A land parcel cannot be sold straightaway to just anyone, particularly to a person from outside of the ejido community. If a land parcel is to be sold, it must be offered first to other ejidatarios and next to non-ejido members with rights to hold ejido land; a prime example here would be the widow of an ejidatario. Even if a certificate is granted, the land parcel itself as a physical property still may not be sold. Technically, if the assembly of ejidatarios agrees, a certificate might be sold but not the land itself.

18. While common understanding of the religious landscape of Yucatán is that the majority are Catholics, this may not be the case on a local level. Evangelical Christianity is quite popular in small towns throughout Yucatán. The most common denominations are Presbyterian and Pentecostal.

19. It is interesting to note how the hotel is described in advertisements. The hacienda is alternately dated as colonial, seventeenth century, and eighteenth century. In fact, it is a nineteenth-century establishment that functioned into the twentieth. The articles show photos of the church tower that very clearly says "1909," while the descriptions label the house as "colonial."

20. The largest single case of privatization in Mexico was with the state's divestiture of the financial Banamex-Accival (Schamis 2002: 121). In 2001 Banamex-Accival was willingly acquired by the multinational CitiGroup in the largest financial merger to date between the United States and Latin America.

21. At the end of my fieldwork, it was unclear how the newly reconstructed building would be used. While plans called for an archaeological museum, short-term uses may include housing for the archaeological project while the main house undergoes reconstruction.

CHAPTER SIX

1. According to most recent dating estimates by archaeologists, the site was occupied from 200 BCE to 1250 CE .

2. See Ashmore and Knapp 1999; Bender 1993, 1998; Bender and Winer 2001; Tilley 1994.

3. The phrase *el otro lado* is more commonly used throughout Mexico to refer to the United States.

4. In the 2001 season, the comisario ejidal, Don Ramón, was nearing the end of his three-year term and apparently was willing to have his secretary handle the relations with the archaeologists. Thus the secretary, Don Marcelino, became the "point person" for the archaeologists in Kochol.

5. Workers ranged in age from mid-teens to mid-sixties, with the occasional septuagenarian.

6. Milpa harvesting does not generally coincide with the archaeology season, as it takes place in the fall, while papaya harvesting is a nearly constant activity.

7. Don Oligario prepared his field but never ended up actually planting the papaya trees.

8. For the co-director in residence during the period of my fieldwork, related anxieties existed. After three seasons of excavation, there is little to show to impress a non-academic audience. In turn, I witnessed him express to the group a desire to forgo the mandated consolidation in favor of further excavation. The hope was that the crew would find more "goodies" to attract the attention of potential patrons.

9. The director stated: *Los proyectos arqueológicos tienen una función. Los arqueólogos extranjeros, su función es hacer cuestiones de tipo de arqueología académica. La cuestión ya de proyectos de desarrollo tendrían que tener otro tipo de orientaciones y otro tipo de autorizaciones. Porque digamos, no es una cuestión. . . . El proyecto arqueológico es un proyecto que se autoriza, es un proyecto de carácter académico.*

10. In Pisté, for example, the word *alux* did not even have to be mentioned to elicit alux stories. The closer I paid attention, I found that discussions that included anything about ruins, culture, history, or "Maya" provoked tellings of alux experiences.

REFERENCES

Abram, Simone, Jacqueline Waldren, and Donald MacLeod, eds. 1997. *Tourists and Tourism*. London: Berg.

Abreu Gómez, Ermilo. 1940/1983. *Canek*. Reprint, Mexico City: Dante.

Agence France Presse. 2004. "Wal-Mart Opens in Shadow of Mexican Pyramids." November 6.

Alba, Richard D. 1985. *Italian Americans: Into the Twilight of Ethnicity*. Englewood Cliffs, N.J.: Prentice Hall.

Anderson, Benedict. 1983. *Imagined Communities*. London: Verso.

Aplin, Graeme. 2002. *Heritage: Identification, Conservation, and Management*. New York: Oxford University Press.

Ardren, Traci. 2002. "Conversations About the Production of Archaeological Knowledge and Community Museums at Chunchucmil and Kochol, Yucatán, México." *World Archaeology* 34, no. 2: 379–400.

Ashmore, Wendy, and A. Bernard Knapp, eds. 1999. *Archaeologies of Landscape*. Malden, Mass.: Blackwell.

Atkinson, John A., Iain Banks, and Jerry O'Sullivan, eds. 1996. *Nationalism and Archaeology*. Glasgow, Scotland: Cruithne Press.

Ayres, William S., and Rufino Mauricio. 1999. "Definition, Ownership, and Conservation of Indigenous Landscapes at Salapwuk, Pohnpei, Micronesia." In *The Archaeology and Anthropology of Landscape*. Ed. Peter Ucko and Robert Layton. New York: Routledge.

Babb, Sarah. 2001. *Managing Mexico: Economists from Nationalism to Neoliberalism*. Princeton, N.J.: Princeton University Press.

Baer, Werner, and Joseph L. Love, eds. 2000. *Liberalization and Its Consequences*. Northampton, Mass.: Edward Elgar.

Baños Ramírez, Othón. 1989. *Yucatán: Ejidos sin Campesinos*. Mérida: Universidad Autónoma de Yucatán.

———. 1996. *Neoliberalismo, reorganización y subsistencia rural. El caso de la zona henequenera de Yucatán: 1980–1992*. Mérida: Universidad Autónoma de Yucatán.

———. 1998. "PROCEDE: Gateway to Modernization of the Ejido? The Case of Yucatán." In *The Future Role of the Ejido in Rural Mexico*. Ed. Richard Snyder and Gabriel Torres. La Jolla: Center for U.S.-Mexican Studies, University of California, San Diego.

Bartra, Roger. 2002. *Blood, Ink, and Culture: Miseries and Splendors from the Post-Mexican Condition.* Trans. Mark Healey. Durham, N.C.: Duke University Press.

Bartu, Ayfer. 1997. "Reading the Past." PhD diss., University of California, Berkeley.

———. 2000. "Where is Çatalhöyük? Multiple Sites in the Construction of an Archaeological Site." In *Towards a Reflexive Method in Archaeology: The Example at Çatalhöyük.* Ed. Ian Hodder. Cambridge, England: McDonald Institute for Archaeological Research.

Baudrillard, Jean. 1983. *Simulations.* New York: Semiotext(e).

Bauman, Zygmunt. 1991. *Modernity and Ambivalence.* Cambridge, England: Blackwell.

Beaucage, Pierre. 1998. "The Third Wave of Modernization: Liberalism, Salinismo, and Indigenous Peasants in México." In *The Third Wave of Modernization in Latin America.* Ed. Lynne Phillips. Wilmington, Del.: Scholarly Resources.

Bender, Barbara, ed. 1993. *Landscape: Politics and Perspectives.* Oxford, England: Berg.

———. 1998. *Stonehenge: Making Space.* Oxford, England: Berg.

Bender, Barbara, and Margot Winer, eds. 2001. *Contested Landscapes: Movement, Exile, and Place.* Oxford, England: Berg.

Bennett, Tony. 1995. *The Birth of the Museum.* New York: Routledge.

Black, Jeremy. 1997. *Maps and Politics.* Chicago: University of Chicago Press.

Boissevain, Jeremy, ed. 1996. *Coping with Tourists.* New York: Berghahn Books.

Bonfil Batalla, Guillermo. 1996. *México Profundo.* Austin: University of Texas Press.

———. 1997. "Nuestro patrimonio cultural: un laberinto de significados." In *El Patrimonio Nacional de México.* Vol. 1. Ed. Enrique Florescano. Mexico City: Consejo Nacional para la Cultura y Las Artes, Fondo de Cultura Económica.

Boston Globe. 1926. Column. October 25.

Bourdieu, Pierre. 1990. *Outline of a Theory of Practice.* Cambridge: Cambridge University Press.

Bracamonte y Sosa, Pedro. 1985. "Sirvientes y ganado en las haciendas yucatecas (1821–1847)." *Boletín de la Escuela de Ciencias Antropológicas de la Universidad Autónoma de Yucatán* 12, no. 70 (January–February).

———. 1987. "El consumo de fuerza de trabajo en dos haciendas henequeneras de Yucatán (1921)." *Boletín de la Escuela de Ciencias Antropológicas de la Universidad Autónoma de Yucatán* 15, no. 85 (July–August).

———. 1989. "Amos y sirvientes. Las haciendas de Yucatán: 1800–1860." Master's thesis, Universidad Autónoma de Yucatán, Facultad de Ciencias Sociales, Mérida.

Brannon, Jeffery, and Eric Baklanoff. 1987. *Agrarian Reform and Public Enterprise in Mexico: the Political Economy of Yucatán's Henequen Industry.* Tuscaloosa: University of Alabama Press.

Brannon, Jeffrey, and Gilbert Joseph. 1991. *Land, Labor, and Capital in Modern Yucatán.* Tuscaloosa: University of Alabama Press.

Brown, Denise. 1999. "Mayas and Tourists in the Maya World." *Human Organization* 58: 295–304.

Brunhouse, Robert L. 1971. *Sylvanus G. Morley and the World of the Ancient Mayas.* Norman: University of Oklahoma Press.

———. 1973. *In Search of the Maya: the First Archaeologists.* Albuquerque: University of New Mexico Press.

Caftanzoglou, Roxane. 2001. "The Shadow of the Sacred Rock: Contrasting Discourses of Place Under the Acropolis." In *Contested Landscapes.* Ed. Barbara Bender and Margot Winer. Oxford, England: Berg.

Castañeda, Quetzil. 1996. *In the Museum of Maya Culture: Touring Chichén Itzá.* Minneapolis: University of Minnesota Press.

———. 1998. "On the Correct Training of Indios at the Handicraft Market at Chichén Itzá." *Journal of Latin American Anthropology* 2, no. 2: 106–143.

Charnay, Desiré. 1887. *The Ancient Cities of the New World, Being Travels and Explorations in México and Central America, from 1857–1882.* Trans. J. Gonimo and H. S. Conant. New York: Harper.

Chippendale, Christopher. 1983. *Stonehenge Complete.* London: Thames and Hudson.

Clancy, Michael. 1999. "Tourism and Development: Evidence from Mexico." *Annals of Tourism Research* 26, no. 1: 1–20.

Cleere, Henry F., ed. 1984. *Approaches to the Archaeological Heritage: A Comparative Study of World Cultural Resource Management Systems.* Cambridge: Cambridge University Press.

———. 1989. *Archaeological Heritage Management in the Modern World.* London: Unwin Hyman.

Colegio Mexicano de Antropólogos. 2000. Carta a la Comisión de Cultura del Equipo de Transición del Presidente Electo Vicente Fox. At http://morgan.iia.unam.mx/usr/Patrimonio/Articulos/2000/Octubre2000/2Fox.html. (Accessed February 1, 2001.)

Collier, George. 1994. *Basta!: Land and the Zapatista Rebellion in Chiapas.* Oakland, Calif.: Food First Books.

Colwell, C. 1997. "Deleuze and Foucault: Series, Event, Genealogy." *Theory and Event* 1, no. 2.

Consejo Nacional de Población (CONAPO). 1993. *Indicadores socioeconómicos e índice de marginación municipal, 1990.* Mexico City: CONAPO.

Constitución Política de los Estados Unidos Mexicanos. 1917/1998. Mexico City: Porrúa.

Corbett, Jack, and Nelly Robles García. 1996. *Cultural Resource Management in Mexico.* At http://crm.cr.nps.gov/archive/17-4/17-4-4.pdf.

Cornelius, Wayne, and David Mhyre, eds. 1998. *Transformation of Rural Mexico.* La Jolla: Center for U.S.-Mexican Studies, University of California, San Diego.

Corner, John, and Sylvia Harvey, eds. 1991. *Enterprise and Heritage.* New York: Routledge.

Dahlin, Bruce, Traci Ardren, and Travis Stanton. 2000. Introduction to *Pakbeh Regional Economy Program Report of the 2000 Field Season.* Ed. Travis Stanton. Jamestown, N.Y.: Jamestown Community College.

de Certeau, M. 1984. *The Practice of Everyday Life.* Berkeley: University of California Press.

Deleuze, Gilles, and Felix Guattari. 1983. *Anti-Oedipus.* Trans. Robert Hurley, Mark Seem, and Helen Lane. Minneapolis: University of Minnesota Press.

———. 1987. *A Thousand Plateaus: Capitalism and Schizophrenia.* Trans. Brian Massumi. Minneapolis: University of Minnesota Press.

Desmond, Lawrence Gustave, and Phyllis Mauch Messenger. 1988. *A Dream of Maya.* Albuquerque: University of New Mexico Press.

Diario de Yucatán. 1926. Column. September 19.

Edgeworth, Matt, ed. 2006. *Ethnographies of Archaeological Practice: Cultural Encounters, Material Reflections.* Walnut Creek, Calif.: Altamira Press.

Elden, Stuart. 2001. *Mapping the Present: Heidegger, Foucault and the Project of a Spatial History.* New York: Continuum.

Fallaw, Ben. 2001. *Cárdenas Compromised: The Failure of Reform in Postrevolutionary Yucatán.* Durham, N.C.: Duke University Press.

Fernández Garza, Mauricio. 1999. "Iniciativa de decreto que reforma la fracción XXV del artículo 73 constitucional." At http://www.cddhcu.gob.mx/cronica57/contenido/cont10/cultu1.htm.

Florescano, Enrique, ed. 1997. *El Patrimonio Nacional de México.* 2 vols. Mexico City: Consejo Nacional para la Cultura y Las Artes, Fondo de Cultura Económica.

Folan, William J. 1970. "The Sacred Cenote of Chichén Itzá, Yucatán." In *National Geographic Society Research Reports: 1960–61 Projects.* Washington, D.C.: National Geographic Society.

Foucault, Michel. 1967/1986. "Of Other Spaces." Reproduced in *Diacritics* 16 (Spring): 22–27.

———. 1977. *Discipline and Punish.* New York: Vintage.

———. 1980. "Questions on Geography." In *Power/Knowledge: Selected Interviews and Other Writings, 1972–1977.* Ed. Colin Gordon. New York: Pantheon.

———. 1984. "Space, Knowledge, Power." In *The Foucault Reader.* Ed. Paul Rabinow. London: Penguin.

Gabbert, Wolfgang. 2000. "Race Mixture, Civilization, and Exclusion: Elite Discourse and the Indian in Nineteenth-Century Yucatán." Paper presented at A Country Unlike Any Other? New Perspectives on History and Anthropology in Yucatán conference, Yale University, November 4.

Gamio, Manuel. 1916/1960. *Forjando Patria.* Reprint, Mexico City: Porrúa.

García Canclini, Nestor. 1997. "Los usos sociales del patrimonio cultural." In *El Patrimonio Nacional de México.* Ed. Enrique Florescano. Mexico City: Consejo Nacional para la Cultura e las Artes.

García Quintanilla, Alejandra. 1986. *Los tiempos en Yucatán: los hombres, las mujeres, y la naturaleza (siglo XIX)*. Mexico City: Claves Latinoamericanas.

Gathercole, Peter, and David Lowenthal, eds. 1990. *The Politics of the Past*. London: Unwin Hyman.

Gatopardo. N.d. "Hacienda Santa Rosa: La Reliquia de Uxmal." At http://www.gatopardo.com/noticia.php3?nt = 577.

Greenspan, Anders. 2002. *Creating Colonial Williamsburg*. Washington, D.C.: Smithsonian Institution Press.

Hall, Stuart. 1996. "Who Needs Identity?" In *Questions of Cultural Identity*. Ed. Stuart Hall and Paul du Gay. Thousand Oaks, Calif.: Sage.

Handler, Richard, and Eric Gable. 1997. *The New History in an Old Museum: Creating the Past at Colonial Williamsburg*. Durham, N.C.: Duke University Press.

Harvey, David. 1989. *The Condition of Postmodernity*. Cambridge, Mass.: Blackwell.

———. 2001. *Spaces of Capital*. New York: Routledge.

Herzfeld, Michael. 1991. *A Place in History*. Princeton, N.J.: Princeton University Press.

———. 1996. "Monumental Indifference?" *Archaeological Dialogues* 3, no. 2: 120–123.

Hewison, Robert. 1987. *The Heritage Industry*. London: Methuen.

Himpele, Jeff, and Quetzil Castañeda. 1997. *Incidents of Travel in Chichén Itzá*. Film. Watertown, Mass.: Documentary Educational Resources.

Hirsch, Eric, and Michael O'Hanlon, eds. 1995. *The Anthropology of Landscape: Perspectives on Place and Space*. Oxford, England: Clarendon Press.

Hobsbawm, Eric, and Terence Ranger. 1983. *The Invention of Tradition*. New York: Cambridge University Press.

Hodder, Ian. 1983. *The Present Past: An Introduction to Anthropology for Archaeologists*. New York: Pica Press.

———. 1991. *Reading the Past*. New York: Cambridge University Press.

———, ed. 1996. *On the Surface: Çatalhöyük 1993–95*. Cambridge, England: McDonald Institute for Archaeological Research.

———. 1998. "The Past as Passion and Play." In *Archaeology Under Fire*. Ed. Lynn Meskell. New York: Routledge.

———, ed. 2000. *Towards a Reflexive Method in Archaeology: The Example at Çatalhöyük*. Cambridge, England: McDonald Institute for Archaeological Research.

———. 2003. "Archaeological Reflexivity and the 'Local' Voice." *Anthropological Quarterly* 76, no. 1: 55–69.

Hooper-Greenhill, Eileen. 1992. *Museums and the Shaping of Knowledge*. New York: Routledge.

———. 2000. *Museums and the Interpretation of Visual Culture*. London: Routledge.

Instituto Nacional de Antropología e Historia (INAH). 1995. Ley Federal Sobre Monumentos y Zonas Arqueológicos, Artísticos e Históricos. At www.inah.gob.mx.

————. 2004. Home page. At www.inah.gob.mx.

Instituto Nacional Estadístico, Geográfico e Informático (INEGI). 2000. *Estadísticas de Población*. At http://www.inegi.gob.mx.

Instituto Nacional Indigenista (INI). 2000. "The Peninsular Mayas: A Socio-Economic Analysis." In *Perfil Indígena de México*. At http://cdi.gob.mx/ini/perfiles.

Joseph, Gilbert. 1982. *Revolution from Without: Yucatan, Mexico, and the United States 1880–1924*. New York: Cambridge University Press.

————. 1986. *Rediscovering the Past at Mexico's Periphery*. Tuscaloosa: University of Alabama Press.

Joseph, Gilbert, and Allen Wells. 1996. *Summer of Discontent, Seasons of Upheaval*. Stanford, Calif.: Stanford University Press.

Juárez, Ana. 2002. "Ongoing Struggles: Mayas and Immigrants in Tourist Era Tulum." *Journal of Latin American Anthropology* 7, no. 1: 34–67.

Kaplan, Flora. 1996. *Museums and the Making of Ourselves*. London: Leicester.

Karetnikova, Inga. 1991. *Mexico According to Eisenstein*. Albuquerque: University of New Mexico Press.

Kelly, Robert. 2003. Letter to Secretary of Defense on Protection of Antiquities in Iraq. At http://saa.org.

Kirk, C. Rodney 1975. "San Antonio: From Henequen Hacienda To Plantation Ejido." PhD diss., Michigan State University.

Kirshenblatt-Gimblett, Barbara. 1998. *Destination Culture*. Berkeley: University of California Press.

Kohl, Philip. 1998. "Nationalism and Archaeology." *Annual Review of Anthropology* 27: 223–246.

Kohl, Philip, and Clare Fawcett. 1995. *Nationalism, Politics, and the Practice of Archaeology*. New York: Cambridge University Press.

Korzybski, Alfred. 1941. *Science and Sanity*. New York: Science Press.

Lefebvre, Henri. 1974/1991. *The Production of Space*. Trans. Donald Nicholson-Smith. Malden, Mass.: Blackwell.

Lister, Robert H., and Florence C. Lister. 1970. *In Search of Maya Glyphs*. Santa Fe: University of New Mexico Press.

Lorenzo, José Luis. 1984. "México." In *Approaches to the Archaeological Heritage: A Comparative Study of World Cultural Resource Management Systems*. Ed. Henry F. Cleere. Cambridge: Cambridge University Press.

————. 1998. *La arqueología y México*. Mexico City: INAH.

Lowenthal, David. 1985. *The Past Is a Foreign Country*. Cambridge: Cambridge University Press.

————. 1996. *Possessed by the Past: The Heritage Crusade and the Spoils of History*. New York: Free Press.

Lustig, Nora. 1998. *Mexico: The Remaking of an Economy*. Washington, D.C.: Brookings Institute Press.

MacCannell, Dean. 1989. *The Tourist*. New York: Schoken.

MacDonald, Sharon, and Gordon Fyfe, eds. 1996. *Theorizing Museums*. Oxford, England: Blackwell.

Maler, Teobert. 1932. *Impresiones de viaje a las ruinas de Cobá y Chichén Itzá*. Mérida.

Marcus, George. 1998. "Ethnography in/of the World System." In *Ethnography Through Thick and Thin*. Princeton, N.J.: Princeton University Press.

Maudslay, Alfred P. 1889–1902. *Biologia Centrali-Americana*. London: Taylor and Francis.

Mayor, Frederico. 1988. "A Patrimony for All." *UNESCO Courier*, August, 4–5.

McManamon, Francis, and Alf Hatton. 2000. *Cultural Resource Management in Contemporary Society*. London: Routledge.

Melé, Patrice. 1998a. "La protección del patrimonio histórico en México: Prácticas locales y competencias federales." *Mexican Studies/Estudios Mexicanos* 14, no. 1: 71–104.

———. 1998b. "Sacralizar el espacio urbano: El centro de las ciudades mexicanas como patrimonio mundial no removable." *Alteridades* 8, no. 16 (July–December): 11–26.

Meskell, Lynn. 2002. "Negative Heritage and Past Mastering in Archaeology." *Anthropological Quarterly* 75, no. 3: 557–574.

Millet Cámara, Luis. 1984. *Hacienda y cambio social en Yucatán*. Mérida: Maldonado/INAH.

Morgan, David. 1992. *Discovering Men*. New York: Routledge.

Morley, Sylvanus G. 1925. "Chichén Itzá, an Ancient American Mecca." *National Geographic*, January, 63–91.

———. 1943. "Archaeological Investigations of the Carnegie Institution of Washington in the Maya Area of Middle America, During the Past Twenty-eight Years." *American Philosophical Society Proceedings* 86: 208–219.

Morris, Earl. 1931. *The Temple of the Warriors at Chichén Itzá*. Carnegie Institution of Washington Publication 406.

Moscardo, Gianna. 1996. "Mindful Visitors: Heritage and Tourism." *Annals of Tourism Research* 23, no. 2: 376–397.

New 7 Wonders. 2005. At http://www.new7wonders.com.

New York Times. 1921. "Sack American's Estate." May 27.

———. 1923. "Tells of Wonders in Ruins of Yucatan." March 6.

———. 1926a. "Mexico Investigates Ex-American Consul." July 11.

———. 1926b. "Mexico to Attach Ex-Consul's Ranch." September 6.

———. 1935. "E.H. Thompson Dies; Found Maya Ruins." May 12.

Nuryanti, Wiendu. 1996. "Heritage and Postmodern Tourism." *Annals of Tourism Research* 23, no. 2: 249–260.

Olivé Negrete, Julio Cesar. 1980. "Pensamiento legal sobre arqueología." In *Arqueología y derecho en México*. Ed. Jaime Litvak King, Luis González, and María del Refugio González. Mexico City: Universidad Nacional Autónoma de México.

———. 1991. "Para la historia de la arqueología mexicana: El caso Thompson." *Arqueología* 5: 119–127.

———. 1995. "Estado, nación y patrimonio." In *El patrimonio sitiado*. Mexico City: Trabajadores Académicos del INAH, Delegación DIIAI1, Sección X del SNTE.

———. 2001. "Retrospectiva y perspectiva en material de legislación sobre patrimonio cultural." In *Patrimonio histórico y cultural de México*. Ed. María Elena Morales Anduaga and Francisco J. Zamora Quintana. Mexico City: INAH.

Orlandi, Lorraine. 2002. "Pile of Rocks Sends Mexican Indian to Prison." *Reuters*. October 10.

Oyuela-Caycedo, Augusto. 1994. *History of Latin American Archaeology*. Brookfield, Vt.: Avebury/Ashgate.

Patch, Robert. 1976. "La formación de estancias y haciendas en Yucatán durante la colonia." *Boletín de la Escuela de Ciencias Antropológicas de la UADY* 4, no. 19: 21–61.

Paul, Carlos. 2002. "Proyectan elaborar la Cartografía de Recursos Culturales de Mexico." *La Jornada*, March 19. At http://www.jornada.unam.mx/2002/mar02/020319/05an2cul.php?origen = cultura.html.

Pearce, Susan. 1994. *Interpreting Objects and Collections*. London: Routledge.

Peraza López, María Elena, and Lourdes Rejón Patrón. 1989. *El comercio de artesanías en Chichén Itzá y algunos efectos del turismo en la región*. Mérida: INAH Centro Regional de Yucatán.

La Prensa (Mexico City). 1921. Column. May 27.

Prentice, Richard C. 1994. *Tourism and Heritage Attractions*. London: Routledge.

Quintal Avilés, Ella F. 1995. "Apropriación y destrucción del patrimonio cultural. Comunidades Mayas y turismo en el oriente de Yucatán." In *El patrimonio sitiado*. Mexico City: Trabajadores Académicos del INAH, Delegación DIIAI1, Sección X del SNTE.

Randall, Laura. 1996. *Reforming Mexico's Agrarian Reform*. London: M. E. Sharpe.

Re Cruz, Alicia. 1996. *The Two Milpas of Chan Kom*. Albany: State University of New York Press.

Redfield, Robert. 1930. *Tepoztlán: A Mexican Village*. Chicago: University of Chicago Press.

———. 1932. "Maya Archaeology as the Mayas See It." *Sociologus* 8: 299–309.

———. 1941. *The Folk Culture of Yucatán*. Chicago: University of Chicago Press.

———. 1950. *A Village That Chose Progress: Chan Kom Revisited*. Chicago: University of Chicago Press.

Redfield, Robert, and Alfonso Villa Rojas. 1934. *Chan Kom: A Maya Village*. Carnegie Institution of Washington Publication 448.

———. 1990. *Chan Kom: A Maya Village*. Reprint, Prospect Heights, Ill.: Waveland Press.

Reed, Alma. 1923a. "The Waiting Ghosts of the Maya." *New York Times*, March 18.

———. 1923b. "On the Track of the Maya's Secret." *New York Times*, April 6.

———. 1923c. "The Well of the Maya's Human Sacrifice." *New York Times,* April 8.

Reed, Nelson. 1964. *The Caste War of Yucatán.* Stanford, Calif.: Stanford University Press.

Robles García, Nelly. 2000. *The Management of Archaeological Resources in Mexico: Oaxaca as a Case Study.* Trans. Jack Corbett. Society for American Archaeology. At http://www.saa.org/Publications.

Robles García, Nelly, and Jack Corbett. 2001. "Problemática social de manajo de recursos arqueológicos." In *Patrimonio histórico y cultural de México.* Ed. María Elena Morales Anduaga and Francisco J. Zamora Quintana. Mexico City: INAH.

Rugeley, Terry. 1996. *Yucatan's Maya Peasantry and the Origins of the Caste War.* Austin: University of Texas Press.

Ruz Lhullier, Alberto. 1970. *The Civilization of the Ancient Maya.* Mexico City: INAH.

Sabido Méndez, Arcadio. 1995. "Los Hombres del Poder: Monopolios, oligarquía y riqueza, Yucatán: 1880–1990." Mérida: Universidad Autónoma de Yucatán.

Salinas-León, Roberto. 1996. "Between Mercantilism and Markets: an Analysis of Privatization in Mexico." In *The Privatization Process.* Ed. Terry L. Anderson and Peter J. Hill. Landham, Md.: Rowman and Littlefield.

Sánchez Caero, Oscar Fidel. 1995. "Delimitación de zonas arqueológicas: historia y protección." In *El patrimonio sitiado.* Mexico City: Trabajadores Académicos del INAH, Delegación DIIAI1, Sección X del SNTE.

Schamis, Hector E. 2002. *Re-Forming the State: The Politics of Privatization in Latin America and Europe.* Ann Arbor: University of Michigan Press.

Schávelzon, Daniel. 1990. *La Conservación del Patrimonio Cultural en America Latina.* Buenos Aires: Getty Grant Program.

Secretaría de Desarollo Social (SEDESOL). 2000. "Perfil Maya de Yucatán: Desarollo Social." At http://www.sedesol.gob.mx.

Selwyn, Tom. 1996. *The Tourist Image.* Indianapolis: John Wiley and Sons.

Shankland, David. 1996. "Çatalhöyük: The Anthropology of an Archaeological Presence." In *On the Surface: Çatalhöyük 1993–95.* Ed. Ian Hodder. Cambridge, England: McDonald Institute for Archaeological Research.

———. 1999. "Integrating the Past: Folklore, Mounds, and People at Çatalhöyük." In *Archaeology and Folklore.* Ed. Amy Gazin-Schwartz and Cornelius Holtorf. London: Routledge.

———. 2000. "Villagers and the Distant Past." In *Towards Reflexive Method in Archaeology: The Example at Çatalhöyük.* Ed. Ian Hodder. Cambridge, England: McDonald Institute for Archaeological Research.

Silberman, Neil. 1989. *Between Past and Present.* New York: Henry Holt.

Skeates, Robin. 2000. *Debating the Archaeological Heritage.* London: Duckworth.

Snyder, Richard, and Gabriel Torres, eds. 1998. *The Future Role of the Ejido in Rural Mexico.* La Jolla: Center for U.S.-Mexican Studies, University of California, San Diego.

Stanton, Travis, ed. 2000. *Pakbeh Regional Economy Program Report of the 2000 Field Season*. Jamestown, N.Y.: Jamestown Community College.

Steggerda, Morris. 1941. *Maya Indians of Yucatán*. Carnegie Institution of Washington Publication 531.

Stephens, John Lloyd. 1843/1963. *Incidents of Travel in Yucatán*. Vol. 2. Reprint, New York: Dover.

Stevenson, Mark. 2004. "Officials Say Wal-Mart Store Won't Disturb Mexican Ruins." Associated Press, October 2.

Stone, Peter, and Brian L. Molyneaux, eds. 1994. *The Presented Past: Heritage, Museums, and Education*. New York: Routledge.

Stone, Peter, and Phillippe G. Planel. 1999. *The Constructed Past: Archaeology, Education, and the Public*. New York: Routledge.

Strickon, Arnold. 1965. "Hacienda and Plantation in Yucatán." *América Indígena* 25, no. 1 (January): 35–63.

Teo, Peggy, and Brenda S. A. Yeoh. 1997. "Remaking Local Heritage for Tourism." *Annals of Tourism Research* 24, no. 1: 192–213.

Thompson, Edward H. 1929. "Forty Years of Research in Yucatán." *Proceedings of the American Antiquarian Society*. Worcester, Mass.

———. 1932/1965. *People of the Serpent*. Reprint, New York: Capricorn Books.

Tilley, Christopher. 1994. *A Phenomenology of Landscape*. Oxford, England: Berg.

Topik, Steven C., and Allen Wells, eds. 1998. *The Second Conquest of Latin America: Coffee, Henequen, and Oil During the Export Boom, 1850–1930*. Austin: Institute of Latin American Studies, University of Texas Press.

Tozzer, Alfred. 1941. *Landa's Relación de las cosas de Yucatán: A Translation*. Papers of the Peabody Museum of American Archaeology and Ethnology, vol. 18. Harvard University.

Turner, John Kenneth. 1910. *Barbarous México*. Chicago: Charles H. Kerr.

Ucko, Peter J. 1994. Foreword. In *The Presented Past: Heritage, Museums, and Education*. Ed. Peter Stone and Brian L. Molyneaux. London: Routledge.

———. 1995. "Introduction: Archaeological Interpretation in a World Context." In *Theory in Archaeology: A World Perspective*. Ed. Peter J. Ucko. London: Routledge.

Ucko, Peter J., and Robert Layton, eds. 1999. *The Archaeology and Anthropology of Landscape*. New York: Routledge.

United Nations Educational, Scientific, and Cultural Organization (UNESCO). 1972. Convention Concerning the Protection of the World Cultural and Natural Heritage. At http://whc.unesco.org.

———. 2002. "Buddhas of Bamiyan: A Crime Against Culture." *New Courier*, October, 48–49.

Urry, John. 1990. *The Tourist Gaze*. London: Sage.

———. 2001. "Globalizing the Tourist Gaze." Department of Sociology, Lancaster University, England. At http://www.lancs.ac.uk.

Van den Berghe, Pierre. 1995. "Marketing Mayas: Ethnic Tourism Promotion in Mexico." *Annals of Tourism Research* 22, no. 3: 568–588.

Varguez Pasos, Luis A. 1999. *Identidad, henequen, y trabajo: Los desfibradoras de Yucatán.* Mexico City: Colegio de México, Centro de Estudios Sociológicos.

Vázquez Leon, Luis. 1994. "Mexico: The Institutionalization of Archaeology, 1885–1942." In *History of Latin American Archaeology.* Ed. Augusto Oyuela-Caycedo. Brookfield, Vt.: Avebury.

Vázquez Olvera, Carlos. 1995. "El museo y su nueva relación con los sectores sociales." In *El patrimonio sitiado.* Mexico City: Trabajadores Académicos del INAH, Delegación DIIAI1, Sección X del SNTE.

Vidal, Miriam. 2004. "Chocan activistas y vendedores en Teotihuacán." *El Universal Online.* Mexico City. November 8.

Villanueva Mukul, Eric. 1980. "Los campesinos henequeneros." *Boletin EDUAdY* 8: 40–87.

———. 1984. *Así tomamos la tierra: Henequen y haciendas en Yucatán durante el Porfiriato.* Mérida: Maldonado Editores and INAH.

Von Hagen, Victor Wolfgang. 1947. *Maya Explorer.* Norman: University of Oklahoma Press.

Walsh, Kevin. 1992. *The Representation of the Past: Museums and Heritage in the Post-Modern World.* New York: Routledge.

Wells, Allen. 1985. *Yucatan's Gilded Age: Haciendas, Henequen, and International Harvester 1860–1915.* Albuquerque: University of New Mexico Press.

———. 1998. "Henequen." In *The Second Conquest of Latin America: Coffee, Henequen, and Oil During the Export Boom, 1850–1930.* Ed. Steven C. Topik and Allen Wells. Austin: Institute of Latin American Studies, University of Texas Press.

Willard, T. A. 1926. *The City of the Sacred Well.* New York: Century.

World Bank. 2001. "Mexico: World Bank Presents Five-Point Development Plan." Press release. May 22. At http://web.worldbank.org/WBSITE/EXTERNAL/NEWS/0,,contentMDK:20014770~menuPK:34466~pagePK:64003015~piPK:64003012~theSitePK:4607,00.html.

Woodward, Christopher. 2001. *In Ruins.* New York: Pantheon Books.

Worcester (Massachusetts) Daily Telegraph. 1911. Column. October 31.

Zoomers, Annelies. 2000. "Land in Latin America: New Context, New Claims, New Concepts." In *Current Land Policy in Latin America: Regulating Land Tenure Under Neoliberalism.* Ed. Annalies Zoomers and Gemma van der Haar. Amsterdam: KIT and Iberoamericana/Vervuert Verlag.

OFFICES OF PUBLIC RECORDS

CAM-RAN, Comisión Agraria Mixta, Registro Agrario Nacional. Mérida.
RPP, Registro Público de Propiedad. Mérida.

INDEX

Abreu Gómez, Ermilo, 141, 150
Acropolis (Athens), 13
Agave fourcroydes. *See* henequen
alux, 198–200, 224n10
Alvarado, Salvador, 151
ambivalence, 2, 9, 10, 27, 33, 34,
    36, 43, 54, 66, 99, 207–209; and
    modernity, 3, 10, 215n1; between
    social actors, 7, 31; toward ruins,
    6, 41, 62, 137, 174, 179, 203–204
American Antiquarian Society, 71, 74,
    217n2
antiguos. *See* custodios
antiquities, 36
archaeological sites: as assemblages, 7,
    176; legislation regarding, 37–38,
    42, 93–94; living in, 13, 92–94;
    ownership of, 40–41; private sec-
    tor involvement in, 14, 91–92;
    provenance of, 26; and social rela-
    tions, 7, 90; spatiality of, 24, 28,
    55; tourism development of, 17;
    zoning of, 179–181. *See also names*
    of individual sites
archaeology: ethics of, 147; history of
    (Mexico), 42–43; and nationalism,
    42–44. *See also* Chichén Itzá;
    Chunchucmil
asociación civil, 129–130

Bamiyan Buddha statues, 51
Banamex, 166, 167, 169–170

Barbachano family, 82, 84, 88, 123,
    127, 131, 219n19
Barbachano Peón, Fernando, 82–85,
    87, 131, 219n15
Bartu, Ayfer, 13
Baudrillard, Jean, 30
Bauman, Zygmunt, 29, 53, 207, 215n1
Bender, Barbara, 12, 177, 214n6
Bonfil Batalla, Guillermo, 44
Butler, Judith, 25

Campeche, 153, 207
Cancún, 16, 62, 122, 125, 127
Canek, 141
Cárdenas, Lázaro, 40, 44, 150, 157,
    213n3
Carnegie Institution of Washington
    (CIW), 59, 76, 85–87, 138; and
    contract with Mexican government,
    86, 88, 102, 219n20; and rental
    agreement with E. Thompson, 87.
    See also Project Chichén Itzá
cartography. *See* mapping
casta divina, 151, 152
Castañeda, Quetzil, 12, 22, 62, 122,
    214n12, 220n6
Caste War, 69, 70, 72, 143, 154,
    217n1 (chap. 3)
Çatalhöyük, 12, 13, 214n12
Catherwood, Frederick, 42, 67
Catholic Church, 201
cha-chaac, 197